The Prime Minister Has It In Mind......

by

Leslie Stowe MBE LL.B

Edited by

David J. Miller

Cover design by

Adele Griffiths

Published by

Abernant Publishing
Alltmawr Fach
Builth Wells
Powys LD2 3LJ

Printed and bound
in the United Kingdom by

Think Ink Fine Art Printers
11-13 Philip Road
Ipswich
Suffolk IP2 8BH

ISBN: 978-1-909196-08-7

First published 2013

Acknowledgements

From Street Urchin to Buckingham Palace:

An anthology of memories which become more precious as age takes its toll. It is humbly dedicated to my children and grandchildren in the hope that they never have to experience poverty and the deprivations of war.

Also to my wife Ann who supported and encouraged me throughout our married life.

My thanks also to Sue Stothard who instructed me in the skills of computer use and without whom this book would never have been completed.

To Hazel Aslett, my friend for many years who spent many hours proof reading the draft of the book.

Preface

The Postman cometh

The very formal looking envelope bore the crest of 10 Downing Street.

I was curious but holding the title of President of the Police Superintendents' Association of England & Wales, I had visited Downing Street on more than one occasion, the most recent having been a few weeks previously for a discussion on crime prevention measures hosted by the Home Secretary Douglas Hurd. I assumed that the correspondence may have had some reference to that meeting.

I had collected the morning newspapers as usual and on my return, my wife handed me the envelope together with the other post and waited for me to reveal the contents. As I read, I held my breath, probably my pulse rate increased at the information before me:

"The Prime Minister has asked me to inform you in strict confidence, that she has it in mind, on the occasion of the forthcoming list of Birthday Honours, to submit your name to the Queen with a recommendation that Her Majesty may be graciously pleased to approve that you be appointed a Member of the Order of the British Empire."

Momentarily I became paralysed and my wife took the letter from me to read it herself. With a shout so loud the neighbours must have heard as she exploded -"Darling!!" Together we read and re-read the letter with the unspoken question "Why me?"

The letter continued that if it was agreeable to me I was to notify the Prime Minister's Office by return of post and if The Queen accepted the recommendation, the announcement would be promulgated in the Birthday Honours List.

As the significance of the honour penetrated my brain, I completed the acceptance form and took it immediately by hand to 10 Downing Street; I could not chance that the Royal Mail would let me down for such an important letter.

The letter was dated 1st May 1987; the Birthday Honours would not be announced until the official birthday of the Queen, on the second Saturday in June, the occasion of the traditional Trooping the Colour on Horseguards' Parade. Those subsequent six weeks required both my wife and I to contain our excitement and felt that we were duty bound not to reveal our secret. After all it would be a terrible anticlimax and disappointment if, for some reason officialdom had a change of heart.

If a week in politics is a long time, 6 weeks to keep such a secret was a very long time.

At that time I was a Chief Superintendent in the Metropolitan Police with the responsibility to represent 400 or so Superintendents and Chief Superintendents in both the Metropolitan and City of London Forces, a position I could never have foreseen 37 years before when I decided I wanted to be a Police Officer.

Contents

Chapter 1. The Approach of War

In the years just prior to the outbreak of the Second World War, life was not easy. In a council estate in the Birmingham suburb of Erdington, youngest of 12 children it would have been easy for me to think that I was in a disadvantaged family. Easy that is but for the fact that other families were also 'hard up' and found difficulty to make ends meet on meagre incomes. In fact at that time, our way of life was normal because we knew nothing different. My parents had married in 1910 and it was considered normal for families to consist of many children but even so I think I must have been somewhat of a surprise to my mother when I appeared in her 45th year and I was destined to be the last.

My father was a metal stamper by occupation, not a well paid job and it required him to leave home just after 6.00am each morning and travel on the tram across to the other side of the city where he was employed by the firm of W. Dingley, 77 Warstone Lane, Hockley. returning home at about 6.30pm. Of course I was too young to appreciate the problems but I knew from his conversations with my mother that any workers who had not 'clocked in' by 8.00am when the factory gates were closed, were denied the opportunity to work that day with the consequent loss of earnings and possibly 'the sack'. No trade union muscle to represent them in those days!

The long hours and physical demands of his job probably accounted for his frequent spells of poor health. At a time when a visit by the doctor cost two shillings and six pence (which prudent spending could have provided a substantial meal for the whole family) there was a tendency to hope that home nursing would suffice and avoid the necessity for days away from work with the ever present threat of losing his job. A visit to the doctor's surgery was a modest six pence but that was still a drain on a very tight household budget. I remember many occasions when my mother applied hot poultices to his chest and words such as 'pleurisy', 'shingles' and 'consumption' could be overheard but meant nothing to me.

The pressure which many workers faced to keep their jobs required my father to go to work whatever the weather and in those early days of my childhood it seemed that in the winter months snow fell more regularly and he would trudge through heaped snow with brown paper wrapped round his trouser legs presumably to provide some meagre protection. His food for the day would consist of his 'snap' – a sandwich or two which was unlikely to be more than bread and margarine and a small amount of tea and sugar.

A few years later when I was older, I was able to realise that those heavy falls of snow were the means by which an enterprising youngster could earn a few pennies by sweeping the snow from the pathways of neighbours' houses supplementing income of pennies earned by 'running errands'. I remember that we usually swept the snow into piles in the gutter which restricted the road width and it would have been more sensible to heap it on the edge of the pavement. However, we did not think of that solution.

This atmosphere of family life was not enhanced by my father's drinking habits. Pay day was traditionally Friday and when he handed over his pay packet, it would be minus that needed for his 2 or 3 pints per day and his tobacco. From the remainder my mother was expected to finance the normal expenses of rent (often avoided until the following week if possible); food, coal supplies, clothing and the regular visit to the pawnbroker's shop to redeem articles pawned earlier in the week to provide a few shillings to last out until Friday. Then the downward spiraling of expenses exceeding income would continue with pay day, shortage of money and moral despair.

I was expected to go to the local public house off licence and queue awaiting opening time to buy his pint or two. I and the other persons waiting for the much sought after drink would take our own bottles which would be formally sealed with a small sticky label intended to prevent children drinking it on the way home. Childhood curiosity would naturally lead to the occasional illicit 'swig' but I found the taste not to my liking. The beer was usually referred to as 'arms and legs' – because it had no body, a consequence of shortage of every commodity due to the war years. I would have been 6 or 7 years old when I commenced my journeys to the pub which today would be illegal but was not unusual at that time. On one occasion when I went to the pub, I was accompanied by a neighbour's little dog of which I was particularly fond. Unfortunately when we were in the road which was a bus route she ran into the road directly under the wheels of the bus. It was a sickening sight and the horror in seeing it remained with me for a long time.

His regular demands for money to buy drink caused many unpleasant arguments at home. He would borrow money from my mother which she had carefully saved for other necessities; when I was old enough to have pocket money (six pennies per week) he would 'borrow' that and very seldom would it be repaid. If he had been drinking or if he was denied the money to purchase his drink, he would often become violent and I remember one particular incident when he struck at a family member, missed and hit the wall resulting in extensive bruising and swelling. It is etched so firmly on my memory that I made an early resolve that I would never allow myself to follow his example.

When I recall my childhood years with the benefit of survival and my own experience of life I realise that not only did I not love or respect my father but that he never showed love or consideration for my mother or his family. I can never remember any single instance when he gave my mother a kiss or exhibited any affection. I never saw him hold her hand, embrace her, give her a present or make any personal sacrifice in her favour.

Looking back over the years with a deeper understanding of human pressures and frailties it may be easier to appreciate the difficulties faced by so many families of that age. I know that when my parents married, there would have been an income scarcely sufficient to meet basic obligations. Denied the advice from medical sources which would be considered normal practice in post war years, unexpected or unwanted pregnancies occurred with depressing frequency creating more pressure on the bread winner. The daily drudgery of rising early, commuting to engage in physically demanding work for minimal wages and a return home to inadequate food and inadequate heating supplies with children who expected to be fed and clothed would all be factors to create a feeling of despair. Perhaps the hazy anaesthetic effect of drink was the working man's solution.

My parents never had a holiday. In fact I could recall only one occasion when they had a single day away from home together. Holidays were an expense that was out of the question. The first time that I went away from home for a holiday was at the age of 11 years. More of that later.

For all his shortcomings, my father had qualities which I did seek to emulate. He was skilled in carpentry and much of the furniture in the house was hand made from timber and plywood which he obtained at little cost. He taught me some basic skills in the use of tools, in particular the art of fret saw artistry which enabled me to become the envy of school friends. He also hand repaired shoes with leather or rubber when available or if necessity dictated, expedient use of cardboard to line the inside of the shoe to cover holes in the soles. His workshop, or rather work bench was in the kitchen of the house, which together with the gas stove, gas boiler and a mangle which folded down to make a table top, left little space to move in the tiny area.

The kitchen also included the 'coal hole' and when delivered, the sacks of coal would be carried by the coal man through the living room, into the kitchen and humped into the coal hole. It was one of my jobs to regularly sort the coal from the slack which was taken outside, and to place boards across the door of the coal hole to prevent coal spilling onto the kitchen floor.

The coal was an absolute essential for not only did it provide a fire to heat the room but the fire was set in the range which included the grate, an oven and a flat top which enabled my mother to cook in the oven and also on top of the range where the kettle or pots would be placed. In the oven were two iron removable shelves which were invaluable in the winter months to wrap in a blanket and place in the beds. Hot water bottles were for the 'well off'! Black leading the range to keep it looking smart was a frequent ritual which was often delegated to me.

At times when coal was unavailable, a visit to the gas works was necessary. The journey was about 5 miles and an old pram or trolley would be pushed carrying the precious sack of coke, the prize for queuing for long periods, hoping that there would be sufficient left as the other customers were served.

Our home was a 3 bedroom terrace house with a bathroom and internal toilet, a far cry from my parents' previous home which had been a 'back-to-back' house in the socially deprived area of Winson Green in Birmingham.

The house was in a small Grove of 16 houses, 'Grove' being the identification of the postal location, not an indication of tree lined beauty. It was a cul de sac with a tiny circular island at the closed end providing a spot which imaginative children including myself could transform into a desert island, dig holes in the dusty earth, trace with our fingers road patterns for our cars (I can only remember ever possessing one – a red lorry with solid brass wheels) and in November, build our bonfire. A gas lamp post was located on the kerb and provided a useful wicket for our cricket games, the bowling crease measured from the kerb of the island. In addition to the 'bowled out', 'caught' or 'LBW', there was another means by which the batsman could lose his wicket. 'Out in gardens' was the penalty where the batsman was required to retrieve the ball if he hit it into a neighbour's garden. If the ball could not be retrieved, the miscreant would virtually become a social pariah.

It was a community of its own; everyone knew everybody and probably knew everyone else's business! Anyone who did not live there, including residents of another 'Grove' across the other side of the dividing road were strangers to be treated with suspicion.

Naturally we never ventured in the other 'groves' without very good reason. This community atmosphere was an accepted part of life; front doors would be left 'on the jar' whilst visiting neighbour's houses without fear of unlawful intrusion. The rent collector and milk man would carry leather satchels containing their money on a strap round their neck without the likelihood of having it stolen; householders would leave the money to be collected on the doorstep with a note for the authorised collector. Most houses left a door key hanging on a piece of string easily accessible through the letter box to ensure that the householder would not be locked out if they forgot to take their key with them. It was common knowledge but there never were any unlawful entries.

In this environment of simple pleasures and basic needs, I was always excited and pleased to see the various delivery men with their horses and carts. The coal man, the Co-op milk man, the baker and greengrocer all delivered their goods from the carts drawn by magnificent shire horses. As a special treat when not at school, I was allowed to give the milkman's horse a bucket of water, release his bit and feed him a crust of bread. Another milkman who delivered from a local farm had a dainty two wheeled cart and dispensed milk from a churn using a pint measure on a long handle. A special favourite of mine was a magnificent horse which pulled a huge two wheeled Corporation cart collecting refuse. Another frequent visitor to the area was the 'rag and bone man' and although I cannot ever remember that he collected bones, his horse drawn cart was always well laden with old clothes exchanged for a few pennies or perhaps a small goldfish in a jar.

The public highways were not the only place that these beautiful animals could be seen at work. Within a short walking distance was the canal, a point of irresistible attraction to children and the object of many warnings from parents which of course made it an even greater attraction. It was a regular feature of the canal to see the barge horses towing barges laden with loads of coal and other commodities The horses would be unharnessed at points where the canal passed through a tunnel and the barge power would then depend on the crew members lying on their backs and 'walking' along the tunnel roof. At the far end of the tunnel, the horse would again be harnessed.

It is perhaps sad to reflect that in the name of progress these powerful gentle equine giants are no longer to be seen in our neighbourhoods but at least one aspect of this feature of yesteryear has been restored in that horse drawn hearses for funeral processions are now frequently seen in the present day. Whereas they were a regular feature of life before the war, their reintroduction provides a particular dignity to a solemn occasion but still attracts attention as something unusual in modern life.

The dependence on horse power had one important benefit for householders. Everyone who boasted a garden would compete with each other to collect horse droppings from the road to provide manure for their gardens.

It was on one occasion when waiting for my friends the horses to arrive that I suffered a serious accident. I was standing on the front garden gate and fell off banging my head on the path causing a nasty wound to my head. I remember being violently sick and my head bleeding profusely. An ambulance in army camouflage with a red cross on the side arrived and I was taken to hospital for stitches to be inserted. The scar of that injury has never completely disappeared but the lesson was never learned not to swing on gates or climb trees etc. and I probably experienced many more falls in the process of growing up.

It was not the only occasion that I had an accident and the other could have proved far more serious. At a time when my age would have classed me as a toddler, I reached up to the table and pulled a pot of tea over my upper arm. The scald scar over the whole of the biceps on my right arm has always served to remind me of the potential danger when pots or kettles containing liquid are within easy reach of children.

Other aspects of life in my childhood thankfully would certainly no longer be acceptable. It was normal for the refuse and coal ash from houses to be deposited in dustbins usually kept in the rear gardens. Dustmen would empty the contents into large open metal baths which were carried on their shoulders to the dust cart where the contents would be heaved into the interior resulting in clouds of dust and debris dropping onto the roadway.

Similarly the drains would be maintained in what would now be considered entirely unhygienic conditions. Our grove had two drains located in the closed end which were always a threat for our tennis ball when we were playing. We were threatened or perhaps warned by our parents to keep away from the drains because of the possibility of catching 'the fever' but if the wayward ball dropped through the large gap set in the kerb, there was no alternative but for two determined youngsters to heave the drain cover out and for one of them to lean down towards the filthy water and retrieve the ball.

Periodically the drains were cleared of excessive sludge. Two men would remove the drain covers and using large ladle type implements on long handles, would drag from the drains large amounts of sludge which would be emptied into a lorry. It is a matter of speculation whether this was a serious health hazard but like so many aspects of life at the time, it was considered to be perfectly normal and something of a spectator sport for us scruffy, [not very clean] children who had little entertainment outside their own imaginations.

Of course the possession of a ball, any ball, elevated its owner to a status justifying a degree of hero worship and the owner would dictate the game to be played. If it was to be cricket, obviously a bat would be required and many gardens fenced in by 3' high palings would develop unexplained gaps when a cricket bat was needed.

Another game which we played and resulted in the mysterious gaps in garden fencing was 'tip-cat' where a short piece of wood about 6" long and tapered at each end, would be placed on the ground and the pointed end struck with a baton causing the smaller piece to cart wheel into the air. The object of the game was to hit it as far as possible and run on a prescribed course before the 'opposition' could retrieve it. This game and 'whip and top' though they provided many hours of pleasure for us could not possibly be expected to survive when more sophisticated children's games became available.

Other games which for us were perfectly normal to occupy our leisure time would probably bewilder our grandchildren who would consider them to be stupid or a waste of time when their own normal diversions would be television, play stations and electrical toys. The game of marbles (or the peculiar terminology of our age – glarnies) was a game of skill where the attractive coloured glass spheres were tossed by the players towards a scooped out hole in the earth of the island in our grove. Depending on the number of marbles available, we would nominate 2, 3 or more to be wagered against our opponent. A marble twice the size of the others was a 'two-er' and a much sought after prize. Whoever tossed into the hole more marbles than his opponent would then be first to flick the others into the hole with his [grubby] finger. It was a game where winner takes all.

Hop scotch was another game where we used chalk (probably 'borrowed' from school) to draw on the road a pattern of 'beds' which we won for successfully negotiating the pattern of lines hopping on one foot whilst kicking a smooth piece of stone or brick with the other. This game was guaranteed to scuff our shoes and bring criticism from our parents who would wonder how long the footwear could last before having to be replaced.

The alternative to playing in the street, particularly when irritated neighbours voiced their disapproval was to go to the local park which was near to our school about half a mile from home. The park consisted of neatly laid out gardens and a play area where we had swings, a round-a-bout and horizontal bars on which we could climb and swing, never giving a thought to the possible injury if we fell onto the hard concrete. There was also a small drinking fountain with a metal cup tethered by a metal chain. I never knew of a single instance where a child suffered any injury and the days of claiming compensation from negligent councils would not be a part of life for many years in the future.

There were other hazards in the park however in that supervision of the park was the responsibility of the Park Keeper, a man who seemed to have the ability to appear the moment any child misbehaved in any way whatsoever. What penalties he could have imposed we never knew but it was sufficient for us to imagine the threat.

Playing out in the street always included the risk of damaging clothing when shoes would be scuffed, trousers torn or articles lost if carelessly discarded to provide a goal post etc. With no spare cash, providing replacements was the cause of constant worry for my mother. To be given cast off clothing was normal and I never forgot the humiliation I experienced when I had a 'new' pair of shoes which were actually the cast off bootees from a girl. However, at that time there was no alternative, bootees or barefoot which would have been even more humiliating. There were occasions when we qualified for clothing provided by some organisation which in later years under the umbrella of the welfare state would be regarded as part of the social services.

There was little stigma in having to attend the distribution centres because so many other families were in similar circumstances. To be given the necessary piece of paper to be exchanged for clothing was to indicate that we were the lucky ones. If no money was available for the tram ride to the city centre, a four mile walk was necessary and I remember on one occasion on the wearying return journey a motorist offered my mother and I a lift. What absolute luxury – to ride in a motor car for the first time in my life!

Because I was the youngest and likely to be at home more than my brothers and sisters, I was often expected to help with the family chores. Wash day was usually once a week and necessitated that the mangle in the kitchen, normally used as a table top, had to be swung into its upright position to expose the rollers used to squeeze the water from the clothes. The wash tub was a large wooden cask kept in the back yard and always had to be filled with water to prevent the wooden panels shrinking and thereby leaking. It would be my job to empty the water which had been there since last wash day and fill it with hot water boiled in the gas heated 'copper' in the kitchen. If it was a dry day the wringer would be man-handled outside and if it was a wet day, the tub would be brought into the kitchen. In days when washing machines were an unknown commodity, the washing was placed into the tub and a washing 'dolly' was used to bang the clothes repeatedly. After the wash, I would have to turn the handle of the wringer whist my mother threaded the clothes through. It would never have occurred to me that I was doing tasks that I should not have been expected to do. This was an age when children did as they were told and I expect my playmates also had to help in the home. However I remember that some of the families who could afford a galvanised metal tub, did not have the weekly chore of filling it with water after every wash day.

However, if the needs must, children can often make their own entertainment and in my imagination, the brim full wash tub became a lake where I could sail little canoes made from garden pea shells carefully opened along the 'wrong' side, the two sides held open with a small piece of match stick. The water was also a diving pool for wooden figures fashioned from my mother's dolly pegs plunging into the water from the 6' high fence which separated our yard from the next door house.

Wash day invariably included folding the sheets when with mother at one end, me at the other, the sheets were folded along their length so that they could be passed through the rollers of the mangle and then folded again and passed through until as much water as possible was squeezed out. Afterwards I would hold one end of the sheet to keep it clear of the ground whilst mother pegged it onto the clothes line. If it rained, there would be a mad scamper to retrieve the partially dried clothes and take in the line because to leave it out was likely to run the risk of it rotting and breaking under the weight of the washed clothes. I sometimes wonder if the availability of labour saving devices, with so much taken for granted in later life, perhaps reduced the opportunity for character building duties of our children.

Life tended to be very basic, few luxuries and with constant reminders to economise, recycle and avoid waste at any cost, it was only to be expected that in many households, certainly in ours, newspapers such as the 'Radio Times' were torn into a suitable size to be used as toilet paper. I feel certain that no amount of imagination could produce an advertisement depicting a golden retriever puppy extolling the virtues of the soft luxurious feel of newspaper on baby's bottom!

Even in times of poverty and war time economy families still tried to maintain some aspects of normality, one of which was the celebration of Christmas. Even with the shortage of money, my mother saved a few shillings every week which were handed to one of the neighbours who acted as treasurer for what was known as a 'Diddlum Club'. The money was carefully safeguarded until a few days before Christmas when the pay-out was made and a few precious pounds were available to buy Christmas presents. Although Christmas presents were those costing very little money a friend of the family sometimes brought me presents and one year I was presented with a pedal car in the shape of an aeroplane with very tiny wings and tail-plane but it was my pride and joy until I grew too big to use it.

Our house was normally decorated with streamers which we made by cutting coloured paper into strips and folded into links fastened together with paste made from water and flour. We did have a few coloured paper decorations which were carefully saved from year to year but I cannot remember that we ever had a natural Christmas tree merely a small artificial one about 3 feet tall with little branches which folded down. Presents for members of the family were always very sparse but because we did not expect any greater celebration, we accepted that it was normal.

As a special treat on Christmas day sometimes for dinner we had a chicken which would require to be plucked and dressed. With a spirit of inventiveness I used the feathers to fashion an Indian war Brave's head dress and with a branch cut from our privet hedge fashioned into a bow, arrows made from the Golden Rod flower stems, the garden and road outside the house became the prairies and canyons of the wild west.

Christmas time was also the time of pantomimes and in some way, my mother saved the few shillings to take me to either the Birmingham Hippodrome or the Aston Hippodrome. I cannot remember a year when we didn't enjoy this treat.

The Family

Although I was the youngest of such a large family, several of my siblings did not survive infancy and my earliest childhood days were shared with two sisters who slept in the second largest bedroom and my brother Alfred who occupied the smallest bedroom with me until he was called for military service in the army shortly after the outbreak of war. When he was demobilised from the Army he married very shortly afterwards and consequently did not resume permanent residence at home. During his military service one of his fellow service men was Gilbert Dodd a qualified doctor and a member of the Salvation Army. During their friendship he influenced Alf to the point where he also decided to join 'The Army' which indirectly was to influence my own future life.

In the summer school holidays in 1946 Gilbert invited Violet and me to spend a week's holiday at his home in Paignton. I was 11 years old and it was the first time I had ever been away from home for a holiday.

Other members of my family were to be found in various parts of the city, my eldest sister Kate living almost in the city centre in what would now be described as a slum area. She had a large family and when my mother took me to visit her, at such a tender age, I did not appreciate the squalor endemic in the area and I saw nothing wrong in the fact that her husband kept a large number of rabbits in individual cages, in the attic of their house.

Kate provided the first contact with my family of the Salvation Army although I was not to learn of that fact until many years later. Joining the 'Sally Army' did not meet with the approval of my father who destroyed her uniform and thereafter was not a welcomed visitor to her home. The influence of the Salvation Army was to prove a very important factor in my life in later years. Sadly, Kate died in 1942 followed shortly afterwards by her youngest son, Brian, who fell into the nearby canal and drowned.

Another sister, Lily, the second eldest, lived in the north of the city which required a journey of about one hour's duration on the No 11 Outer Circle 'bus route. I always enjoyed a visit to her home with my mother and one of the attractions at their house was a coal cellar which provided many opportunities with my nephew Ronald, for childhood fantasies and imagination. I did not attach any significance to the fact that my father never accompanied us to Lily's home and it was not until many years later I discovered his drunken behaviour on one visit had resulted in him being considered an unwelcome guest for the future.

Lily had a daughter Jean, 2 years older than I and a son Ronald, a year or so younger. When I was about 4 years old, Ronald and I were page boys at the wedding of a friend of Lily's. We were dressed in lime green silk like suits with white shoes. In adulthood, it stretches my imagination to wonder why we did not object to such outfits.

Perhaps unintentionally, Jean was to play an important role in my subsequent educational development. When she was old enough she was admitted to a local grammar school which had a very good reputation and the family connection subsequently dictated which school I would attend if possible.

A third sister, Esther, known to us all as Etty , was apparently entrapped in an unhappy marriage and left her husband in 1943 to live with us in our tiny, overcrowded house. The only place in which she could sleep was on a sofa in the main living room. In all honesty, my memory is rather vague as to how she managed but I do know that she was in very poor health due to tuberculosis and died in 1944 one Saturday morning when I was alone in the house with her. My mother was in a neighbour's house and knowing that something was wrong, I desperately tried to attract her attention by waving a small flag in the window. I attended Etty's funeral but was so distressed that in my immaturity I vowed never to attend another. The subsequent years would prove how immature that vow had been.

My eldest brother, David was always something of a mystery to me. He lived near to our family home but due to some domestic dispute which was never disclosed to me he was an infrequent visitor although my mother often fretted that he stayed away. The image of him which always came to my mind was a photograph of him in scout leader's uniform; shorts, wide brimmed hat and holding with two hands the 6' pole which seemed to be an accepted and expected accoutrement for any scout of that era.

The two sisters who lived at home with me, Violet (Vi) and Ethel in different ways greatly influenced my childhood and adolescent life. Perhaps it was because I was the baby of the family that resulted in Vi taking it upon herself to provide for me the financial support which my parents were unable to give, but more of that later. Ethel on the other hand in 1946 following brother Alf's example was persuaded to join the Salvation Army at which point in her life she decided to use instead, her middle name of Patricia. Her decision to join the Army influenced me shortly afterwards to make a similar choice which I never regretted. Again, more of that later. Alf married another Salvationist.

Whatever the economic constraints on luxuries in the home, I often accompanied my mother on a visit to the city centre travelling on the tram which for part of the journey passed an abattoir where pigs were off-loaded in the main thoroughfare and driven into the slaughter house accompanied by much squealing from the condemned animals. In the city centre we invariably went to Lewis's departmental store and its many attractions included the biscuit counter where racks of square boxes displayed the individual type of biscuit. The prudent housewife however could purchase quantities of broken mixed biscuits at a greatly reduced price and that is what my mother would buy. It did not occur very often but was considered to be a great treat when it did.

In this background of family life, community spirit, and war time deprivations I grew up with friends who attended the same school and shared my playtime activities.

The War Years

I was four years old when war was declared and too young to understand the significance. I did not appreciate the difference between affluence and poverty. I lived with my parents, brothers and sisters, was fed and clothed and that to me was normal therefore the threat of food shortage, the possibility of losing one's home, death and destruction did not enter my infant's comprehension.

In those days of scarcity, shop keepers tended to give priority to their regular customers and consequently families were inclined to retain their patronage even if a long walk was involved, hoping always that the journey would be worth while. It all seemed perfectly natural to a young boy growing up in circumstances where everyone faced the same problems and the relationship between shopkeepers and customers, neighbours and friends all seemed to be based on honesty and good will.

In the early war years with the introduction of rationing, food was scarce and monotonous. Meat was a luxury, eggs were powdered and tasteless, bread was obtained by queuing for long periods at any shop where it could be found, providing that customers had their 'BUs' (bread unit coupons) but always the common thread in our house was that father must have his share even if at the expense of other family members. I recall that many occasions my mother would have nothing left for herself other than the most meagre portion and many were the times that she threatened to 'throw herself in the cut' (canal) or put her head in the gas oven. It was remarkable and a tribute to her motherly instincts that on a basic diet of porridge for breakfast, stews or mashed potatoes and bread and margarine we actually survived apparently none the worse until food became more plentiful and varied.

Even as the war progressed, the change in life was not a change for me and my friends of similar age. What we experienced, to us was normal life because we had no criteria of peace time living with which to compare.

That is not to say that we did not experience various degrees of indoctrination. We all knew that Hitler was a bad man whom we parodied by marching in a 'goose step' with one finger held horizontally under the nose and the other arm held near vertical in an exaggerated salute or chanted rhymes (which did not always receive the approval of our parents!) We were obliged to carry our gas masks in a square cardboard box and at night time, there were the frequent shouts from the local air raid warden to "Put that light out." All houses were obliged to have opaque curtains on their windows and anyone who was indiscreet and allowed a light to shine from the house would be accused of giving assistance to the German bombers.

Bombing was a regular occurrence. Birmingham being an industrial city was an obvious target. In particular we lived about one mile from Castle Bromwich where Spitfire aircraft were produced next to a Royal Air Force airfield. There were frequent occasions when bombs exploded near to my home, the nearest being about 100 yards away. There were many sad occasions when individuals or distressed pathetic family groups would knock at the door asking if we could take them in because they had been bombed out. Our small house was already overcrowded and we could not have offered such help but on one occasion a small dog was accepted as an additional family member after much pleading and tears from me.

In the earlier days of the war, communal air raid shelters were available, the nearest to our home being about ½ mile away at a bus depôt but such facilities were not popular and many families chose to remain in their homes whatever the risk. The impending bombing raid would be announced by the wailing siren and whatever the time of day or night we would be encouraged to go to the shelter. There was an anti aircraft gun battery nearby and whilst the raids were in progress we could hear the repetitive 'crump crump crump' of the guns. One particular gun was larger and louder than the others and was known affectionately as 'Big Bertha'. When we heard 'Big Bertha' we would invariably cheer or voice some encouragement.

Later, all houses were provided with an Anderson shelter which was installed in the garden. It consisted of corrugated metal sheets fastened together to make a little house about 8' x 6' and 6' high with a curved top. It was buried to half its height, set in concrete in the garden and covered with a thick layer of earth in which plants could grow. Ours was covered with a mass of nasturtium plants which were a blaze of orange colour when they were in bloom. Inside the shelter was fitted with bunks. Ours had two bunks each side each about 2' wide and at the closed end, a double width bunk. When the siren was sounded, we would file down the garden path to the shelter which could not have withstood a direct or near miss but did provide some safety from shock waves from the bombs and falling debris.

When the 'All clear' siren was heard we returned to the house and back to our beds. In daylight, with the inquisitive nature of all children we would pay frequent visits to the anti aircraft site and the adjacent search light emplacement. There was also a barrage balloon base nearby and we would watch as these elephantine monstrosities were slowly inflated and allowed to grace the skies tethered on their metal hawsers. Any new bomb sites where houses had stood the previous day became un-chartered territories to be explored. To children of my age and understanding who had never known any difference, this was normal life.

With families living on basic rations there was very little food to spare but nothing was ever thrown away as waste. In our Grove, as in every other street and thoroughfare, 'pig bins' were placed in which householders were expected to scrape all uneaten scraps of food. The contents were collected regularly to be taken to processing plants and turned into food for pigs. The whole farming industry was intensified to provide the necessary food for the nation and most gardens, however small became vegetable plots. I was allocated a tiny patch in our garden as my very own and I always had great delight in cultivating potatoes, beans and other basic necessities which we were able to produce. Even from a very early age I had an ambition to own a municipal allotment but it was to be many years before the wish was realised.

Whether it happened and I never knew or whether it never happened I do not know but I cannot recall that thefts or vandalism occurred at the allotments or in neighbours' gardens. One neighbour kept a few hens which produced fresh eggs but however much a delicacy fresh eggs were, pilfering was unknown. It was not only in respect of waste food that prudence was exercised. Nothing was actually wasted. Newspapers were collected and presumably recycled; any metal, be it metal garden gates or tin cans were vital commodities to be used in the manufacture of tanks and aeroplanes, or so the radio broadcasts would claim.

Old clothing when it was no longer fit to be worn could be cut into narrow strips, threaded through a piece of hessian and the result would be a serviceable rug for floor covering. Such an article would take many hours of laborious cutting and threading but was the means of occupying hours when other activities were not an option.

At a time when television was unknown, entertainment in the home depended on the radio or as we knew it, the wireless. This name was appropriate because the receivers were not wired to a mains electricity supply but relied on electricity from acid filled batteries which had to be taken regularly to a local shop to be recharged. Transistor radios and walkman sets, like television, were completely unknown. Gramophones were a usual feature of households and we had one, the motor of which was wound up with a handle on the side, a metal gramophone needle which had to be replaced from time to time and a large brass trumpet which amplified the sound from the record. It had to be expected that at sometime whilst the record was playing the music would become distorted indicating that the motor needed winding.

My memories of the radio programmes which we heard other than news bulletins giving details of the war progress, are mainly of the light entertainment variety. 'Workers' Playtime' broadcast at mid day, 'In Town Tonight' in the evening and my favourite – 'Children's Hour' are the ones which still bring back thoughts of days when simple pleasures were probably the most endearing. One programme which I enjoyed was 'Itma' featuring a comedian named Tommy Handley. The show included characters who achieved national icon status. Colonel Chinstrap with his phrase "I don't mind if I do, Sir." Mr.s. Mopp with her "Can I do you now Sir?" were fictional characters who became part of our lives. Strangely, without any logic to my child's mind, my father would not allow the programme if he was in the house, dismissing it as 'Tommyrot'. Many years later almost as latter day rebellion, I included in my cassette tape collection, recorded Itma programmes. It was disappointing that the humour of the programmes which in war time was hilarious, no longer had the same appeal.

As an alternative to the entertainment available in the home there were other attractions for the inquisitive child. One diversion for me was to go to the 'main road'. It was in fact what I would later know as an 'A' class road, the A38 but to me it was the main road where buses, trams and heavy goods vehicles could be seen. A regular feature was convoys of military vehicles including tanks and Bren Gun Carriers roaring along on their metal tracks. On the roads where these convoys travelled, there were large concrete round blocks which apparently were placed in strategic locations and if an invasion of Axis Forces did occur the blocks would be used to hamper progress.

Also to be seen in lines like silent sentinels along the road side were smoke screen canisters. These were dustbin size contraptions with a smoke stack intended to burn oil and produce dense smoke to obscure the neighbourhood in the event of bombing attacks. Many years later when environmentalists brought pressure to create smokeless zones such a war time invention would have been completely unacceptable.

Other structures which appeared and became semi permanent features of our neighbourhood were the static water tanks. Where our Grove branched off the adjacent road, a black tank appeared. It was about 10' square and 4' deep. It was filled with water which provided an immediately accessible supply for the local fire fighters with their stirrup pumps if ever the need should have arisen following a bombing raid. We never experienced any damage caused by incendiary bombs and instead of the use for which they were intended, the tanks became yet another opportunity for children's adventures and parental admonishment.

The aeroplanes at Castle Bromwich had a special fascination for me and particularly during school holidays I would take myself off to watch the Tiger Moth aircraft taking off and landing as pilots learned to fly. On the opposite side of the road to the airfield was a factory where Spitfires were assembled and if I was very fortunate, I occasionally saw these magnificent machines wheeled across from factory to runway. As with thousands of other aircraft enthusiasts, I have never tired of hearing the awesome roar of their engines. Because the airfield would have been a target for enemy bombers and because our home was relatively near, it was understandable that our neighbourhood occasionally suffered the consequences of poor bomb aiming by the aircrews. As a child I could not possibly have known that Royal Air Force Castle Bromwich would play a very important part in my future life.

Also near to my home was Sutton Park, a large area of unspoiled natural beauty which was regarded as a natural choice for a special day out for families, Sunday School outings and youth organisations' activities. However, during the war it provided the location for prisoners of war camp, the occupants of which could often be seen in their distinctive uniforms when they were used on working parties. I don't think it ever occurred to us when we saw them that they were dangerous men and perhaps in all honesty, they weren't.

There were several other parks more easily accessible than Sutton Park each with their own attraction. Pype Hayes Park justified a ride on the No 79 tram for the princely sum of one half penny or as we called it, "an ape-nie". At this park there was a small lake where we occasionally saw fishermen and beyond a barbed wire fence, the irresistible attraction – a river where we could use fishing nets to catch tiddlers. I am quite sure that the correct name was something different but to us, the little fish in our jam jars were tiddlers. Those of us who were more adventurous would discard shoes and socks to paddle in the water ever mindful of the threat from the dreaded "toe biters". On reflection, these small crayfish were never known actually to bite any one's toe but children's imagination would change the inoffensive little crustacean into a creature as terrible as a piranha.

The mood of the day would dictate the park to be visited and another venue for our adventures was Ward End Park. This was a little further afield, nearer 2 miles and a bus ride followed by a one mile walk was necessary to reach our goal. What then was the attraction of this particular place? It was a very high helter-skelter slide and a boating lake where on very rare occasions, some kind adult would offer to take us for a ride. Because it was such a long journey to this park, we would often take a picnic consisting of a bread and jam sandwich together with a bottle of cold tea. Oh the gastronomic delights of the children of yesteryear!

In the summer months, some of the parks provided entertainment, when under a marquee, artistes who would probably never achieve fame in the music halls, together with the firm favourites Punch and Judy, performed. Whether they did so without payment I never knew and it was immaterial for children who were always prepared to take full advantage of anything on offer.

Open air activities and self made entertainment were occasionally supplemented by a visit to the cinema but as children we could only gain admittance to films identified as 'U' category (suitable for children). If we wanted to see an 'A' category (no children unless accompanied by an adult) we had one of two choices; the first was to go with our parent or adult sibling (my parents never visited the cinema) or the alternative would be to stand at the entrance of the cinema and solicit some adult to take us in. In an age when the words 'paedophile', 'social worker', and 'counsellor' were unknown, this seemed to be a perfectly natural choice and sometimes, the condescending adult would even pay for our ticket

Towards the end of the war the local cinema started a children's Saturday morning programme where for the princely sum of six pence (my total week's pocket money when I had pocket money) we created mayhem and a great deal of noise watching our film favourites and heroes of the day.

 Probably my favourite leisure activity was swimming. I qualified for a free pass to the local swimming baths when I achieved the minimum distance required (probably one length of the bath) and particularly during school holidays every day that I could do so, I went swimming. Although the local baths were only one mile from home and therefore easily accessible, there was an extra attraction to visit others in the City.

Although these childhood activities served as a diversion for us from the true horrors of war, there were ever constant reminders: the incessant need to queue for everything from vegetables in the greengrocer's shop to coke for the fire; the shortage of public transport; the nightly patrol of the Air Raid Wardens; the regular departure of my father to the factory premises where he worked to be on duty through the night as his fire watching duty; the billboards which questioned "Is your journey really necessary?" or reminded us "Careless talk costs lives."

Of course as children, we did not understand the full implications of these Governmental messages and even when at the cinema we watched Pathe News or British Movitone news reels, the scenes of warfare were entertainment rather than current affairs but in any event, for us, it was normal life because we had experienced no other. One character of the war years which did have a lasting impression for us was Mr. Chad. Mr. Chad was a cartoon feature showing the top half of a man's face peering over a wall saying "Wot, no ...." referring to the absence of some commodity such as potatoes, beer, or whatever was in particularly short supply. Why it made a lasting impression for us was that we could easily draw the figure ourselves and insert whatever it was that we claimed was in short supply.

In the closing months of 1944 and early 1945 even for children it was obvious that the war was likely to finish soon and we became increasingly excited probably not because we knew that hostilities would cease but because there would be a street party to celebrate. During the months leading to the armistice, my mother earned a small amount of money with 'out work' from a local factory. Large rolls of cloth printed with rows and rows of the Union flag would be delivered to the house and I would help her to cut the rolls into strips and then into small individual flags. How many hundreds or even thousands we produced I could not estimate but I do know that they were to be available for the forthcoming celebrations.

Even when the war with Germany ended, it did not necessarily indicate that husbands and sons, fathers and brothers would immediately return home. There were those of course who would never return home. There were those in hospital and there were those who were still on active service either in the army of occupation or fighting in the Far East where it was to be several more months before Japan capitulated. For the returning service personnel however, there were unashamed, unrestricted demonstrations of welcome. Every street was festooned with bunting, flags of every description and banners proclaiming 'Welcome Home ....' with the name of the service man or woman.

When they had returned home, the service men and women were still required to wear uniform and another feature of the time to remind us that normality was not fully restored was the sight of military police – the dreaded 'Red caps' patrolling the railway stations and main streets in the city centre or sometimes they were to be seen knocking at a door making enquiries for service personnel who were absent without leave. It never crossed my mind that a few years in the future I would be held in equally low esteem when I joined the ranks of the Royal Air Force Police and became identified as a 'Snowdrop'.

The resilience of the population to food shortages and other hardships together with the determination to celebrate culminated in what the children had eagerly anticipated for months – the street party. How it was possible to produce large quantities of sandwiches, cakes, jelly and blancmange was a tribute to ingenuity, initiative and the saving for a rainy day philosophy. On the appointed day, in the true community spirit, chairs and tables were taken into the street, bed sheets served as table cloths and the whole neighbourhood partied! The whole neighbourhood, that is, except for a few including one little boy who developed a very upset tummy and instead of joining my friends outside, I was confined to a bed which was made up for me on a sofa with the front door of the house left open so that I could watch what was going on. When the Far East conflict finished there was another party and fortunately I was able to enjoy that one.

Although the war brought many hardships and shortages, life continued and those not involved in military service had to cover for those who were. It did not occur to me until many years later that at our school there were no male teachers other than the somewhat elderly Head Teacher. In peace time, 40 or 50 years later Governments would express their intentions to reduce the class sizes in schools from unacceptable levels of 30 or so. At my school for the end of term report in July 1945 (immediately after the war in Europe finished and a few weeks before the Far East war ceased) I was 4th out of a class of 52. In December of that year I was 6th out of 50 and one year later when it would have been expected that normality was returning, I was 5th out of 43. Why there were fewer pupils I do not know but certainly, there were no extra teachers.

Chapter 2. School Life

School was Birches Green infants and junior school, a little over ½ mile from my home. With very little vehicular traffic on the roads, any suggestion of danger in allowing children to walk to school unaccompanied was not a consideration. Child molesters were unknown and I cannot remember one single incident of any of my contemporaries suffering any misfortune. Because we were unaccompanied by parents, we could dilly dally on the way, balance precariously on irate householders' garden fences, tease each other and not be accused of bullying and often arrive at school dishevelled and barely in time before the whistle for assembly was blown and we lined up on the playground in our respective class formations. Depending on the mood of the teacher in charge lateness may have brought a verbal reprimand or a stroke of the cane. Either was a salutary warning not to repeat the indiscretion.

Another diversion on the way to school was to search for pieces of shrapnel from bombs which may have fallen in the neighbourhood the previous night. The social standing of any boy could be enhanced depending on the size of his piece or pieces of shrapnel to be exhibited to his peers.

I can distinctly remember the first and second days at school. Toilets were outside at the far end of the playground. On the first day, like every other little boy I needed to use the facility and did so without further thought. The second day, instead of using the boys' toilet, I used the girls and was somewhat bewildered that they were different. Whether or not I was reprimanded by a teacher, an embarrassed little girl or some other reason I do not remember but I never made the mistake again and gradually learned that there are differences between little boys and little girls. Anyway it was much more sensible to use the boys' toilet where competitions could be held to see who could pee highest up the wall.

There was one other little problem or misunderstanding that I had to overcome. It was not made clear to me when I started school that children were expected to remain there until told to go home. On at least one occasion I decided that I had had enough and went home at morning playtime. Whilst my mother was not pleased, I never did find out what the teacher thought of my part time attendance. Not only did I quickly learn the rudiments of school attendance but I also became aware of the dreaded 'School Board Man' an official apparently with terrifying powers to search out children who were absent from school and to take appropriate action. I never did encounter this bogeyman personally but the knowledge of his existence was sufficient to guarantee compliance with the requirement to go to school.

Overall, school had no particular significance for me. It was something that everyone did; we were sent to school, we came home and went to school the next day. It was normal life. We were not aware of any political pressures as to which school we attended or the significance of examinations. We were taught in classes of about 50 children and periodically we had examinations or tests, and we took the results home to our parents. Such were the shortages of materials in the war years that we were given pieces of paper which may have been torn off a note pad; we wrote down in our best writing 'Arithmetic', 'Spelling' 'History' etc and handed them to the teacher who wrote the appropriate mark of our test, added appropriate comments, folded the paper over and stuck it with a piece of sticky paper for us to take home. Woe betide any pupil who was found to have tampered with the seal!

There were simple rules to follow at school. We were expected to learn to the best of our ability and we were expected to respect the teachers. Talking in class was not encouraged and infringements likely to be punished. I remember one occasion when we were required to write an essay on making a cup of tea, or at least that was the central theme. At one point I turned to the boy sharing the double desk and whispered that I had written "you but the tea in the pot" instead of "you put the tea in the pot". He probably giggled but it was the justification for the teacher – Miss Oakley standing me in front of the class and demonstrating the use of her cane. Corporal punishment however was infrequent and modest means of helping us to concentrate on what was expected of us. At the age of eleven we all left junior school with a good command of the basic requirements of reading, writing and arithmetic.

School however, was also a time of learning by practical means. One bright sunny day we were led out into the playground where we formed a circle round the headmaster. He had a single cricket stump in a wooden base which he stood upright and solemnly drew a line with a piece of chalk along the shadow of the stump. An hour later we were again taken into the playground where we excitedly watched the headmaster draw a second line marking the shadow. That demonstrated the relative movement of the earth and sun and that we could make our own sundial, something we did on another day.

Outdoor activities at school were not always strictly educational. In the winter months if there had been a heavy fall of snow, we were sometimes allowed to participate in snow ball fights supervised by the teachers or were allowed to create slides on the icy playground surface. Health and Safety legislation was unknown and the thought of claiming compensation for a minor injury was never a consideration.

One day I was told by my teacher, Mrs. Radford, that the headmaster wanted to see me. Full of trepidation, not knowing what wrong doing had been attributed to me, I nervously obeyed. He produced an empty strip of paper which had contained 5 Aspro tablets and had apparently been found in my possession. I had not realised that showing my class mates how clever I was, being able to chew and swallow Aspro tablets I was endangering my health. That was the only occasion when [naively] I ventured into drug taking. I was nine years old.

The Church featured in my life from the earliest days of my memory. I attended an Evangelical Church about 2 miles from my home but why I experienced my earliest days of Sunday school at that particular place I do not know. In later years a chapel about 5 minutes walk from home was opened and I spent many happy years there. I enjoyed learning passages from the Bible some of which I could repeat 60 years later. I always thought that the beauty of the language was lost in the modern translations.

The Grammar School

September 1946 was the commencement of a very important period of my life; a pupil at George Dixon Grammar School in the Edgbaston district of Birmingham. Edgbaston was an area of contrasts where families of great wealth living in large mansion type houses, identified their addresses as being in 'Edgbarston'. On the opposite side of some of the thoroughfares the identification referred to Edgbasston' where the less salubrious residents often provided the street walkers or 'Ladies of the Night' profession. Admittedly I was not to learn of this division of the social classes until 20 years later when I worked as a police officer in the same district.

George Dixon Grammar School had a separate boys' and girls' school and was acknowledged to be one of the best in the city. My mother's earnest desire that I should attend was fostered by the knowledge that my niece Jean, daughter of my eldest sister Lily, was also a pupil at the same school. It was 10 miles from my home and necessitated leaving home at about 7.30am to make sure that I could catch a bus in time to arrive at school in good time. I would not return home until at the earliest, 5.30pm

The school was proud of its history and achievements, committed to maintain the standards deemed appropriate to groom pupils for their role in society. Competition was encouraged and the division into 'Houses' named Normans, Saxons, Britons and Danes allowed pupils to strive to the best of their ability in sporting events, selection for rugger and cricket teams etc for the honour of their House. I was allocated to Britons and whilst I never achieved selection for school teams, my swimming ability produced many points for the House. Included in our swimming instruction was learning life saving skills and in my final year at school I achieved the Bronze Medallion award.

The Birmingham Corporation provided a facility to assist pupils' travel costs and plastic tokens in lieu of money were supplied for use on the public transport. Ironically my home was a few hundred yards beyond the arbitrary radius from the school for assisted travel which caused much financial hardship to my parents. After repeated requests a concession was made and I received the necessary payments. Eventually I received as a birthday present a bicycle which gave me complete independence from public transport.

School uniform was compulsory and consisted of a green blazer with a red badge on the breast pocket, green cap with a similar badge and school tie. Grey socks were required to complement the grey trousers. Together with a satchel, the whole outfit was an enormous financial burden. I was only to learn later that without the support of my sister Violet, it would not have been possible. Not only was school uniform compulsory but we were expected to be appropriately dressed when travelling to and from school. Being so readily identified with the school, woe betides us if our behaviour reflected adversely. Undignified conduct in the bus queues, failing to offer a seat to a standing adult on a crowded bus, not wearing one's school cap or neglecting to acknowledge a member of staff in the street were considered breaches of school discipline which seemed to have an unerring certainty of transmission to school.

The satchel was a recognised accoutrement of all pupils at the school and it was not until 3 or 4 years later that the availability of government surplus stocks of army haversacks etc encouraged some of my contemporaries to break the mould.

In addition to the uniform we were expected to possess suitable kit for school sporting activities which included physical training in the gymnasium (anyone forgetting their plimsolls could borrow a pair from the school supply but invariably resulted in a smack across the bottom with one of the borrowed shoes) Corporal punishment it may have been but was accepted as normal. Swimming shorts, rugby kit etc. were also required and although the family budget did not stretch to the purchase of a rugby shirt in red and green hoops (I had to use an army surplus khaki pullover) I was the proud possessor of rugby boots made of soft leather whereas all other members of my school form had hard leather football boots. It would be considered patronising to identify the family member who purchased them for me but the reader can surely guess.

The much maligned 'school dinners' were available but even though the cost would be considered reasonable, I took sandwiches for my lunch. The wide variety of pre-packed sandwiches available in the supermarkets many years later was not an option and it was much more likely that the contents would be the less imaginative strawberry jam or the readily available fish paste. In the immediate post war years, all schools were supplied with bottles of milk 1/3rd of a pint in size and one for every pupil. Of course some would not drink the milk (although some schools appointed 'milk monitors' whose duties were to make sure that their class members drank their milk.) but it was permissible to leave it until lunchtime rather than the recognised morning milk break.

At some point in my school development, lunch time sandwiches were superseded by taking school dinners which were subsidised and I soon realised that acting as a monitor and serving the other pupils with their meal would justify an enhanced portion for personal consumption. Whether sandwich or cooked meals, after our lunch we were obliged to leave the building and go to the playing fields. To reach the field, we processed along a narrow pathway which passed the girls' school and they lined their classrooms probably making the same sort of teenager comments about the boys as the boys made about the girls.

The lunch time activities on the playing field were such that youthful energies could be expended and games which had the potential for physical injury were considered perfectly normal. Thank goodness healthy exercise and youthful exuberance had not been overtaken by the paranoia associated with the 'compensation culture' of later years. I cannot remember any incident which did cause reprimand from our teachers or an imposition of restrictions on our activities. Neither can I recall any evidence of bullying although teasing was expected and accepted. One of my contemporaries was nick-named 'Taxi' because he had protruding ears and at that time there was a popular song the first line of which was "Got big ears, got big ears, like a taxi with the doors wide open." If he was distressed he certainly never gave any indication to that effect.

The girls' playing field adjoined that of the boys' but any thoughts of romantic liaisons were frustrated by prefects from the boys' school who maintained a 20 yards separation area. Fortunately this morality patrol did not extend to activities beyond the normal school hours and tales of [claimed] sexual conquests achieved the previous evening by the more worldly wise boys were frequent topics of conversation during the following day. I realised many years later that in this particular aspect of adolescence, I was definitely at the bottom of the class!

Whereas it may be considered normal for children to have friends at home and attend the same school, as a pupil at the grammar school my friends at school lived in a wide area of the city whilst my friends at home went to local schools. This may have proved an advantage in that arriving home from school in the early evening with perhaps one or one and a half hour's homework to complete, the distraction of wanting to join my friends at home was not a problem. They presumably enjoyed their extra curriculum activities without having the wish to share them with me. This is not to say that I had no leisure activities and in fact enjoyed an adequate social life and pursued my favourite hobbies. Every day when I returned home from school my mother invariably asked three questions: "Have you seen Jean (Lily's daughter)?"; "What did you have for dinner?" And "What homework have you got?" The amount of time to complete homework was sometimes reduced if I had managed to conspire with friends travelling home on the bus.

Although I had received good reports from junior school for my academic ability, it would be fair to say that the early days at grammar school were a struggle. Maths, Chemistry and French were particularly taxing but English language, Scriptural Knowledge, Geography and Art became favourite subjects. The teachers obviously greatly influenced our thinking particularly in English Language lessons. Fountain pens rather than the newly introduced ball point pens were compulsory to ensure good hand writing, precise punctuation was expected at all times and the disapproving use of tedious abbreviations, set patterns which never changed for me. The fountain pen has always been my preferred writing implement and the use of expressions such as 'uni' instead of university, 'prezzies' and not presents continue to be anathema to me. The expression 'dumbing down' was not familiar to me but it does seem that the richness of our language has been sacrificed on the altar of modernisation.

The school had strong Christian worship principles and the Headmaster, Mr.. Rumsby was an ordained minister. Every morning there was a short service in the school hall and on Thursdays, we filed from the school to St Germain's church which was adjoining the school. We would normally have a full length Anglican Church service with a visiting preacher. The school choir was under the direction of our music and religious subject's teacher, Mr. Geoffrey Fletcher who was also the organist at one of Birmingham's principal churches, St Martin's in the Bull Ring. In an age when racism had little significance for school children I often wondered why two of our class mates were excused morning service and one day when curiosity could be restrained no longer they told me that they were Jews. No one, including the two boys ever made any issue of their religion.

I enjoyed singing and when I was selected as a boy soprano with the choir I still recall, 60 years later, the pleasure which I had from participating in such pieces as the classic 'Magnificat' or 'Nunc Dimitis'. Choir practice was on Monday evenings for one hour or more which meant a very long day before arriving home. The school choir also provided the training which allowed me to sing solo at my local church.

Unfortunately in the last few weeks of my first year, I was absent for 6 weeks with a little medical condition which adults euphemistically refer to as 'water work' problems and necessitated what for me was an embarrassing operation in hospital and a week in a convalescent home. That break resulted in my being 34th out of 35th in the form position and I lost ground in mathematics from which I never recovered completely and algebra and trigonometry always proved difficult. My own children and grandchildren had the benefit of calculators and computers which made my difficult subjects obsolete.

Following the 34th out of 35th result I tried to re-establish my more realistic capabilities and in the next term's exam results I moved up to 23rd position in the form. This achievement was marked by the award of a book prize for progress. I never really accepted that this was justified but the encouragement it stimulated subsequently moved me up to 9th in the form and eventually 1st although I slipped slightly in the ratings afterwards.

At that time, there seemed to be minimal complications in assessing the development of pupils. Examinations were held in spring, summer and autumn. With a final examination for the School Leaving Certificate. This examination was changed in 1951 to the two-tier General Certificate of Education in 'O' level and 'A' level. At the age of 16, pupils who achieved suitable passes in 'O' level would be allowed to continue into the sixth form where they could sit for their 'A' levels and progress to university. I achieved 4 '0' levels but had no ambition to continue schooling after the minimum leaving age of 16. I wanted the opportunity to earn my own living.

School reports in those days were succinct, using language which was clear and could be easily understood. "A keen worker"; "Satisfactory progress"; "He has worked well" would have been typical comments all contained in a single page. How different from the school reports brought home by my grandchildren which were impersonal, generated from computers, verbose and extending to 20 pages or more designed to give the impression that no pupil was below the desired standard of achievement. The insatiable demands of central Governmental Departments presumably demanded such changes to complement policies which generated increasingly confusing changes in testing of pupils.

A straight forward pass or fail in an examination was clear and unambiguous. 50 years later when the General Certificate of Education became the General School Certificate of Education results in the examinations were identified by letters of the alphabet in descending order from A starred, down to G all of which were considered passes. Similarly there developed much distrust from the public generally that the quality of examinations had deteriorated, exacerbated by the publicity generated from examination results which were reviewed and amended after complaints from disenchanted pupils.

The years of austerity affected every facet of life including school. Economy in the use of commodities was the rule and profligacy or waste was deplored. Exercise books were provided but a replacement could only be obtained after the form master had checked that it was full and signed the back cover which was torn off when the replacement was issued. This precluded the possibility of using the same full exercise book to obtain repeat issues.

School outings were virtually unknown. My children, grand children and their peers would experience trips to foreign countries as normal school activities but the only outing ever organised from my school whilst I was a pupil was to a local beauty spot known as Clent Hills about 20 miles away. We were required to pay the small amount of 5 shillings (an amount which would equate to the cost of 10 loaves of bread) and I remember my form master making an offer to sell his coat to provide the necessary money if any pupil was unable to pay himself.

Whilst there is a euphemism that school days are the happiest days of your life, on the whole I think my school days provided more happy memories than disappointing ones. At junior school, Miss Chapman, a pleasant young woman cycled to school and sometimes I was allowed to push her cycle for her when she dismounted. Miss Oakley was a stern woman who was authorised to use the cane, which she did when it suited her mood and

Mrs Radford, who was a matronly type of person who treated us as would a mother to her children

At grammar school Mr.. Showell was our woodwork teacher and his workshop gave me endless pleasure for his lessons. When cutting wood he had two basic rules which lived with me forever – "Always cut to cut lines and always cut on the waste side of the wood." One morning at school assembly it was announced that he had died suddenly I was very upset. Another sudden death was that of our art teacher, Mr. Brooks and again, because I was keen on his lessons, I was similarly upset.

Mr. Walker was the fearsome deputy head teacher. Of rotund physical appearance he was known throughout the school by the pupils as "Piggy Walker" but his reputation for use of the cane ensured that when he was addressed by school boys it was always the respectful "Sir."

Mr. Varley was the French teacher who loathed the smell of oranges and one day when I was somewhat thoughtless and peeled one of the forbidden fruits in the classroom, he walked in, we stood as was the normal practice and he demanded to know who was the recalcitrant boy, I owned up and was severely punished with a flick of his gown across my face causing stifled sniggers from the other boys. He then harangued us for several minutes about the offensive smell

Mr. Dillworth was our geography teacher and our form master for one year. He was also responsible supervising our lessons at the swimming baths for which we had to take a short bus ride. He was a popular teacher and we often speculated about his lunch time recreation activities because he would appear from the direction the school kitchen with a percolator of coffee and disappear into the school secretary' office.

Mr. Geoffrey Fletcher was our teacher of divinity, music, choir master and was also the organist at St Martin's in the Bull Ring, one of the churches which a group of us would visit often after the Salvation Army Services on Sunday evenings.

Chapter 3. Beyond School

The years at grammar school were important in formulating my future life in more ways than academic learning. In 1946 my brother Alfred returned home from military service. He had served in Burma with a doctor, Gilbert Dodd with whom he established a close friendship. Gilbert influenced Alf to become interested in The Salvation Army and on his demobilisation, Alf joined the local Corps. Alf was my soldier hero and I, together with my youngest sister Pat, also developed an interest in 'The Army'.

Pat changed her affections from the local Corps to the central Corps known as The Citadel which boasted a youth club, The Torchbearers, catering for teenagers. Influenced by Pat I joined the Torchbearers where I formed friendships with many persons who were to remain friends for many years and where I met a young girl, Ann Madden, who was eventually to become my wife.

Ann had been a member of the Salvation Army all her life as were her parents and grandparents. From the time I joined the Torchbearers' Youth Club it was perhaps a short, almost inevitable step to joining the Salvation Army as a junior soldier where I could enjoy my singing interest and learn to play a band instrument. The choice was the euphonium and that instrument has remained my favourite with its rich mellow tone. My mentor in learning to play was a man renowned for his virtuosity, Alf Watts whose skills I yearned to emulate.

With hindsight, I shudder to think what torments I gave to the neighbours where I lived when I practised but perhaps youthful enthusiasm overrode other considerations. Admittedly I used to place a pillow over the bell of the instrument to muffle the sound but I expect the neighbourly disturbance was still more than tactful.

The Army became an ever increasingly important factor in my life. Sundays were totally committed to Army activities attending open air meetings morning and evenings and indoor meetings morning afternoon and evening. I used to take food with me so that I could have lunch and tea at the Citadel where the meetings were held and practise my euphonium if I could do so without annoying the others who also stayed for their meals. I was expected to attend band practice evenings and because I cycled to school, from my home, I found it practical to go straight from school to the Citadel, do my home work and a little additional practice before the full band practice. In time I graduated from the junior band and became a member of the senior band. That opened up wider horizons including visits to other towns where we were hosted by members of the local corps.

Becoming a member of the Salvation Army band necessitated wearing uniform the expense of which was certainly beyond our family means. Several of the Salvationists were very helpful and a tunic from one, cap from another and overcoat from yet another solved the problem. I do recall that when needing a new pair of trousers, it was a choice between a grey pair for school uniform and a dark blue pair suitable for Army uniform. The Army uniform won but I had to wear the dark blue for school and the mis-match with other school choir members resulted in my being removed from the front row of the trebles because I looked out of place.

Whilst I formed lasting friendships with many of the Salvationists one person in particular influenced me to make a decision which was to affect my future life completely. He was the bandmaster, known affectionately as Bert Langworthy. Bert had been a policeman and when I was 14 years old, suggested to me that I might wish to join the police myself. That suggestion which I accepted was one which I was never to regret and subsequently resulted in nearly 40 years police service.

Because open air meetings were a normal activity for the Salvation Army, Sunday evenings were always something special. The open air meetings were held in the Bull Ring and although the market stalls were not trading on Sundays we always attracted large crowds with many people attending week after week. After the service, the band would march back to the Citadel, a distance of about 1 mile with the uniform ladies following our march and many non-members following us to our indoor service. There is no doubt that the Salvation Army were a popular sight on the streets of Birmingham and I never felt inhibited from wearing the uniform.

I also attended Corps Cadets' instruction given by one of the ladies of the Corps who held the title Corps Cadet Guardian. This was intended to teach not only Bible study but Doctrine of the Salvation Army. Although I was personally interested, with only 2 or 3 others attending and a less than imaginative instructor it was difficult to maintain enthusiasm.

I never thought that one day I would take on the role of instructor but when I was asked to become Corps Cadet Guardian, I agreed and made one or two dramatic changes. Instead of holding the Corps Cadets' instruction on a mid-week evening at the Citadel, Ann and I decided that our home being within a mile of the Citadel, we could hold our classes on Sundays after the normal afternoon meetings. The change was popular and whereas the previous attendance at classes may have been 2 or 3, our Sunday classes at our home increased the numbers to 12 – 13.

Whilst I would have never identified myself as a 'Bible Puncher', from the earliest age, I had strong Christian principles which I would like to think helped to develop my character and integrity. Although of limited intrinsic value or interest to a prospective employer, I consider my success in the O level GCE in Scriptural Knowledge at school was appropriate and a reflection on my personal beliefs. I never once considered that these beliefs and police work were incompatible and I have never been inhibited from acknowledging my Army background.

Working for a Living

I left school in the last week of July 1951 and commenced employment as a Police Cadet with the Birmingham City Police one week later such was my eagerness to earn my own living and make some contribution to the family finances. Perhaps it was my new found independence where I was a wage earner or possibly my father was becoming mellower as he aged, but I was conscious that he frequently made comments which suggested he was proud of my modest achievements.

There were 50 cadets employed by the Birmingham City Police, a Force of 2,000 officers and their training consisted of 4 monthly attachments to various departments or police stations. On two afternoons in each week we undertook army style drill and physical training. We also received first aid training and swimming which included life saving techniques. In life saving, whilst at school I had reached "Bronze Medallion" standard and it was relatively easy to progress to "Bronze Cross" and "Award of Merit". Not once in my life have I ever found it necessary to put my qualifications to the test but I often wonder how competent I would have been in an emergency.

My first attachment was to the Criminal Investigation Department and although my father expressed his congratulations saying that it was obviously a special job, the reality was working as a filing clerk, duplicating information crime sheets, running errands and acting as a general "Gofer" (Go for this and go for that). Duplicating the crime information sheets was time consuming and laborious requiring one person to collate the individual messages giving details of crimes committed. The typist would type the information on waxed stencils which I would then wrap round the ink drum of a duplicating machine and 'run off' the appropriate number of copies required to distribute to all police stations and departments. The first few copies produced by the duplicating machine were always indistinct and would be discarded. One day I was summoned to the officer in charge of the CID Clerks who showed me a large pile of discarded copies retrieved from the copying room.

The Chief Inspector left me frightened and in no doubt whatsoever that it was waste that could not be tolerated and that if I ever repeated the practice my career with Birmingham City Police would be short lived. He quite reasonably pointed out that a few sheets of paper could be used over and over again if the only requirement was to stimulate the flow of ink on the roller. It should be remembered that the year was 1951; a brief 6 years after the end of World War 2 when the country as a whole was struggling to recover from the enormous cost and devastation. During the war, not only was nothing wasted but recycling of every commodity was encouraged on pain of prosecution for failing to do so. Those attitudes persisted for years afterwards and the lesson I learned from my reprimand was to avoid waste whenever possible.

Although the work of filing case papers was routine and monotonous, there was always the diversion of reading juicy details of interesting cases and the opportunity to meet face to face with famous detectives.

My 4 month term in the CID Clerks was followed by a posting to a Divisional Police Headquarters where duties manning the telephone switchboard were relieved by opportunities to accompany officers on motor patrol and school crossing patrols. Many such activities would almost certainly be in contravention of the rules and regulations of proverbial red tape and would not be permitted in an age of "compensation culture", Health and Safety restrictions, or union demarcation issues etc. Fortunately the only limitation for me was the consent of the office sergeant and the agreement of friendly constables prepared to take me with them. I loved it.

One such diversion was to accompany the duty constable on the 'dispatch' run. Each division was allocated a small van which was used to collect correspondence from all of the stations on the respective divisions, take it to the divisional headquarters where it was sorted. Correspondence for headquarters and other divisions was taken to Force Headquarters where it was again sorted and then the vans would take their own divisional correspondence back to their divisions where it was again sorted and distributed to the individual stations. This cumbersome labour intensive system was time consuming and a far cry from the computerised systems which in later years would dominate every aspect of communications but in the period of my Police Cadet Service was regarded as a much sort after privilege and provided a sound grounding in geographical knowledge of the city.

One particular requirement at the police station where I was employed was to signal the commencement of two minutes silence at 11.0am on 11th November, to commemorate the end of hostilities after the Second World War. That was 1951; traffic ceased to move and the population stood silent. I was allowed to connect two electric wires which fired a maroon in a sand filled dust bin in the station car park. Sadly these simple acts of remembrance did not survive for many years afterwards.

Further postings included the Traffic and Communications Department, Aliens' Registration Office and the Recruiting Department. The Sergeant in the Recruiting Office was also responsible for deciding which individual cadet would be posted to particular police stations or departments. On completion of the term in the Recruiting, I was posted to the police station approximately 1 mile from my home; I wonder how that happened?

Most police stations and the Force Headquarters had a snooker table and in common with many of my contemporaries, I developed skills on the green baize which may have indicated that the duties for which we were paid were not too onerous, allowing time for these other pursuits and improving my table tennis skills in competition against some of the more competent police officers.

This two year period of my life provided much job satisfaction and formed a solid foundation for my ambition to become a police officer, a decision I never regretted until the day I retired. If there was any disappointment at all it was that the pay was very low, paid monthly and in order to give my mother a reasonable amount for my keep, there was very little left for personal expenses. The bicycle which had served me well in my school days was an equally important feature of my life as a police cadet providing me with reliable transport.

Chapter 4. Military Service

In 1953 with few exceptions, National Military Service was compulsory for all young men when they attained 18 years. When approaching my 18th birthday, I receive many words of advice from ex service men who recommended their own army regiments but the khaki uniform held no attraction for me and when the appointed day arrived, it was to the Royal Air Force that I offered my loyalty.

From a reception at a Royal Air Force establishment in Gloucester where I was 'kitted out' I was posted to R.A.F.Cardington in Bedfordshire which was a holding Unit for new entrants pending postings to various recruit training centres. The brief period of stay at Cardington scarcely allowed for friendships to develop but some of those fledgling contacts reappeared many times in the following 3 years of Royal Air Force service.

My posting from Cardington was to RAF West Kirby in Cheshire, which the doom mongers would have us believe was the most oppressive of the recruit training centres but whether the reputation was justified is purely subjective. Certainly as soon as I arrived with my fellow recruits, we were left in no doubt whatsoever that discipline was the order of the day and no concessions were allowed. We were not allowed to walk anywhere, we had to march and perhaps my drill experience in the police cadets bore me in good stead from the onset whilst my companions in the first few days were constantly harangued for their inability to march correctly.

Early experiences included the 'voluntary' offers to become blood donors with the encouragement from our drill instructors – "We need blood donors; all cowards one pace backwards march!" Obviously the whole intake of recruits became blood donors which, on reflection was very commendable. After this enforced induction I became a regular donor on return to 'Civvy Street' until reaching the age when I was deemed to be too old.

Of course there were 'volunteers' and 'volunteers'. Apart from the enforced volunteering we were given an opportunity to volunteer for specialised commitments which would be rewarded by modest additions to pay. With a weekly pay of about £1 the temptation for more money was a strong inducement. One such offer was to take part in a research programme at Porton Down Laboratories, a high security Government Establishment. At this time we lived in a period referred to as 'The Cold War' when the western world expected nuclear missiles to be fired from Soviet countries who anticipated similar aggression from NATO (North Atlantic Treaty Organisation) countries. The research programme was intended to determine how to survive a nuclear attack but I decided that it held no attraction for me.

Tragically, some individuals who did volunteer suffered terrible consequences after they were subjected to experiments which included exposure to toxic gases and liquids. One individual died whilst the experiments were taking place and 50 years were to pass before a second inquest determined that the airman had been unlawfully killed by the Ministry of Defence, overturning an inquest in 1953 which had returned a 'death by misadventure' verdict..

I have often wondered what would have happened to me if I had volunteered to take the small additional supplement to my weekly wage in return for inclusion in the experiments.

My early days a RAF recruit training changed somewhat dramatically when at some point it was learned that I was able to play the euphonium. I was immediately drafted into the Station band and thereafter, most mornings whilst my fellow recruits endured rifle range training and other activities, I was ensconced with my fellow musicians practising for the occasions when the band was required to perform at Station parades etc.

This was not to say that I never ventured onto the firing range but those occasions were only with the permission of the Band Master, a delightful Flight Sergeant who was in the twilight years of his career but fiercely protective of his band and band members. Their duties took priority over every other commitment.

The practices and performances with the band provided a wonderful balance against the incessant barrack and kit inspections petty criticisms from junior officers hoping to impress their subordinates and pressures from non commissioned officers which verged on what in later years would be regarded as bullying.

During this period of national service which was only 8 years after the end of the war, commodities were still in short supply and with my fellow recruits I would scour the refuse areas to find cardboard cartons to be cut into suitable shapes to ensure that our kit inspections displayed socks, shirts, underclothing all neatly squared off in precise and acceptable shapes.

Although discipline was rigid and sometimes overbearing, living in the same dormitory hut with 9 other men, a strong sense of comradeship developed. We all depended on each other. Floors were scrupulously polished, toilets impeccably cleaned and billet surrounds meticulously tidied knowing that any defects would bring retribution on everyone.

After 8 weeks of intense training we were posted to various other locations for further training in our respective trades. Having been accepted for the Royal Air Force Police I was sent to Netheravon, a bleak location on Salisbury Plain 20 miles from Salisbury.

Salisbury Plain in winter can be inhospitable outside the cloistered huts and buildings of the camp itself. The billets always seemed to be at a lower temperature than would be acceptable in civilian life and meals were served in a mess more akin to a barn than an eating establishment but complaining was not encouraged and the conditions were accepted as part of Service life.

Instruction in our forthcoming police duties was given in classrooms approximately half a mile from the residential quarters and continuing the practice learned at recruit training, we marched along the featureless road several times a day. Netheravon is near to Boscombe Down, which was a classified establishment having a reputation for top secret experiments and military developments. It was not unusual to experience military aircraft flying at low level and perhaps to relieve his tedium our escorting NCO would scream at his recruits to dive into the ditch at the side of the road.

The NCO explained that the object of responding immediately without question was for our safety because had they been hostile aircraft we would have been dead men otherwise. After the second or third such experience we were more sceptical and regarded it as his warped sense of humour.

All police recruits who successfully passed the initial training were qualified to become Station Police but those considered suitable undertook further training to qualify as Provost Police. An essential element of this further training was to drive four-wheeled motor vehicles or motor cycles. I was allocated to motor cycles and whilst our instructors rode superb Triumph 110 machines the trainees were expected to master their techniques on Royal Enfield 350 motor bikes.

The road along which were marched daily was bounded by a ditch on one side and ploughed fields on the other. Never having ridden a motor cycle before, it wasn't long before I found myself trying to ride across the ploughed field and when the engine stalled realised that pushing a motor cycle over ploughed land is extremely difficult.

Having successfully completed the Police training course we were visited by the Assistant Provost Marshall who was anxious to select personnel for a top secret establishment in Cornwall. I applied but when I was interviewed and disclosed my police cadet background in Birmingham, I was posted to No 7 RAF Police Headquarters at Castle Bromwich scarcely one mile from my home and the location of many happy childhood memories. To enhance the pleasure, one of my beloved Spitfires stood silent guard at the gate of the airfield. Perhaps Service life wasn't too bad after all.

I was posted to the security section of the police detachment under the command of a Flight Lieutenant and our duties required that we test the security of RAF establishments throughout central England and Wales. Our methods included gaining access by subterfuge or straight forward burglary techniques although we were not allowed to commit structural damage. It was only 8 years since the war had finished and espionage and subversive political infiltration were still concerns for cold war Britain. We were expected to identify any breaches in physical security of RAF establishments, particularly if the sites were classified.

Not all our checks went according to plan. One day our commanding officer gave me and one of my colleagues a brief. We were to go to a classified RAF establishment in north Wales. We were told that this site stored 'eggs' whether they were Easter eggs or chicken's eggs was for us to find out. Security at the site was in the hands of the Air Ministry Police which suggested that we were unlikely to gain entry by subterfuge. We therefore decided on a burglary approach.

Arriving at the site some time after midnight, dressed in dark clothing, we scaled the perimeter wire and made our way to the hangers where we believed the 'eggs' were stored. We found that the huge sliding doors of the hangers did not fit flush, leaving a gap sufficiently wide to squeeze through. As I was about to gain access by this means, I was grabbed from behind, unceremoniously forced to the ground and I found myself looking up at two Air Ministry Police Officers armed with pick axe handles. I considered that it was not appropriate to argue and accompanied them to the guardroom where my colleague and

I were eventually allowed to establish our credentials. Obviously we had confirmed the effectiveness of their security arrangements and learned that the 'eggs' which were stored in the hangers were quantities of highly toxic gasses which required that anyone entering must wear protective clothing and masks. Perhaps we were fortunate that we had been caught.

These security checks covering a large geographical area obviously required the use of a vehicle and on this particular occasion my colleague suggested I drive back to our base over 100 miles away. It was in the early hours of the morning and when we arrived back safely there was some casual conversation about how long I had been driving and when he realised I had never driven before and did not hold a licence he realised his mistake.

Another aspect of our duties was to carry out vetting procedures on persons seeking employment at RAF establishments. Anyone with extremist political affiliations could be considered as security risks and it was our responsibility to identify any such trends.

It was whilst serving at Castle Bromwich that my friendship with a young woman at the Salvation Army gradually developed into a marriage which was to survive over 50 years.

Love Will Find a Way

In Birmingham there was one bus route which skirted the perimeter of the city and after a few miles, diverted through some of the inner suburbs until reaching its terminal point in the city centre. This bus route was tailor made for the development of my love life. One of the young ladies at the Salvation Army and I had been friends for 4 or 5 years but had gradually become attracted to each other. She was a student nurse with no other ambition at that time than to pursue her career as far as possible and attain the highest level in her profession.

The number 28 bus passed the front gate of RAF Castle Bromwich and conveniently also passed the gates of the hospital 6 or 7 miles away, where my young lady, Ann Madden, worked. Discipline for student nurses at the hospital dictated that they must be in their quarters by 10.00pm otherwise they would be locked out and later required to give their explanations to the Matron. Ann's tour of duty usually finished at 8.30pm and if lucky we could be on a bus into the city centre by about 8.50pm

On such a tight time schedule, all that we could do was call at a coffee house, order "two coffees, one black no sugar" a precious few minutes for our private conversation, then board the bus back to the hospital. It was at this point that I realised I had latent athletic capabilities which in later years would become an important factor in my life. Many of the bus routes in Birmingham had 'Bundy clocks'; points on the journey where the driver was required to insert a key to activate the machinery which would record the time at which he was at that point. Many years later technology would produce the tachograph which served the same purpose.

When Ann and I alighted from the bus at the hospital as near 10.00pm as we dared for a goodnight kiss, I knew that about ¾ mile further down the bus route, there was a Bundy clock and if I ran fast enough, I could expect to catch the same bus so that I could return to RAF Castle Bromwich without having to wait another ½ hour for the next bus.

Of course there were occasions when our courtship was not quite so rushed, particularly on Sundays when we would normally spend most of the day at The Army or travelling from her home to the Services. Even so there was very little opportunity to share each other's private company unless we went to a theatre or similar attraction. However at some point it was possible for me to "pop the question" and determine that we both wanted to get married. There could be no question of a lavish wedding, a hugely expensive engagement ring or any of the other extravagancies which we could not afford.

In September 1954 accompanied by her parents, we visited the nearby town of Leamington Spa where there was some sort of festival taking place which included scenes from the children's story book 'Alice in Wonderland'. It may not have been everyone's idea of a romantic venue but we actually became engaged, a diamond ring placed on her finger in the rabbit hole.

Obviously the good fortune which had arranged my posting so close to my fiancée was about to desert me and shortly afterwards I learned that I was to be posted to RAF Steamer Point in Aden. If the limited time we had spent together because of her nurse's duties were testing times, the following 2 years would prove to be much more testing for young love

The Barren Rocks of Aden

Situated on the most southern tip of the Arabian Peninsula, the port of Aden had been a British Protectorate since 1839 until the British withdrew in 1967 and became known as South Yemen. Rudyard Kipling described it as "the barrack stove of Arabia" and with temperatures rising to 120 degrees Fahrenheit, it is easy to understand why.

When I boarded the Avro York aircraft at RAF Lynham, I was delighted to meet Peter Green, one of my fellow recruits from RAF Police training days who was also posted to Aden. A brief stop-over in Malta and then in the middle of the night we touched down at Waddi Halfa, a remote airfield in the Sudan. We were served a meal which included some sort of meat but the myriads of small flies that were everywhere, including on our food made me realise that I was not at all hungry. We took off and the next occasion we set foot on soil was at RAF Khormaksar, approximately 10 miles from Steamer Point. I distinctly recall making a comment to fellow passengers that the aircraft felt and sounded as though it was falling to pieces and it was no surprise to me that very shortly afterwards the YORK was withdrawn from service.

In 1954, the port was still a very important staging post and a large variety of ships including many troop ships berthed for refuelling or to take on or discharge cargo. The local post office displayed schedules of ships' arrivals which provided some interest for the Service personnel outside their normal duties. Across a narrow bay lay the oil refinery Little Aden which provided opportunity to mix with non-native civilians. Other than the RAF bases, the only other acknowledged centre of population was the town of Crater which, as the name suggests had developed in the extinct crater adjacent to the highest peak in the area – mount Sham- Sam. Although there was no specific bar on travelling further afield, the Yemen border was very close and as the political tensions increased such excursions were discouraged.

Apart from the incessant heat, Aden was dry. In almost 2 years I experienced only one short downpour of rain which caused so much excitement that many ran out into the street in sheer exuberance. Without rain, it may have been difficult to understand why there was such lush vegetation in the ornamental gardens principal of which was Queen Victoria Gardens dominated by a statue of Her Majesty. The mystery of the water supply was quickly solved when we realised that the suction vehicles which emptied the cess pits, pumped the water onto the gardens. It may be questioned whether the perfume of the plants benefited as did the roots.

One feature of RAF Steamer Point was the Detention Barracks and whilst my colleagues undertook other duties including town patrols in the 'off-limits' areas, I was allocated to the DB. Although I held the rank of corporal on arrival, I was shortly afterwards promoted to sergeant and took charge of the Establishment. At that time the majority of Service personnel were airmen but there was also a strong contingent of soldiers who provided the majority of our temporary residents.

Religious persuasions were acknowledged in three broad categories: Roman Catholic, Church of England and PMUB. At first I was puzzled by this terminology until I realised the initials referred to 'Presbyterian, Methodist and United Board', in other words, everyone of the Christian faith who were not R.C. or C of E. The PMUB church was located up a hill which was barren of any vegetation and no more than a large cave, appropriately known as 'The Church in the Rock'. Our minister was from the Church of Scotland and one other regular member of the Church was a Salvationist from Chester-le-Street in County Durham.

From somewhere, he had acquired a large collection of Salvation Army band records and we played them frequently on the local Services broadcasting network. The music of the bands brought us just a little nearer home in our minds if not in body.

My sister Vi sent me a beautiful Bible for my birthday whilst I was serving in Aden and without embarrassment I left it in full view on my bedside locker together with a small Salvation Army flag on a miniature flag pole. I never experienced any animosity and when detainees in the Detention Barracks asked to attend Church services it was natural that I would be their escort.

Driving a vehicle was a necessity and within a few months I had persuaded my superior officers that I should have driving lessons which were undertaken in an Austin 3 ton truck instructed by a corporal from the Mechanical Transport section. Because I had driven in the UK, albeit as an unlicensed driver, I quickly qualified even though on one occasion in the narrow back streets I had clipped a camel cart and my instructor insisted that I should not stop but drive as quickly as possible away from the scene of the mishap.

Driving duties included a requirement to convey one of the Police Officers for night duty at X Group which was a storage area for ammunition and explosives. His duties were to supervise local 'chowkidars' employed as security guards armed only with pick-axe handles. Although the political situation was not of great concern at that time, the situation was to change dramatically within a few years involving bloody military action and the withdrawal of the British from Aden. I can only assume that security at X Group had been improved since my service there.

Although Aden did not feature regularly in the world Press there were occasions when my relatives and friends at home could appreciate what was happening. One such incident was when Aden was due to be visited by the Bishop of Khartoum. His aircraft was intended to land at Khormaksar where the runway finished a few hundred yards short of the water of the bay. Unfortunately the pilot touched down short of the runway and we were treated to the spectacle of an air-sea rescue. Probably the pride of the pilot was the only serious damage.

A much more serious incident occurred when the wife of a Wing Commander was paddling in the sea with her infant son. Sharks were prevalent in the area and every day local fishermen could be seen with long poles over their shoulder from which dangled sharks of various sizes. Sadly a shark attacked the woman who died from her injuries. That occurrence caused not only headlines for the world Press but also fomented political unrest when agitators claimed that native fishermen were killed every day by sharks but no one was interested. When a white woman was killed, it was headline news.

The lido area where we swam or sun bathed was also an attraction for troops on the visiting troop ship and was protected by a large area of shark netting.

With few activities to occupy us, I found relief from boredom by my letter writing. I wrote to my mother and sisters regularly and wrote every day to Ann. Because the postal delivery system was spasmodic, I would sometimes receive 2 or 3 letters from her on one day and perhaps a whole week with no letters.

It was in one of her letters that I received news that hit me like a severe blow. The hospital at which Ann worked specialised in the treatment of tuberculosis and her letter was to inform me that she had been diagnosed with the disease and would require surgery. The operation would result in the removal of part of one of her lungs and she was likely to be in hospital and convalescing for many months.

I approached my senior officers with a request that I be granted compassionate leave but was refused. There was little I could do to alter the situation. I could not be home to comfort and reassure her and had to depend on letter writing to remind her that I loved her. The emotional pain subsided with the passage of time but the underlying anxiety remained.

Although my duties were mainly in the Detention Barracks I was also required to investigate allegations or suspicions of offences committed by service personnel. One particular incident involved the theft of money from an airman's billet. My enquiries identified the culprit and he was charged and a Courts Martial was convened. Unfortunately it was towards the end of my normal tour of overseas service and my repatriation date was postponed. Wanting to return home to Ann as soon as possible, waiting for the court procedure was an unwelcome extension to my time in Aden.

However, the day of departure eventually arrived and because there were no service flights available, I was booked on to a BOAC Argonaut aircraft as civilian passenger. Certainly the flight home was more comfortable than the Avro York but I had to purchase a new outfit of civilian clothing because I was not permitted to fly home in my uniform.

Ann had spent months in hospital and convalescence at home but she was on the platform at New Street railway Station to welcome me and for the first time in my life I travelled in a black cab to take her home to my parents.

Chapter 5. Return to Civilian Life

As soon as possible after demobilisation I applied to join the Birmingham City Police which I expected to be a mere formality. However I had to undergo various medical checks etc which included a visit to the Radiography Unit of the main hospital. With her own experience still very much part of her everyday life, I think that Ann was more worried than I was when I was recalled for further X-rays. Whatever had been the problem with the first check, nothing was detected on the subsequent visit and shortly afterwards I was accepted as a probationary constable.

The initial training was at a police establishment in Staffordshire which had also been used during the war years as a camp for prisoners of war. It would be disingenuous to suggest that the trainee police officers were subjected to similar restriction of liberty as the previous occupants but we might well have been because we were miles from the nearest town of Stoke-on-Trent with no individuals having their own transport.

The training establishment accommodated police officers from 15 or 16 other police forces and because our responsibilities would involve different duties depending on whether we were from a city or county force, we were required to have an understanding of legislation from diseases of animals to Town Police Clauses offences much of which would be totally irrelevant in later life.

My particular intake was divided into 2 and in every examination which we were required to pass, I was top of the class. In the other half of the intake the top student was a police woman: Joy Glanville who was to become a lifelong friend and for whom a few years later I would take on the role of matchmaker.

From the following intake of recruits I struck up a friendship with Malcolm Pinder who was a few years older than I and had been a merchant seaman. Malcolm confided in me that he was attracted to Joy and because we were class mates it was not long before Joy confided that she would like to get to know my friend Malcolm. One of the problems was that Joy's up-bringing had been on a higher social level than Malcolm's which both of them considered to be a likely barrier. In the age old adage of 'Love will find a way' not only did they marry but lived next door to Ann and me when we were housed in police accommodation.

The recruit training included physical exercise and Wednesday afternoons were sports afternoons. Various activities were encouraged with varying degrees of compulsion and whereas cross country running was considered by some as the punishment event, for me, it was the preferred choice. I found that I could complete the 3 mile course in sufficiently good time to join a volley ball game whilst the other runners were finishing. From that moment my cards were marked by the physical training instructor who was also a cross country running enthusiast and had provided a running trophy for competition in his own Force. In subsequent years he and I were regular competitors representing our respective Forces in cross country competitions.

Having completed basic training we all returned to our respective police forces where in Birmingham we undertook further local training which consisted of part beat work and part classroom work learning local bye-laws and procedures.

At this time I lived in single men's accommodation at Edward Road Police station along with 6 or 7 other constables including Malcolm. The area which we policed included busy shopping locations, notoriously troublesome pubs and Balsall Heath, one of Birmingham's red light districts. For any police officer with determination and an inquisitive nature, the scope for positive police work was endless.

Whilst at the recruit training school having developed an interest and some degree of success in cross-country running I was quickly identified as a recruit for the City Police cross-country team and one of the established members, John Thomas, persuaded me to join him as a member of Small Heath Harriers. The club was in the top flight of athletic clubs and the competitions in which I was included as a member enabled me to extend my running ability. I was frequently included in Small Heath Harriers teams for road relay races including the Manchester to Blackpool; Bristol to Weston; London to Brighton and also in the county and National cross-country championships. With the experience I gained I developed a reputation as the man to beat in our inter-police teams' competitions. We undertook frequent engagements against Staffordshire, Worcestershire County, Worcester City, Warwickshire, Northampton Borough, Northamptonshire County and local RAF stations.

It was not only cross-country running which was encouraged by the Force but every year there was an inter-division athletics afternoon which included a 1 mile race for the 'Black' trophy, a ½ mile race for the Alan Paley cup and a medley relay, This consisted of 4 runners, the first completing 880 yards, the second and third runners each competing 220 yards and the fourth runner running 440 yards.

In 1959 at the City Police Sports ground, Tally Ho! I lined up for the 1 mile race with my very good friend Goff Chambers who was a member of Birchfield Harriers with whom I had served in the Royal Air Force Police at castle Bromwich. Goff and I regularly trained together but on the running track, no quarter was asked or given; we were rivals. There were other runners in the race but the result was never in doubt, the winner would be Goff or me. Goff was second and I carried off the winner's trophy – 'The Black Trophy' which had been donated by a member of the Force of that name.

In the 880 yards, Goff was anxious to turn the tables but with less than 220 yards to the finishing line, I surprised him with a sudden burst and again, Goff was relegated to second place. That added 'The Alan Paley' cup to my collection the award having been donated by the father of a constable who had died in tragic circumstances. The medley relay was the final event of the afternoon and my Division's team consisted of me for the 880 yards, two very good sprinters, Les Handley and Bob Twyford for the 2 x 220 yards and a young constable, Jim Murphy who we had pressured into completing the team because we had no one else. Jim did not consider himself a runner and was doubtful that he could run 440 yards.

For the third time that afternoon, Goff and I lined up for the start of the race and matched each other for the first lap, Goff always slightly ahead. I knew that if our team was to win, I had to make a special effort and with 300 yards to go, completely outwitted Goff by putting in my sprint finish. I was able to open a lead of 30 – 40 yards when I handed the baton to the first of our sprinters Bob Twyford who extended the lead to almost 100 yards which was maintained when he handed over to Les Handley. Although Jim had insisted that he couldn't run, he ran his heart out, stumbling the last 10 – 15 yards to snatch victory from Goff's team.

In addition to the inter-Divisional sports events the Midland Police Championships provided competition between the Police Forces in athletic competitions. As would be expected with the competition more intense, my successes were fewer than in the local events but in the Midland Police competitions made the 3 mile event my speciality winning in successive years. Although Birmingham City Police always entered teams in the National Police Championships I never achieved any outstanding results other than finishing 9th one year in the National cross-country championships, an event in which an international star, Police Constable Stan Eldon always excelled.

However, as an athlete, until the day I die, I will remain Birmingham City Police one mile and half mile champion and also the Midlands Police three mile champion because subsequent to my achievements 1 mile and half mile races were replaced by metric measurements (other than the Emsley Car Mile) and Birmingham City Police ceased to exist when it was incorporated into the West Midlands Police.

The ability to run was to prove an advantage on many occasions during my police career.

The First Arrest

Police pay in 1956 was not generous and any opportunity to work overtime was always welcomed. One night, Malcolm and I had worked our normal tour of duty from 2.00pm until 10.00pm and donning civilian raincoats over our uniforms, carried out a patrol and observations in the shopping area where burglaries were occurring far too frequently. After a fruitless 4 hours, we mounted our cycles to ride the 2 miles back to our beds. We saw two men walking in the opposite direction and at 2.30am it seemed that something was not quite right. It took only a few minutes questioning for them to admit they had just burgled a house. Brendan and Alfred Lynch were their names which I think will remain in my memory for ever. We returned to the station where more experienced officers took over the investigation on our behalf and two probationary constables with barely 2 months service had notched their first success.

Other successes followed but on occasions fate decreed otherwise. One night I was walking along a dark alleyway towards the road when a male person stepped out ahead of me, pulled his raincoat open and a young woman walking past him screamed and ran away. I should have run towards him before I shouted but I didn't and he had the advantage of several yards as he escaped and I missed my first indecent exposure arrest.

Walking the beat included duties which allowed ready contact with members of the public, none more so than school crossing duties which on the early turn shift required the police officers to be at the school crossing to see the children safely in, out at lunch time and back into school after lunch. Not much time for other police work but emphasised one of the principles of policing – protection of life when children and their parents could identify with the friendly policeman. However even such a routine commitment could produce unforeseen problems and one day whilst standing in the middle of the road whilst the children crossed I glanced over my shoulder to check that the traffic was suitably controlled.

What I saw made me think I was dreaming. Filling the whole of the width of the road was a herd of cattle. There must have been some mistake; I was on patrol barely one mile from the centre of England's second city, not in some rural farmland area. What no one had told me was that it was still the practice to bring cattle by rail, unload them at nearby sidings and drive them down this particular street to the abattoir which was about half a mile away. In fact that occasion was probably the last and shortly afterwards the practice was discontinued.

If my early successes were likely to create some feeling of self importance it was shattered one day when standing at the street corner, tall and athletically slim, a lady paused, eyed me up and down then said "I shouldn't stand too close to that drain love; you might slip down the cracks." I soon learned that she was one of the 'characters' of the district, salt of the earth and a valuable source of gossip and information. She knew all of the policemen by name and I was added to her extended family of friends.

Other useful contacts were cultivated by the 'put ups' – shop keepers who were prepared to provide a cup of tea or a place where officers could hide away for a cigarette. If the sergeant caught us indulging in such practices we could expect to be for the proverbial high jump.

Although most police stations had permanent civilian cooks to provide meals for the officers, night duties always required that one officer would be detailed for canteen duty. Refreshment times would be at 1.00am and 2.00am but an astute constable could stretch the time off the streets from perhaps 11.30pm until 4.00am and the basic skills of preparing meals for his contemporaries was good training for future life.

Although I could not officially drive, it seemed that I was frequently posted as observer to the area cars when the regular crew men were unavailable. Those duties extended my experience because we were expected to deal with a range of duties not possible for a foot patrol officer. Road traffic accidents, violent disturbances, stolen car chases, house fires, in fact any and every occasion when police would be called. Those were the days when police cars were black with a bell, many years before the 'blues and twos' of the multi coloured patrol vehicles and indeed the days when police officers always wore helmets or caps and did not carry firearms.

On the occasion of one such tour of duty I found myself dealing with my first fatal accident. The death of a young motor cyclist who had collided with a motor car required the professionalism to deal with the matter in hand whilst observing the need for compassion to those involved and their relatives.

It was necessary to escort the body to the mortuary for the purpose of proving continuity that the body taken from the scene was the one to be the subject of the coroner's inquest. Having never actually handled a cadaver previously I was cautiously attempting very gently to lift the body out of the casket in which it had been conveyed. At that point my very experienced colleague gave me valuable advice. "That is not a human being it is just a lump of meat and bone so pick it up." Whilst the comment may have seemed somewhat crude the logic was that in such circumstances sentimentality must not interfere with the need to undertake the job in hand. There were to be many occasions in the future when that advice was to become second nature.

Informing relatives of the death of their loved one is never easy and again with the advice of more experienced officers, the practice would be to call on the neighbour initially to get some idea of how the intended recipient of bad news would take it. My first "death message" was to inform a lady that her elderly husband had died in hospital and following the advice given I called on the next door neighbour and asked if Mrs. Jones lived next door. Not only did she live next door but she was actually in the house at which I was making the enquiry. Realising that I would have to deliver the information there and then, I did so and was amazed at the response – "About bleeding time, I wondered how long it would be!"

It may have been a little black humour but at least I had overcome the uncertainty and embarrassment of my first death message with no emotional breakdown to deal with.

In those early days of police experience in Birmingham, police constables were required to patrol a specified area referred to as 'beats' and would be given usually 4 'points' at which the sergeant could rendezvous with the constable. These points would normally be located at a public telephone box or a police pillar known colloquially as a 'blue boy' which had a public telephone to use in the case of an emergency and also a police phone inside the locked side of the 'blue boy' the pillar being surmounted by a blue lamp which would flash if the local station needed to attract the attention of the patrolling officer.

Not only were areas of the beats specifically identified but the patrolling constable was expected to remain on that beat, no so much as crossing a road onto another beat other than for very good reason. Of course human nature would always interfere with disciplinary restrictions and particularly on night duty it was normal practice for constables on adjoining beats to meet and spend some time gossiping with each other providing the sergeant, or worse still the inspector, was not on the prowl.

On one such occasion at about 3.00am, my pal, Ron Brotherhood and I were sharing a few minutes of illicit conversation when a young boy, perhaps 10 or 11 years old ran towards us and breathlessly gasped "Quick, mom's having the baby." Both of us were equally inexperienced and looking nervously at each other, I breathed a sigh of relief when the boy gave his address which was on Ron's side of the road.

Whilst I summoned an ambulance, using the 'blue boy' Ron went to the address and assisted in the emergency birth which resulted in him looking very pale and ready to faint when I again met up with him at the address. So, Ron had experienced the value of an oft expressed myth – the piece of string suggested by some 'old salts' to be added to the list of 'appointments' which we would produce when parading for duty - truncheon, handcuffs, first aid pouch and torch if on night duty. Ron was the only person I ever knew who may have benefited from that advice but the parents named the child after Ron. He subsequently received a commendation and award of 2 guineas from the Watch Committee (our Police Authority) for action at childbirth. Personally I found this rather amusing because our first aid training stipulated the least done the better other than placing the child between the mother's legs.

Walking the beat was not just an aimless wandering and a conscientious officer would develop his own skills, walking on the outside of the pavement during daylight hours when he could be seen and talk to people and close to the building line at night so that he would not be seen too readily. He would also look up and it is surprising what can be seen at night for an inquisitive gazer!

We were also expected to check premises to make sure they were properly secured. Standing in a darkened doorway, during the hours of darkness virtually invisible when wearing a cape, many were the times a person has walked past and a few paces further on suddenly realised with a start that there had been an apparently bodyless face looking at them from the doorway. The effect could be enhanced if the policeman made a moan or cough. This misguided sense of humour was almost my undoing on one occasion when a young woman ran down the road screaming after such an experience.

Apart from these modest diversions, checking not only the front of buildings but also the rear could have unexpected consequences. On one occasion another colleague, Gordon Laws, was patrolling his beat and went up an alleyway between two buildings. For whatever reason I never learned but a resident living opposite noticed the officer and realised after some time that he had not reappeared. There could have been many explanations but the lady concerned thought it was so unusual that she dialled 999.

We found Gordon at the back of the premises with a knife embedded in his back. He was still alive but suffered such serious injury that he was partially paralysed and after many months of convalescence was relocated to permanent office duties. The perpetrator of the assault was eventually traced and sentenced to a long term of imprisonment.

Speaking to people on the street always seemed to me to be an obvious and natural part of my duties and I learned a valuable lesson in developing this skill at about 12.50am one night. The streets were deserted and recalling an old adage that only thieves and policemen walked the streets at the dead of night, I saw a man who roused my suspicions. The only justification was that it was 12.50am. My initial approach to him must have been arrogant or at least brusque and he resented my manner. Maintaining my presumed authority I questioned him as to his identity and where he lived. As I persisted, he commented that he supposed I would want to check that his address was correct and determined not to lose face I agreed.

He lived about a mile from the point at which I had stopped him and during the walk we developed a more friendly rapport and he made one very important comment. He said that if only my first words to him had been "Good evening," his reaction to me would have been more co-operative. I never forgot those words of wisdom and vowed that unless the situation dictated otherwise, a friendly approach was always likely to prove more productive. Using this approach I found that I could stop a potential suspect, ascertain all I needed to know about him or her and send them on their way without them even realising they had been interrogated. Of course if my questioning revealed some criminal activity it was then a case of "You're nicked," although I cannot honestly remember ever using that expression.

The hour of receiving my valued advice was significant. Officers on night duty would go to their police station for refreshments at 1.00am or 2.00am. On this particular occasion I was due to take mine at 1.00am, in fact that had been my intention when I stopped the man on the street. When I did not report at the police station at the appointed time and neither did I appear at 2.00am my sergeant and inspector, perhaps fearing another Gordon Laws type incident instigated a search for me. When I walked into the station at about 2.30am the reception was not immediately welcoming but after explanation, instead of disciplinary proceedings I was allowed to eat my overcooked bacon egg and beans which had been left in the oven by whoever was duty cook that night.

Every officer would develop his own skills, whether they were 'hunches' sixth sense' or whatever and I always thought that if I was walking along behind an individual who appeared nervous at my closeness, if he turned left down a side street, I would turn left; if he then turned left again, there was something odd and worth investigating. Of course not all criminals turn left and left again but the principle held good and on many occasions I found that my suspect had pockets full of coins stolen from a gas meter by way of burglary and I was able to arrange overnight accommodation in the cells.

On one occasion I actually assisted a burglar who was leaving premises through a window and I steadied him as he dropped the last few feet. I cannot now recall his comment but I think it may have been an expression of bad luck and you can never find a copper when you want one.

In my early days as a constable, using initiative was expected which provided the opportunity to experience unusual incidents. The police station's area where I was based was dissected by a railway line which was a constant source of worry with children trespassing. One day in an effort to identify the children I boarded a steam locomotive at the nearby sidings and rode on the footplate to the point where the youngsters regularly congregated. It may be an under-statement to say that they were surprised when the engine shuddered to a halt and a police constable jumped down to take their names and addresses. However we were more concerned to prevent a serious accident than to pursue trespassing offences.

By the time my probationary 2 years had passed, I had developed a reasonable reputation as a thief taker and although I had never made any representation to be considered for the Criminal Investigation Department, one day my chief inspector told me he had put my name forward to be an Aid to CID. Such appointments would not normally be offered to a constable so young in service and would expect to be for an initial 6 months during which suitability for permanent transfer would be assessed. When I replied that I had not applied he left me in no doubt that I was to do so promptly. I wondered if he had already made the necessary arrangements having overlooked the fact that I hadn't made any overtures.

Transfer to CID Duties

I had mixed feelings about CID duties. My impression was that detective officers spent too much time in pubs and worked many hours more than their uniform colleagues. However it was apparent that some of my senior officers considered that widening my horizons would be to my benefit. I was posted to the same police station where I had worked as a uniform constable and where I had lived for the first few months of my police career, Edward Road, an area I knew well.

The permanent CID officers were Detective Sergeant Cyril Edwards who had a no-nonsense approach to catching criminals whether there was supportive evidence or not; Gordon Lauder a pleasant Scot who was generous to his friends but resolutely tight fisted in the company of any outside his close circle of acquaintances and Bill Coates, a dour Brummie whose only characteristic which remains in my mind is when he announced his mother-in-law had disowned him after his wife became pregnant only weeks after giving birth to another child.

Before I was assigned to any CID duties an opportunity was given to take a police driving course which I immediately accepted. There were 12 students on the course, 3 trainees and one instructor in each of 4 cars operating out of the central garage at Duke Street (a few yards from where my sister Kate had lived in my childhood days.)

We spent the first week in the classroom learning the basic functions of a car and its component parts and were expected to learn the Highway Code off by heart. There were 3 basic principles to be remembered; (1) learn the Highway code and always drive according to its requirements; (2) never take anything for granted; a person with his hand out of the window may not be signalling his intention to turn right but indicating where his mother-in-law lived or if it was a woman driver, she may be drying her nail polish and (3) if you had an accident it was your fault because you should always be ready for the unexpected.

When we reached the point of driving a car, I had scarcely moved a few yards when I was told to stop and the instructor asked me if I was a qualified driver. I explained that I had driven in the Royal Air Force but did not hold a British driving licence. He made it clear to me that I could forget anything I thought I knew because he would teach me to drive properly.

We drove many miles on the public roads during which time we would have to give a commentary on what we were doing and what we observed but for specialised skills we went to my old haunts – RAF Castle Bromwich. The buildings were long since demolished but the vast openness with its perimeter track remained and provided scope for intricate movements weaving in and out of bollards, reversing into narrow spaces and smooth gear changes. When stationary the instructor would place a tumbler full of water on the bonnet of the car and the exercise was to accelerate through the gears to about 30mph and then brake to a halt without spilling the water. At the end of the 4 weeks course was the inevitable exam but I was then qualified to drive cars.

One of the police stations adjacent to Edward Road was Speedwell Road, well into the red light area and haunt of prostitutes and their pimps. To widen my CID experience I was attached for a short time and my colleagues there were a jovial Welsh Detective Sergeant Cyril Morgan, proud owner of a wire haired terrier and Charlie Lloyd, the equally proud owner of two dachshunds which would prove significant to me some time later.

Whilst I undertook my duties at Edward Road and Speedwell Road to the best of my ability I was never comfortable when frequenting pubs. However on one occasion, 23rd December 1959, Cyril Morgan, Charlie Lloyd and I went to another area of Birmingham to meet up with CID colleagues known to Cyril. Whilst there at about 7.45pm we received a message asking Cyril to contact Speedwell Road station. The call was to tell him that a woman had been attacked outside the Young Women's Christian Association hostel which was near to the station. This was 2 days before Christmas and the CID officers' priority perhaps normally would be to finish their festive drinks. However other factors dictated a different response.

The Stephanie Baird Murder

At that time I lived with Ann, my wife approximately half a mile from the YWCA and Ann worked night duty at a nursing home about 200 yards from the YWCA in Wheeley's Road. It was a quiet, poorly lit road with few people likely to be using it at 7.45pm, which was about the time Ann would have been cycling past the hostel to the nursing home. The awful thought crossed my mind that the victim of the attack could possibly be Ann and when I expressed my fear to Cyril, thoughts of finishing our drinks were forgotten in a hectic dash to the scene of the incident.

The YWCA hostel was a large Victorian style house set in its own grounds, with many rooms and a sun lounge extension at the side where the residents had laundering and ironing facilities. The story which was related to us by two uniform officers who had responded to the initial call would negate any Christmas festivities for the police, horrify the nation and create an atmosphere nearing hysteria in the locality.

The date was significant because with Christmas only 2 days away, many of the young women residents had left the hostel to join relatives or friends and many of the rooms were unoccupied. One woman who was still in residence was alone in the sun lounge ironing her clothes when she heard the door giving access to the garden open and she turned to see a man moving towards her. She screamed, ran away and the man turned and fled. She suffered some minor injury but was very frightened and there was every justification in the emergency call to the police which was relayed to Cyril Morgan as an attack on a young woman.

The two police officers who responded to the call reassured the victim and the few other persons in the house thinking that they were dealing with a peeping Tom type of incident. However, it was to their credit that they carried out their responsibilities assiduously and decided to search the grounds. In addition to the rooms in the house, there were some single storey type buildings divided into other rooms for individual occupancy. The officers checked the exterior using their torches to peer into the interiors.

Most of the rooms were empty, some with the curtains drawn but in one, the scene before them would result in nightmares for both of them. Half on, half off the single bed was the partially clothed decapitated body of a woman with her torso horribly mutilated and clothing, bed linen, walls and floor covered with blood. It was obvious they were dealing with more than a peeping Tom incident.

Because we had responded promptly to the initial call, Cyril, Charlie and I were the first CID officers on the scene but very quickly were joined by others from the Crime Squad and senior investigating officers including the frightening Detective Superintendent Gerry Baumber, a man with a fearsome reputation of ruthless efficiency.

The crime scene was immediately sealed and I was deputed to await the arrival of the Police Pathologist and make sure that he was taken without delay to the senior investigating officer.

Police dogs had been summoned to search the grounds but it was apparent from the original confrontation with the woman in the sun lounge that the intruder had run down the path to the road making the possibility of tracking him somewhat remote. Scenes of Crime officers also arrived and a significant footprint was found outside the window of the room where the woman's body lay. It was of a moulded rubber sole with a distinctive bar pattern across the heel.

A murder incident room was established at Speedwell Road Police Station and other investigating officers drafted in to assist. In Birmingham at that time, murders which would require extensive enquiries were few and far between and when they did occur, a Force wide message would be disseminated requiring all available CID officers to respond. The consequence was that there may have been some initial 'organised chaos' but very quickly briefings were held, teams with particular responsibilities organised and emergency feeding facilities arranged.

For the first few days of the investigation no consideration was given to hours to be worked or time off and it was a matter of working literally 'round the clock' until some supervising officer directed his subordinates to go home for some sleep.

It was obvious from the nature of the injuries sustained by the deceased that the assailant was likely to be bloodstained and all 'bus garages were asked to notify the police of any matter giving cause for suspicion. When it was reported that a bus had gone into one of their garages with a pool of congealed blood on the upper deck I was despatched to guard the vehicle until it was thoroughly examined. Although I spent a lonely boring Christmas Eve at least the garage staff on duty were friendly and their canteen provided my necessary feeding requirements.

Eventually the scenes of crime officers finished their examination concluding that the bus garage line of enquiry was one of the many red herrings that would be investigated and eliminated. I was relieved from that duty and as a bonus was allowed to take Christmas Day off.

One line of enquiry which is basic to any detailed investigation is house to house enquiries. Depending on the information sought would dictate the nature of the questions to be asked of the householders. From the onset, Detective Superintendent Baumber directed that house to house enquiries were to be made within a half mile radius of the crime scene. Every male person over the age of 14 was to be accounted for and his movements established for the evening of the murder. Many of the householders, terrified of what they had heard on the news bulletins or read in the newspapers were very reluctant to open their doors until they were absolutely sure of the identity of the police officers. Because I lived within the half mile radius I was required to answer the same questions but I think my alibi was foolproof.

I was allocated to one of these teams but initially after a few days was relocated to work with Cyril Morgan following up enquiries from information submitted to the incident room.

Other teams were briefed to make enquiries at suppliers of footwear to identify the footprint left at the scene; mental hospitals; check on persons recently released from prison and because of the nature of the wounds inflicted, butchers, abattoir workers, surgeons and anyone with the appropriate skill to remove the head from a a body were to be identified and subjected to questioning.

The enquiries on which Cyril and I were engaged were more mundane and far reaching. One particular report which we followed up was from a woman who had been in a bus queue and heard another person in the queue relating that her neighbour had come home on the night of the murder covered in blood. And had burned his clothing in the garden. So vague was the information that we realised the chances of identifying the suspect were almost non-existent. However, Cyril Morgan showing the same dogged determination as his wire haired terrier would have done was not to be beaten.

We knew the identity of the woman who had made the report, and seemingly against all the odds we traced the women in the bus queue and then visited the home of the man who had arrived home in a bloodstained condition. We thought that we were on the point of solving the murder but it proved to be yet another red herring when the man gave a perfectly reasonable explanation of his movements and the cause of his condition.

In the meantime while we were pursuing one false trail after another, the area of house to house enquiries was extended to a one mile radius from the murder scene and everyone carried a picture of the incriminating footprint checked against every suspect print noted in the snow which was with us for several weeks.

The enquiries continued for three weeks and into the fourth and fifth when the senior investigating officer instructed that the house to house enquiries must start again from scratch. Again I was checked out to establish where I had been on the night in question and who I had been with but I was only one of hundreds of men who were required to verify their credentials. Although several weeks had passed most people were able to remember exactly what they were doing because it was the day before Christmas Eve when they were making their Christmas arrangements. Also a copy of the Radio Times and TV Times provided a valuable aide memoir.

During this review there may have been other examples of inadequate checking first time round but one in particular was to prove very significant. At one of the lodging houses within the original half mile radius of the house to house enquiries, an Irish labourer had left his lodgings to go to an address in a northern city. The only verification was from the owner of the lodging house but on the re-visit, it was decided to check out the man's whereabouts. His name was Patrick Joseph Byrne.

When his present address was identified, the local police were asked to check Mr. Byrne's story and within a short time, our investigating officers were informed that he seemed to know more about the murder details than would be expected. They then put him on a train and told him to report to the Birmingham police, a course of action which on reflection may have been considered inappropriate. However, detective officers met him off the train and took him to Speedwell Road Police station. Those of us who were present at the time waited with anxious anticipation until one of the Detective Inspectors announced to us all "We've got him. He's admitted it."

Perhaps not ready to believe that the weeks of painstaking enquiries were over, none of the murder team were anxious to go home but the pubs were closed by the time we were assured that we did actually have our man. Being a very junior officer, obviously I was in no way involved with the questioning of the suspect but at about midnight, when he had been charged with the murder of Stephanie Baird, I was directed to escort him in the prison van to the central lock-up where he would be held until his appearance before the magistrates the following morning.

Patrick Byrne was an Irish labourer living a few minutes walk from the scene of the murder. He was not an experienced butcher or abattoir worker, neither was he a surgeon or skilled in anatomical dissection from any other profession. He had used an ordinary table knife to inflict the injuries.

Although the scene of the crime had been subjected to careful examination by the scenes of crimes officers, it was not until Byrne made his confession that further evidence was brought to light. He told the investigating officer that he had gained access to the building where the rooms were located and had hoisted himself up to peer through the fan light window to watch the woman undressing. His fingerprints were later found on the frame of the fan light window.

However thorough the investigation of any crime may be, there are the occasional strokes of good luck which could never be pre-determined. The footprint outside the room of the deceased was very distinctive and Byrne was questioned about this matter. He said that he had thrown the shoes into the rubbish bin at his lodgings. Although 6 weeks had passed, detectives visited the house and the landlord explained that the bin had been emptied a few days after Christmas. Following a trail long since cold, the detectives traced the crew of the vehicle used to collect the refuse. Much to their amazement, the driver of the vehicle remembered the shoes because they were in such good condition that he had salvaged them for his own use and produced them from the driver's cab. Forensic examination confirmed that they were the shoes which had left the imprint at the scene.

At his subsequent trial, Byrne was convicted of murder but on appeal, the conviction was quashed and a conviction for manslaughter was substituted.

The Beth Peplow Murder

If the Stephanie Baird murder was horrific, the next enquiry in which I was to be engaged was bizarre by comparison.

Kingstanding is an area on the north east side of Birmingham and when the body of a young woman, Elizabeth Peplow was discovered on waste ground with a stocking tied round her neck, the normal 'all available detective officers required' message was broadcast. My colleague Gordon Lauder travelled with me on my motor cycle for whatever briefing would be made.

The enquiry quickly fizzled out when the head of the CID, Detective Chief Superintendent James Haughton (later to become Her Majesty's Chief Inspector of Constabulary) carried out a dramatic experiment. Relying on his deputy Detective Superintendent Baumber to act promptly, Mr. Haughton demonstrated that the injury sustained by Elizabeth (Beth) Peplow was self inflicted. He knotted a stocking round his own neck to prove that once knotted, it was virtually impossible to release the knot and required scissors to remove the stocking.

The enquiries which were made indicated that the unfortunate young woman had fallen out with her boy friend and carried out the throttling on herself to gain attention but it had gone tragically wrong.

Fire Raising and Other Successes

At one point in my relatively short career as a CID officer, the area in which I was working suffered several serious arson attacks. Observations were carried out, enquiries made but without success. The arsonist was not particularly careful and left fingerprints at many of the locations and those of us involved in the enquiries took to carrying with us an enlarged copy of the main prints in order to make a quick comparison of any person whose fingerprints were taken.

One day, with a colleague, I visited a dwelling house in Balsall Heath where a burglary had been reported. Whilst there in the street I found a National Insurance card and although there was nothing to indicate that there was any connection we traced the owner, a young man who admitted that he was responsible for the break-in. There was always a feeling of satisfaction when clearing up a burglary and he was subsequently charged, sent to the central lock-up where his fingerprints were taken and Hey presto! We had caught the fire raiser. Whilst this result was no more than a stroke of luck, the report prepared for our superiors was probably elaborated to emphasise the brilliant detective work which had resulted in clearing up the arson offences.

If some positive results were brought about by good luck, many more were through informants, many of whom were convicted criminals seeking to mitigate their own dishonest activities but other informants acted out of a sense of public duty. One example was an Indian shopkeeper who had been offered a large amount of cigarettes which he suspected had been stolen. He arranged for the suspect to return to his shop with the cigarettes and notified us. When he entered the shop, we confronted him and he immediately took to his heels.

At that time I was the holder of the Birmingham City Police one mile title and the Midlands Police 3 mile and cross country titles and gave chase. There was no contest because I just let him run knowing that I was in far better condition than he was and eventually he sank to his knees gasping for breath whilst my colleague drew up alongside us in the police car and so concluded another successful arrest.

Another series of offences which caused considerable concern were a number of burglaries at factories where the safes were attacked. Together with a colleague I was instructed to patrol in a plain van during the hours of darkness in the area where the crimes were being committed.

In the small hours one morning we drove down a street and were waved down by two young men standing near an entry between two shops. They asked if we could give them a lift with some boxes they needed to move. When we saw that the boxes were several cases of cigarettes they had just stolen from a shop, we obliged by giving them a lift to the police station. If that was bad luck for them and good luck for us it transpired that we had also caught our safe breakers. Lucky, or astute observations?

Patrolling in this non-descript van certainly enabled us to bring about results which may have otherwise not been achieved. One night keeping observations on a road in a popular shopping area, the intruder alarm was activated on a shop which sold televisions and other electrical goods. From the premises, we saw a man and a woman run away and turn down a side road. Driving the van I gave pursuit and as we drew level with them I could quite easily have driven onto the pavement to apprehend them but at that point they both stopped running and they were arrested. They were charged with shop breaking and appeared at Birmingham Assizes before the Lord Chief Justice, Lord Parker. The man was sentenced to imprisonment but the woman who had obviously been under his influence was given a period of probation.

During this series of observations in the plain clothes van, at one point we were stationary in a dark street alongside a cinema which had an alleyway leading to the emergency exits of the building. Whilst there we saw a young couple walking towards us arm in arm and disappear down the alley. It may not have been part of our observations to speculate on the reason but a little later they reappeared and walked off together.

An hour or so later I received a call that I was required at the local police station to assist in enquiries for a rape allegation. In those days, police women were regarded as a specialised section of the Force and a policewoman on call for such allegations was at the station awaiting my arrival. The story outlined to me was that a young woman had been to a dance, travelled home on the bus and when walking down the street to where she lived she had been dragged down the alley at the back of the cinema and raped. Sure enough when I was allowed to see the complainant, I immediately identified her as the woman who I had seen a short time previously. When I told her that I had seen her with her male companion and there had been no indication of a lack of willingness on her part, she admitted that she had indulged in sexual activity with the young man and panicked that she may have been pregnant by someone she didn't know. She had made up the story of the rape to explain to her mother why she was late home.

The clothing which we had submitted for scientific examination was returned to her a few days later when she informed us that everything was OK, she wasn't pregnant and had nothing to worry about.

She apologised for making the false allegation but we took no further action and everyone was satisfied, including the young man presumably.

Although I was beginning to consider myself quite experienced as a CID officer I was selected to attend a Detective Training Course at the Police Training Centre, Ryton-on-Dunsmore. The course lasted for 3 months and together with my colleagues from several police forces as far away as Lancashire County, was instructed in every investigation technique which was available to the police service at that time.

Chapter 6. Marriage and a Family

Whilst my professional life was proceeding favourably there were factors which would have a substantial effect on my family life.

Having become engaged to Ann in 1954 and having experienced the stress of knowing my fiancée had been subjected to serious surgery, there was never any doubt that she and I would be married but in 1956 Police Regulations stipulated that the prospective wife of a policeman must be acceptable in the eyes of the Force. It was also a requirement that where a police officer lived had to be subject to scrutiny. However, there could never have been any question as to Ann's suitability and on 23rd February 1957 we were married at the Salvation Army where we were both soldiers.

My pay in the Royal Air Force and as a young constable gave little opportunity to save and Ann's long period of sickness had reduced her income capabilities. Consequently any suggestion of a lavish wedding was beyond our financial resources but relatives and friends contributed to the cost. Ann's grandmother made the wedding dress and bridesmaid's dress; she also made the three tier wedding cake and a friend offered to produce the wedding photographs as his gift.

On the great day, it snowed, outside photographs were not practical and the only ones which comprised our album were those in the hall. The wedding breakfast was a modest spread, mainly supplied and prepared by our relatives for about 30 guests.

We had arranged to go to London for our honeymoon and having changed out of our wedding clothes made our way to Snow Hill railway station where, much to our surprise and embarrassment, members of the Salvation Army band were awaiting our arrival and played 'Here comes the Bride' to the amusement of other rail passengers on the platform. I remember that on the journey sitting in the railway carriage, I was wearing a new bespoke suit with a blue faint check pattern. Ann was dressed in a red dress and a green coat. A small boy who was also in the carriage had chocolate on his hands and at one point, lurched into me, grabbing my knee and leaving chocolate smears. I was not best pleased.

Sadly, other memories of the honeymoon are very vague. I know we stayed at a small hotel and were surprised and perhaps a little embarrassed that on our first morning in bed together, we were roused by knocking on the bedroom door and found that breakfast had been delivered for us.

We visited the theatre and saw "The Pyjama Game" with Edmund Hockridge as the principal performer, but apart from meeting with an ex-colleague of RAF days, Mike Murphy, who was a police officer in the Metropolitan Police, of other aspects of our brief stay in London I can remember nothing.

As with so many other newlyweds, we experienced difficulty in finding accommodation and Ann's parents allowed us to use a bedroom and a small front room for our sitting room. We were there for about 3 months until we found rooms with an elderly spinster lady which allowed us a little more independence. In 1959 we were allocated a police house in a block of maisonettes near to the city centre, the house where we lived at the time of the YWCA murder. Our finances were still fully stretched and to supplement our income, Ann took a job of office cleaning in a nearby block of offices but I was relieved when after a few months she decided to explore other opportunities and eventually followed her nursing instincts at the nearby nursing home.

Now that we had our own home, we decided it was time to start a family which was to prove easier said than done. Infertility is no respecter of race, class or status and can cause great distress to those it affects. For us, visits to the family doctor were followed by Ann's visits to specialist Units, increasingly intimate and embarrassing tests, discussions with gynaecologists then to hospitalisation and surgical operations which she was to endure for the next 10 years. At one point after all normal options had been explored, the doctor suggested that we should find a puppy dog which would enable Ann to channel her maternal instinct into caring for the puppy. Apparently there was good evidence that women experiencing such frustrations tended to relax psychologically and generate the magical formula to facilitate conception.

We decided that any dog brought into our household would have to be small and smooth coated to reduce the possible shedding of hairs onto my uniform. When I discussed with my CID colleagues the possibility of buying a dog, Charlie Lloyd insisted that if I had a dachshund, I would never want any other breed. Having been so influenced by his passion for his dachshunds, Ann and I found a breeder of dachshunds and went to visit her home where we were shown her most recent litter of puppies.

Out of the half dozen or so which all clamoured for our attention, one drew us like a magnet. She was a tiny red puppy and I held her in one hand captivated and besotted by her appeal. The breeder cautioned us that she had already half promised this particular one to someone else but we could not resist the tiny puppy and after further discussion, little Amanda went home with us. Because she was a pedigree animal we considered it appropriate that she should be registered with the Kennel Club and her official name became 'Lesane Amanda'.

The breeder suggested to us that before long we would want a second dog and although we thought it may have been just sales propaganda, after a few months we realised that two dogs would be company for each other and so Lesane Mitzi, sharing the same father as Amanda, joined our family. The pleasure that the two little companions gave to us was immeasurable although their characters could not have been more different. They played together, chased each other, slept in the same basket sharing the same blanket, but whilst Amanda could be very sedate, almost aloof to the point where we nick-named her Duchess, Mitzi's lower jaw was a little undershot giving an impression of a cheeky grin and she was a little rascal.

There was one occasion when, following our regular practice, we set a tea tray on the hearth rug intending to share tea and buttered scones. When I went into the room, I pointed out to Ann that she had omitted to put butter in the dish, a suggestion which she pointedly rejected, but there was the evidence - an empty butter dish. Some time later a similar incident occurred and we identified the cause. Both dogs had been lying on the rug near the tray but whilst Amanda showed no interest, Mitzi edged forward, her tongue flicked out again, and again giving the impression that she knew she shouldn't but if she took just a little lick, we wouldn't notice. There were similar indiscretions perhaps the most memorable was when Ann had made a buttered torten as a special treat for me and hid it in the bedroom. When we returned from a shopping trip we were greeted with two not so little dachshunds both of whom looked like footballs, having very guilty expressions and upstairs a buttered torten three quarters eaten.

I was taking every opportunity available to me to pursue my athletic interest and we travelled throughout Birmingham and surrounding areas for me to participate in races. We owned a BSA 250cc motor cycle and in order to take the dogs with us, Ann constructed a pillow case type of bag for the dogs using an old blanket into which they would sit. Riding on the pillion she would have one dog balanced on each thigh peeping over my shoulders. Great amusement was caused for other motorists and never once did the dogs fidget or jeopardise our safety.

We decided to have Amanda mated because we had been advised that it would be to the dog's benefit to have a litter but others warned us that Mitzi may prove to be jealous and be a danger to the puppies. Nothing could have been further from the truth. When Amanda returned from her courtship experience, she immediately adopted her dignified matronly attitude. No more chasing up and down the stairs, no more teasing each other with squeaky toys, Amanda was the archetypal mother in waiting. When we realised that Amanda was due to whelp we prepared a box for her suitably protected with newspapers etc for the delivery but when the puppies arrived it was very late in the evening and Ann had decided to take a bath. When the first puppy was delivered, Amanda was so excited she ran into the bathroom and if she could have spoken she would have urged Ann to go and see the puppy, which of course she did, wrapped in her bath robe.

Four other puppies duly arrived and then we witnessed an amazing experience. Mitzi, the spinster aunt immediately took over all responsibilities for cleaning the puppies whilst Amanda stood back as much to indicate that she had completed her duties for the time being. As the puppies gradually grew, both Amanda and Mitzi were ever attentive to their needs.

Unfortunately one puppy a black and tan, was diagnosed with hydrocephalus and was put to sleep but the others stayed with us until they were sufficiently developed to go to new homes and literally from the moment the door closed behind the last one to go, Amanda resumed her previous carefree attitude of chasing Mitzi up and down the stairs squeaky toys and the whole range of activities denied her as a nursing mother.

Whilst the dogs had become our surrogate children and having shared the excitement of the birth of the puppies at the same time we seriously considered the possibility of adoption and Ann having been adopted herself had no inhibitions whilst I had a completely open mind. By a quirk of fate, one of the other police officers living in the same block of maisonettes was married to a lady who worked for an adoption society, and made arrangements for us to be included on their books.

In due course we were interviewed to determine whether we were suitable persons to take on an adopted child. As would be expected the questions were searching and in depth to bring to light any doubtful aspects of our character. Being a 'professional' couple, a police officer and nurse, we had no concern that our social status was beyond reproach and our membership of the Salvation Army was indicative of our moral standing. The only hesitation in our answers was when we were asked if we would be prepared to take twins. It was a question we had never expected and hesitatingly suggested that we would be more comfortable with one child and perhaps consider a second at a later date.

It was only after the interviewing officer had left us that we discussed the question in detail between ourselves and thought that if we were offered twins it would be no different than if they were born to us naturally. We notified the adoption Society that if the occasion arose, we would be prepared to adopt twins and it was a decision that would change our lives for ever.

A Crucial Turning Point - Adoption

As in most professions, experience and advancement is dependent on examinations and the police Service is no exception. Recruit training, progress through two years' probation and subsequent promotion require the all important examinations which in turn demand a commitment to study. I could not take my promotion examinations until 1962 and I was determined to pass as soon as possible. I attended night school classes provided by the Force and also invested in a correspondence course. Came the all important day of the examination and my friends from recruit training, Joy and Malcolm Pinder who had married and were living next door were also intending to sit the examination.

We agreed that following the weeks of study and the stress of taking the examination, the four of us would treat ourselves in the evening to a meal at a restaurant, an extravagance which was seldom a pleasure we could afford. It was co-incidental that we had been notified there had been developments in our application for adoption which was likely to be fulfilled in the near future and I was instructed by the Adoption Society to make a telephone call on the evening we were intending to dine out. With a degree of trepidation I made the call from the restaurant and was informed that everything had been finalised, we were to attend a nursing home in Wolverhampton, about 20 miles away on the following Saturday, that was in three days time. I am sure it was almost an afterthought that I was told that we would be receiving twins, a boy and a girl.

The following 2 days were a flurry of activity because although we had prepared a nursery for one baby, the sudden realisation that we needed two of everything was something on which we had not planned. We went to a city centre multi-store to find a twin pram but we found that they were a rare commodity. We persuade the store to remove the only twin pram from their display in the store and gradually the panic buying and changes of plan rationalised into some sort of adequate preparation.

A local newsvendor who had a stall on the street nearby had become a very close friend and he was the proud possessor of a Rover 75 motor car, a veritable limousine which, without hesitation he insisted I borrow for the journey to Wolverhampton. Although I had become used to using modest, run of the mill cars, this purring emblem of affluence was a dream to drive and entirely appropriate for such an important occasion. I found myself very embarrassed when, having decided to fill up with petrol, I could not find the release mechanism for the petrol filler cap but the problem was soon resolved.

When we actually took possession of the babies, they were 6lb in weight and 10 weeks old.

We never met the mother but we learned subsequently that she was 15 and the father of her babies was also a teenager. It must have taken a great deal of courage and support from her family for her to give birth to the babies and then offer them for adoption. It is impossible to speculate how our lives would have been affected if she had not taken those decisions. That was 1962; 40 years on, social attitudes had changed enormously and consideration for termination of unwanted pregnancies would become commonplace particularly if the mother was under age and expecting twins.

As any parents would be, we were very proud of our babies and on our return to our home, Ann's parents were waiting to greet us and share our happiness. Perhaps one sad aspect was that my own father died shortly before we received Denise and Lloyd into our lives and hearts. The cause of death was recorded as Carcinoma of rectum and 50 years later, I was similarly diagnosed but thankfully medical expertise had improved greatly to ensure my successful treatment.

Attending the Army the following day was a very special occasion and pushing the twin pram the mile or so to the Citadel was a new experience for me but one which was to become a regular commitment for both of us and Ann quickly became identified as the lady with two babies and two dachshunds when she walked out in the street.

Amanda and Mitzi seemed to share in the general excitement of having babies in the house and we frequently found them both in the nursery, quietly keeping an awareness of the children as they slept.

At this time, my father-in-law was the proud owner of a small Morris 8 motor car. One Saturday morning shortly after the excitement of receiving our twins, he arrived in the car which was parked at the rear of the house. It had been freshly cleaned and he asked me what I thought of it. I made some complimentary reply and he then said "It's yours." I could scarcely believe what he had said but he explained that now we had the children we would need a car and he was giving it to us.

As weeks slipped into months we prepared ourselves for a very important point in the adoption procedure. Although the children were de facto ours, we were not legally their parents. We were required to appear before a magistrate acting as Guardian ad Litem who would either formally approve the adoption or, if not satisfied for any reason, reject our application.

The magistrate on this occasion was someone for whom I had a great respect and because of my CID duties had become well acquainted with him. Mr. Hamilton-Baines was a character and frequently injected his own brand of informality to legal proceedings. On this occasion proceedings were reduced to a minimum and he seemed more interested in expressing his own excitement because it was the first time he had ever dealt with an application to adopt twins and had no hesitation in approving the necessary procedure. Personally I have never met any other parents who have done so.

The Salvation Army does not baptise children as do many other churches, instead they hold a similar ceremony which they identify as 'Dedication'. The officers of the Corps, Brigadier and Mrs. Evans agreed to our request and shortly after the court proceedings, our children, Lloyd and Denise, were legally ours and we had given an assurance that they would be brought up in a Christian home.

Summoned to the Assistant Chief Constable

A short time after Amanda's puppies were born I was instructed that the Assistant Chief Constable wanted to see me. For a young constable, to receive such a summons was an indication that something was seriously wrong. I had no idea what personal transgression justified this dramatic call and when I stood before him, frantic with worry, he informed me in his most authoritative manner that a complaint had been made against me.

The block of maisonettes in which we lived together with another 10 – 11 police families was one of several similar blocks on a council estate. All other residents, within the terms of their tenancies, were forbidden to keep dogs in their homes. Someone had complained about my dog (in my explanation I made no mention that in fact I had seven dogs at the time.)

The Assistant Chief Constable informed me that I could not keep the dog and I must get rid of it. Fortunately for me, it was still a requirement of Police Regulations that keeping a dog in a police house required permission from a senior officer. I had made such a request and my report had been approved by my Chief Superintendent.

When I explained the reason why we had decided to keep a dog (I forgot to mention the other dog and five puppies) I added that I would resign rather than lose the dog. His manner softened, thought for a moment then said that as an alternative I would be moved from my maisonette to a house with a garden. I was overjoyed because although we were happy where we lived the thought of more space and a garden was something I could not have anticipated.

It was 18th May 1962, my sister Lily's birthday that we left our city centre maisonette to move into a semi-detached house in the Kings Heath district of Birmingham. Our neighbours were police officers but we were not on an estate in the same way that we had been in the maisonette where we had often received calls for police action.

To be given a 3 bedroom house, garden front and rear, no rent or rates to pay and someone else to take care of repairs and maintenance would probably be a dream come true for any young family. Certainly we were pleased and very excited to move into our new home, courtesy of the Birmingham City Police. We were within walking distance of shops for our every day requirements and a short car or bus ride from a busy shopping High Street. We were also within easy access of fields and woodland where the children and dogs could run and play to their hearts content.

We were also sufficiently close to recreational areas including Cofton Woods and several public parks one of which was Kings Heath Park. Unfortunately that was the scene of an accident when my children were showing their expertise on new bicycles. However Denise showing more enthusiasm than caution lost control as she careered down a hill, falling off and causing damage to her face which in later years justified an operation which she described as 'a nose job'.

One of my hobbies and interests had always been woodwork and found my limited skills adequate to build a climbing frame and slide in the garden for the children and because they were growing out of the cot stage for sleeping, I constructed two bunk beds with a built in wardrobe and chest of drawers under the beds. To facilitate my studies for examinations I also constructed a bookcase inspired by a photograph I had seen in a magazine. It was so designed that it had the appearance of balancing on one slender leg with open shelves. Ann was particularly proud of the bookcase and insisted that whenever we changed houses, the bookcase travelled with us, on each occasion suitably modified to be fitted into the new location.

Many hours were spent in the closed garden shed, building a large doll's house for Denise which I think gave me as much pleasure as my daughter. The shed also provided another opportunity for inventiveness. It was constructed of bricks as part of the house and at the far end of the garden was a large oak tree. I fastened a slim wire hawser to the tree and the other end to the wall of the shed. A large pulley wheel supporting a cross member for handles completed this death defying slide for the children. It gave them great pleasure until one day the brick of the shed wall to which it was fastened became detached and the pulley wheel ride became defunct.

A short distance from our house was a small general provisions store run by a delightful lady, Mrs. Barefoot. We made almost daily visits and our 2 little dachshunds caused endless amusement when they sat up and begged, waiting patiently for their treat, small pieces of cheese given by Mrs. Barefoot. She was generous in other ways too and at a time when I did not own a car, loaned me hers to visit Ann when she was in hospital.

Chapter 7. An Unexpected Development

Although I enjoyed my CID duties (I had been awarded 9 commendations by the Chief Constable) I knew that I would never be a hard drinking, pub frequenting detective, mixing with the underworld. I never relaxed my Christian principles and my family were much more important to me than seemed to be the case with some of my colleagues. When I was asked if I would like to transfer to Special Branch I accepted without hesitation. The type of work appealed to me and was in my blood from my RAF Police days at Castle Bromwich.

It was a relatively small department based at headquarters under the supervision of a Detective Superintendent. Making enquiries, observations and attending political extremists' meetings to identify potential subversive elements in our society was something that appealed to me.

It was whilst I was in Special Branch that I received a summons to see the deputy head of the CID, the fearsome Detective Superintendent Baumber. As with the Assistant Chief Constable's interview, I had no idea the purpose of the call and when I entered his office he asked me if I had applied for the Special Course.

There had been considerable concern expressed from various quarters that the Police Service had depended too much on retired military personnel to fill its senior ranks (perhaps the most notable having been Lord Trenchard appointed Commissioner of the Metropolitan Police in 1931). A Government White Paper recommended that a scheme be set up to identify young officers in the Police Service who were capable of achieving the highest ranks in the Service. I had seen some mention in police publications inviting constables who were successful in the promotion examinations to apply but I had not given the matter any serious thought because I did not consider myself to be suitably eligible.

In the promotion examination I had achieved the top student place in Birmingham Police for which I subsequently received a book prize award from the Chief Constable, Sir Edward Dodd (also later to be appointed Her Majesty's Chief Inspector of Constabulary) and Mr. Baumber wanted to know why I hadn't applied. Whatever my explanation, he made it quite clear that I was to do so immediately. I later learned that out of the 5,000 constables who sat the national promotion examination at the same time, I was in the top 20 of the results nationwide.

I submitted my application which I presume received positive endorsement from my superiors because I was called for interview by my own Chief Constable followed by a further interview with the Commissioner of the City of London Police, Mr. James Page CBE QPM at the City of London Police Headquarters.

Shortly afterwards I was informed that I was to attend the National Police College at Bramshill in Hampshire for an extended interview to assess my suitability for the Special Course. Because the conception of the Course was a new policy, the question of the most suitable selection procedure had still to be resolved. It was undecided whether students should be selected solely as a result of their position in the national promotion examination or whether the extended interview system should be used.

The Metropolitan Police had a promotion system different from provincial Forces. The constables sat an examination based on Metropolitan Police General Orders applicable only to that Force. Those who received the highest pass marks in their examination were guaranteed promotion to sergeant whilst those further down the list waited for vacancies. In all provincial Forces there was a common national examination and a pass in the examination only guaranteed that the constable was considered suitable for promotion when the Chief Constable saw fit to promote them.

To achieve a balance, the composition of the first Special Course was a total of 36; 9 from the Metropolitan police who were the top students; 9 provisional officers who had achieved the top 9 places and the remaining 18 selected by extended interview from the top students from the Metropolitan Police and the provincial Forces. From this first course experiment a decision was made that subsequent courses would select only by extended interviews.

I was one of about 25 for the 2 day interview at the Police College designed to test every aspect of the qualities looked for in a senior officer and although stressful in its intensity I thought that even if I was not selected I had gained a great deal from the experience. One specific question asked was what rank in the police Service, did I think I could achieve. I remember considering very carefully before replying "Assistant Chief Constable." I was pressed as to why I had not said "Chief Constable" and I recall that I said because there were only a small number of Chief Constable posts in the country, I thought it much more realistic in my own self assessment.

On return to Birmingham it was a question of waiting for the result. I suppose I was not convinced that such an opportunity was really within my grasp but began to believe that perhaps a door was opening for me. Eventually I received the call that I was required at the Chief Constable's office where another constable, Sidney Perks and I were informed that we had been selected for the Special Course due to commence at the end of September and would last for 12 months.

Ann gave me every encouragement in spite of the fact that had we two babies barely 8 months old and she would be left more or less on her own with them for a whole year. We weren't to know that in a few months time we would endure one of the coldest winters for decades that water pipes would burst, and we wouldn't have enough money to pay the electricity bills. If we could have looked into the future it may have been that I would have had a different outlook. Fortunately we could not foresee what would happen and as in so many difficult situations, when hardships are overcome, there is a resulting strengthening of character.

The National Police College

The National Police College has been in existence since 1948 when it was established at Ryton-on-Dunsmore Warwickshire and moved to Bramshill in 1962. Bramshill House is a Jacobean mansion standing in 269 acres of land near Hartley Wintney, Hampshire. The present building was completed in 1612 but its history can be traced back to Saxon times and there are many myths and legends including stories of ghosts which are perpetuated to the present day. The main approach road is one mile long, straight and the magnificent house standing on a rise from its surrounds dominates the landscape.

The Special Course was intended for sergeants, and whilst the Metropolitan Police and many of the provisional officers had been confirmed in their rank before attending the college Sidney Perks and I were given the rank of temporary sergeant and whilst the modest increase in pay was welcome, for the whole of the subsequent 12 months we had to anticipate that the substantive rank would remain for the discretion of the chief constable, Sir Derek Capper. Whilst the overall objective of the course was to identify and groom those of us considered suitable for higher rank, the ethos of the college would also improve our social skills and etiquette.

In September 1962 my salary as a temporary sergeant was about £1,000 pa and the normal expense of maintaining a household with two infant children did not allow spare money for luxuries or unnecessary items. All those attending the course had been instructed to obtain their personal copies of various law books including Archbold Criminal Pleading Evidence and Practice, Stone's Justices' Manual and numerous other expensive tomes. Whilst these important reference books were familiar to me, not so for the Metropolitan officers who had achieved their selection for the course as the result of their examinations based on Metropolitan Police General Orders. In addition to this expensive personal library, we would require a dinner suit for the many formal occasions accepted as normal college life.

The Special Course was not only a new venture for the police Service, it was an experiment. There were confusing opinions on the structure and priorities of the training during the following 12 months. The other courses running at the college were for inspectors, chief inspectors and foreign police officers based on a university style approach including lectures, seminars and sporting activities for those who wished to participate. Many of the British officers seemed to regard their attendance at the college as of little value other than to justify any later promotion.

The Special Course was different and to some extent based on Bramshill's near neighbour, Sandhurst Army Officer training establishment. The Commandant of the college at that time was genial retired Major General Jelf who may have had some influence on that initial outlook. The curriculum which we were to follow would include frequent periods of drill supervised by a drill sergeant from a local Force and enforced physical activities supervised by an inspector from another local Force. These diversions were in addition to the two main aspects of study in police law and liberal studies intended to broaden our overall outlook and comprehension of worldwide subjects and politics.

Of the 36 members of the course, 9 were from the Metropolitan police and 27 from Forces as far apart as Northumberland to Exeter, Glamorgan to Peterborough many of which were small and would eventually lose their identities in amalgamations. We were to be divided into three syndicates, "Peel", "Blackstone" and "Romilly" each with our own Chief Inspector tutor, one from the Metropolitan, one from Lincolnshire and one from my own Birmingham Force. The Course Director was the Birmingham Assistant Chief Constable who a few months previously had instructed me to dispose of my dog, Mr. Philip Knights later to become one of the first police officers to sit in the House of Lords as Lord Knight of Edgbaston.

The initial curriculum of the course consisted of four periods of 3 months each followed by 2 weeks leave and a weekend leave every 4 weeks. We would be expected to remain at the college for the other weekends and participate in sporting activities against local teams to broaden our overall horizons. It very quickly became obvious that the Metropolitan police members of the course set their own agenda, departed to their home on Friday afternoons and were never included in the cricket, hockey, football, volley-ball and cross-country teams representing the Special Course in our weekend fixtures. (On our initial briefing for course physical activities I had perhaps naively suggested including cross-country running for which my fellow students showed less enthusiasm than I did.)

The intended purpose of the sporting activities during weekends at the college was obviously intended to develop team building and camaraderie but the "Met Lads" often gave the impression of treating the provincial officers as second class citizens. Certainly those of us who participated in the sporting fixtures against Sandhurst, The Sunday Express and other teams enjoyed the friendship and hospitality provided for the competitors. It also identified that I was a more competent runner than cricket umpire when, acting as square leg umpire and one of our opponents was run out by a mile, I had been distracted, didn't see what happened and gave a decision "not out".

The whole format of the course was experimental and subject to change as we progressed giving justification to the affectionate reference to us as "guinea pigs". One factor which was decided for subsequent courses was that the extended interview system would be used for selection and no one would be selected only as the result of high examination marks. After the first 3 months, the embargo on weekend leave was dropped but many of us could not have afforded the expense of travelling every weekend and those from Durham, Exeter and other far distant locations would have found it impossible to take advantage of the relaxation. Consequently, little changed in that respect, the Met Lads still went home and those left at the college played sport.

There was a wide range of sporting facilities available to everyone on all of the courses including archery which was something new to me but for which I developed an enthusiasm second only to my running activities. However, volley ball was the passion for everyone, competitions arranged and matches played at every possible opportunity. In addition to the provision for outdoor sport, there were snooker tables and a magnificent library. In our private research for the discussion papers we were expected to produce from time to time, the proverbial midnight oil was burned by many of the college students.

There were other activities to take our minds away from studies and every Tuesday evening there was a film show in the main hall of the student block. The incidental music which always played before the film started was "Telstar" or "It might as well rain until September". Although those two tunes have disappeared from the pop music charts, if I ever hear them, my thoughts immediately go back to Bramshill days.

There were other mind broadening activities including the Henry Fielding Society which discussed the importance of Fielding in the legal development of the country and from time to time eminent speakers would be invited.

In addition to our syndicate studies of law and liberal studies, life at the college enabled us to experience and develop the social skills expected of senior officers. Every week we attended a formal dinner, dressed in dinner suits and to which guests were invited. The members of all courses were required to nominate in rotation, a Mess President who would preside at each dinner to uphold the traditions of the Mess procedure. When I was nominated, I sat at the head table flanked by the Commandant and Deputy Commandant. When the formality of the meals reached the point for the Loyal Toast, I stood, banged the gavel 3 times and announced to my Vice President sitting at the far end of the room "Mr. Vice, The Queen." The Vice President would then formally propose a toast to "Her Majesty, Queen Elizabeth." After dinner we would adjourn to the drawing room and bar for the pleasantries of social intercourse. It would also provide an opportunity to take guests on a guided tour of the very historic house.

Although living in an atmosphere of formality and apparent opulence, I found that the expenses of maintaining such standards stressful and Ann, coping by herself with problems of parenthood without my support, similarly had little cash to spare but from time to time managed to send me a few pounds for me to keep my head above water.

At the end of the first 3 months of the course we took 2 weeks leave which coincided with Christmas and New Year. It was to be one of the coldest winters recorded for several decades and snow fell heavily for several weeks. Although I had changed my car from the little Morris to a larger, Vauxhall Velox, it was out of the question to drive back to Bramshill and covered with a tarpaulin, my car was parked on the forecourt of a shopkeeper friend.

Meeting up with Sidney Perks, we travelled by train to Reading railway station where we boarded a mini-bus from the college. We drove along roads which were flanked by banks of snow as was the main drive to the college. It was bitterly cold and I consoled myself that once back in our rooms I could have a hot bath to thaw out. It was not to be because it transpired the central heating had become defective and there was no hot water. I would have readily swapped the potential benefits of the course, further promotion and every advantage of the college on offer if I could have returned home there and then but rational thinking soon replaced my negative outlook.

Although having a chapel at the college, there were no regular services and little encouragement to participate in church activities. Probably I would have had little interest anyway and made contact with the Reading corps of the Salvation Army where I was allowed to play in the band even though I had no Army uniform with me. However these occasions were effectively the end of my participation in Army activities. Having moved home to the Kings Heath district we were then about 5 miles from the Birmingham Citadel and without a car it was impossible for Ann to contemplate the journey, with the twins on the buses. Consequently we transferred our place of worship to a local Methodist church within walking distance and although we continued as Methodists, we never forgot our Army background and maintained contact whenever possible.

During the third term of the course we were seconded to Police Forces other than our own and I was sent to Manchester and Cheshire Forces. Whilst Manchester was very similar in reputation and capabilities as Birmingham, Cheshire seemed to be somewhat antiquated. The Chief Constable at that time was a retired army captain who insisted that the Force use bottle green Rover 75 cars for their fleet even though when compared with other Forces, such vehicles were not the most suitable. However the opportunity to see how the other half lives, proved to be a valuable experience.

Although Ann and I were living virtually in 2 different worlds it was possible for her to visit the college and see for herself not only the historic house itself and accommodation where I lived but also she was able to stroll round the estate with its large lake, home to dozens of Canadian geese and listen to the late night screeching of the peacocks which strutted displaying their wonderful plumage.

At the end of each 3 months term we had to sit examinations in police law and liberal studies. We knew that failure at any point would result in return to our home Forces. The pressures on 35 of the 36 were constant but for one Metropolitan Police officer who was so disdainful of every aspect of the course, his contemporaries queried why he had ever been admitted in the first instance. When he was threatened with dismissal from the course unless he made more effort, his response to point out he was already a substantive sergeant. Consequently it was no surprise when he left our company permanently.

As the completion of the course neared, our apprehensions increased until finally the all-important results were announced. Out of the 36 original students, one had been sent back to his Force, one was considered not to have achieved the necessary standard required and 34 passed, 3 with distinction. Those 3 were Geoffrey Dear (Peterborough), later to be appointed one of Her Majesty's Inspectors of Constabulary and appointed to the House of Lords; David East (Berkshire) was later appointed as Chief Constable South Wales Constabulary and Sidney Pleece (Metropolitan) later appointed Assistant Chief Constable Devon & Cornwall but was denied further promotion, dying at an early age. Many others from that first course also achieved senior ranks and positions in the police Service. For those of us who were accredited a pass, we considered that it was unfair for the one failure to have allowed him to continue for the full duration when it must have been obvious that he was not up to the required standard.

Although the format of the course had been developed over the 12 months in which we were students, no consideration had been given for a suitable recognition for those who had passed with distinction and it was to be a further 3 years before a decision was made.

To perpetuate for posterity the contribution we had made to the further development of the college, everyone subscribed to the cost of a silver plaque inscribed with our names which Sidney Perks and I obtained from the world famous Jewellery Quarter in Birmingham. On subsequent visits to the college I was pleased to pay my personal homage to the plaque on display, a reminder of the many memories which it commemorated. The plaque was on display in the entrance to the main lecture hall and in the same location was a magnificent 9' tall wooden carving of a police constable wearing a helmet and a cape over his shoulder. Although he seemed to be a permanent feature of the Police College, when the National Memorial Arboretum was opened at Alrewas, Staffordshire in 2001 the statue was moved there as part of the Police Memorial.

Chapter 8. Return to the Real World

Although we had received promotion to temporary sergeant and anticipating that successful completion of the course should have ensured confirmation of the rank, when Sidney Perks and I returned to the Birmingham Force, the Chief Constable claimed that he had received no guidance on that matter. He did make it quite clear to us however that we should expect no favoured treatment with regard to promotion merely because of the Special Course. I would not have wanted subsequent promotion other than from my own determination and effort but he also gave an assurance to us that at the appropriate time it would be advantageous to our careers to apply for posts outside Birmingham for which he would give supportive references. Our promotion to sergeant was confirmed within a week and I was posted to the central "A" division, back in uniform.

'A' Division was divided into 2 sub-divisions, Steelhouse Lane and Digbeth. As a uniform sergeant I was expected to supervise 10 – 12 constables and ensure that they patrolled their beats conscientiously and effectively, a role which had been reversed when I was a constable. Although the normal expectation was to walk the beat alone, from the onset of my supervisory responsibilities I made a practice that when I met the constables I would often patrol with them which gave me opportunities to assess their competence and generally get to know them.

On one such occasion soon after I commenced duty at Steelhouse Lane I accompanied a young probationary constable recently out of recruit training and obviously nervous that his sergeant was apparently watching his every move. We noticed a young man who seemed apprehensive and agitated as 2 police officers approached. Whether it was sixth sense, a hunch or that unquantifiable factor, policeman's intuition, we stopped him. It was the young man's bad luck day because after a few minutes chatting to a man in the street which became questioning a suspect, quickly brought a confession that he had just committed a house breaking in the Ward End area of Birmingham.

At my direction, the constable formally arrested and cautioned the suspect, we escorted him to the police station and a young rookie constable with no previous arrests to his credit became the toast of his colleagues for showing initiative in effecting the arrest of a house breaker for an offence which had not even been reported. I would like to think he also realised that sergeants weren't ogres waiting to criticise but whose job was to support and assist less experienced officers.

Of course there were occasions when criticism was justified. One quiet sunny morning at about 7.00am I rendezvoused with a constable at his 'point' which was at a road junction adjacent to a large timber yard. I was greeted by the usual formal acknowledgement "All correct sarge." My response was "What about the fire in the timber yard?" He obviously thought it was some sort of joke until he looked to where I pointed and saw flames and smoke issuing from a stack of timber. What could have been a serious incident was averted by promptly calling the Fire Brigade. It was a lesson learned for that constable who then realised formal "All correct sarge" should have indicated that nothing untoward had been detected on his beat.

Whilst the sergeant's primary responsibilities may have been directed to the supervision of subordinates to ensure they undertook their duties effectively, there always remained the opportunities to experience the surge of adrenalin when the arrest of a criminal was likely. Such an occasion arose when, one November on night duty I was informed by a member of the public that someone was on the roof of factory premises. Personal radios carried by every police officer were not in use at that time and assistance when needed was not always immediately available. My informant was requested to find a telephone and dial 999 whilst I endeavoured to substantiate the original information. Using whatever observation point I could I eventually saw some movement on the roof and when other officers with a police dog arrived we used flashlights in an endeavour pick out our suspects.

We could neither see the men nor satisfy ourselves that we had been mistaken. Fortunately at this time, policing was not hide-bound with Health and Safety paranoia, petty restrictions or political correctness. Using questionable authority I requested the attendance of the Fire Brigade. On arrival they extended a ladder to the roof and accompanied by a fire officer I climbed up. Within a few minutes I found our two suspects crouched in a culvert between the roof parapet and sloping roof. It was November, the temperature was a little above freezing and they had been there for nearly 2 hours. It took great care and much encouragement to take them down the ladder to the relative warmth of the police car taking them to the police station. They were later charged with factory breaking with intent.

Even though I had completed the Special Course the policies were still unclear and in later years, promotion to inspector was a factor built into the syllabus. Not so for the two Birmingham City graduates and we were expected to sit the police examination to be considered for advancement. Fortunately I did not find too much difficulty with the discipline required for study and once again was awarded a book prize when I finished top of the exam results in Birmingham

Most police officers have an abundance of anecdotes as a result of their police work and when related, some border on the incredulous, some humorous. One of my own experiences in the latter category resulted in the court appearance following my arrest of a man for being drunk and disorderly. He duly appeared at court the following morning and to my surprise, pleaded 'not guilty' and was represented by a solicitor. I gave my evidence briefly and concisely – "Drunk and disorderly by urinating your worships." The defending solicitor anxious to challenge the evidence admitted that the man had been urinating but had tried to be discreet by relieving himself in a shop doorway. I replied "Yes sir but he was standing on the kerb and urinating across the pavement into the doorway." The magistrates found the case proved.

My duties at Steelhouse Lane lasted only a few months before I was posted to the Vice Squad based at my old area of operations – Edward Road.

Another View of Life

The Vice Squad consisted of an inspector, 2 sergeants and 6 constables all working in plain clothes. Our principal targets were men living off the immoral earnings of prostitutes – pimps. The traffic and trade in illegal drugs was not so prevalent at that time but was also included in our enquiries. Whatever may be the moral issues of prostitution, it is not illegal but the associated problems which result include abuse of women in its many forms.

Of necessity, our sources of information were the prostitutes, many of whom were completely open as to their activities but were very careful to avoid the pitfalls of arrest for soliciting or unwanted domination by pimps. They would provide the names of pimps who we could target and often facilitated our observations by making sure the pimps were in the right place at the right time for us to monitor the 'girls' handing over their takings or to see the pimps collecting their social security payments. Most of them drove high value cars, frequented betting offices and pubs all of which would provide evidence that they had sources of income which were not from paid employment. Many hours of observations, making notes showing the daily activities of the pimps would allow us to collate all details to justify making arrests for living off immoral earnings.

Of course the information from the prostitutes was not always from a public spirit aspect and it was accepted that the local plain clothes officers who dealt specifically with soliciting offences would be more tolerant of their activities. However it was not only the 'girls' who may have been a little devious on occasions. We had two pimps who were very good informants and many arrests which we made were as the result of information supplied by them. We knew them as Menzie and Dyer who also associated with a third pimp known to us as Freddie. We called Menzie and Dyer to our office one day to tell them word was circulating that the only reason they had never been arrested was that we were receiving bribes from them

We made it quite clear to the two men that we would not permit such unjustified allegations to be made and either they or their associate Freddie would be our next target. Showing remarkable common purpose they both agreed it should be Freddie and for the next few weeks they arranged for him to be at locations where we could monitor his activities. Eventually we had sufficient evidence to surreptitiously gain access to his lodging house, burst into his bedroom (the screws on the door lock had been loosened by Menzie) and pull him naked from the bed he was sharing with his girl friend. As we led him away, he called over his shoulder "Keep hustling Janet," 'hustling' being the colloquial term for soliciting and Janet was the daughter of a local councillor who was not best pleased when he learned of his daughter's activities.

What Menzie and Dyer had failed to appreciate was that all of the observations and surveillance we had carried out with their assistance on Freddie were equally relevant for them and following Freddie's arrest, Menzie and Dyer also appeared before the court. There were no more rumours that we were in their pay.

One particular incident which I investigated by myself concerned a prostitute named Ann Holland and her pimp 'Lumber'. Two other prostitutes told me that they were very worried about Ann. Her pimp had assaulted her and fractured her arm. The treatment she received included a plaster cast to support the broken limb but after one or two days, Lumber had forcibly removed it because it interfered with her earning capabilities. The poor girl was obviously in great pain and unable to attract clients. When she returned to the lodgings she shared with Lumber, he had poured boiling water over her legs and beaten her with a stick until the skin peeled off. I was incensed and eventually located him and arrested him.

Although we had been aware of Lumber's pimping, he had not at that time been a specific target for our enquiries but I was so outraged that I charged him with unlawful wounding and living off immoral earnings (The Crown Prosecution Service was not in existence at that time and decisions on which charges to prefer were the responsibility of the police officer.) I reflected afterwards that possibly I had acted with emotion rather than sensible analysis of the available evidence.

In due course Lumber appeared at the Birmingham Assizes (the Crown Court was not established until several years later) and I was very worried that the paucity, even non-existence of evidence for living off immoral earnings would bring serious criticism. Much to my surprise and relief, Lumber pleaded guilty to both charges and was sentenced to 5 years imprisonment for the unlawful wounding charge and 7 years for living off immoral earnings.

Our enquiries did not always have a successful conclusion and dealing with drug suspects was likely to result in frustration rather than celebration. We had received reliable information that a man known to us would be carrying drugs using a car which we could identify. Together with my team we carried out our surveillance and tailed the car to a petrol filling station. Our suspect was in the driving seat. My colleague approached the driver's door as I went to the passenger side. Suddenly he jumped from the vehicle and ran off with me in close pursuit. After 200 or 300 yards he turned down an entry between two houses and I followed. It was very dark and I heard him trying to climb over the garden gates at the end of the entry. I was about to run forward to tackle him but that invaluable 6th sense stopped me doing so and he escaped over the gates into the gardens of the houses. Our informant later told us that the drug dealer normally carried an axe in his belt the consequences of which could have been very serious for me. You win some and you lose some!

The potential dangers of the duties were brought home to me very forcibly when one of the constables on my team did not report for duty one Monday morning. It transpired that he had been consorting with one of the well known prostitutes married to a drug dealer serving a term of imprisonment. The husband learned of the illicit association and on release from prison, vowed to deal with his wife and her policeman lover. In fleeing from the man, my constable had been involved in a road traffic accident and had submitted an application to the chief superintendent to resign with immediate effect. I never saw him again.

I remained with the Vice Squad for 12 months but was relieved when my tour of duty was completed. The whole sordid business of vice, drugs, humanity dragged to its lowest levels was an experience which I considered alien to my normal principles and I regarded it as a job I was pleased to leave behind every time I went home.

When I returned to normal uniform duties on 'A' division I transferred to the Digbeth sub-division which was located in the markets area of the city which included the abattoir. One of the long serving constables at Digbeth knew most of the street traders and market workers, checking the stalls regularly with an authority which suggested he was the Lord of the manor and they were his serfs. Shortly after my arrival he suggested that I would find it interesting to visit the abattoir, the destination of cattle I had witnessed driven along the street on one of my first days on the beat. With my approval he made the necessary arrangements. There was no doubt that his demeanour indicated that he was a regular visitor and that he expected to be treated as though he was the boss. I was given demonstrations of the slaughter of sheep, pigs and cattle which I found distasteful and bestial in the manner the animals were dispatched. In an age where animals are bred for slaughter, I should not have been surprised but I never made a return visit.

Whilst some of the duties were mundane there were the occasional 'gems' of contacts with members of the public. I was stopped one day by an elderly lady who asked me tentatively if I had found her key. Replying somewhat cautiously I asked for more detail. She explained that a few days previously she had lost her door key, gone to the police station and reported the loss. The desk sergeant had assured her that he would circulate the description and every policeman would look for it. I smiled thinking that whilst there would never be a realistic chance the key would be found whoever the sergeant was, the lady's problem had been treated seriously and she had been given very personal attention. Silently I commended him

I had been at Digbeth for only a few months when the superintendent engaged me in what appeared to be casual conversation one day. He asked me what I was doing the following day and when I replied that I had no specific commitments he replied, "Right, Chief Constable at 10.00am; Watch Committee at 10.15am and don't be late." The Watch Committee were the Police Authority of city and borough Forces and although he did not actually say the words, I knew that promotion was intended.

One Step Up the Ladder

The interview with the Chief Constable was a mere formality to tell me he had recommended to the Watch Committee that I should be promoted to inspector. A few minutes later in a room 2 doors away from the Chief Constable's office I stood in front of members of the Watch Committee to be informed that they accepted the Chief Constable's recommendation and congratulated me on my promotion which was to take immediate effect. A visit to the clothing store which was in the same building to be measured for my new uniform was next and to be issued with my coveted inspector's baton, a leather covered swagger stick approximately 24" long. This was a symbol of the rank and accounted for the frequently used nick-name for an inspector of 'The stick'.

Somewhat to my surprise my posting was to the Sparkhill sub-division of 'F' division which bordered the area I had worked at Edward Road. It was an area I knew well and stretched from a point 3 miles from the city centre to the city boundary at Solihull in Warwickshire. Other than the sub-divisional headquarters at Sparkhill, I had one other station – Robin Hood which was about 2 miles on the same main Stratford Road. It was a frequent practice of mine to pair up with one of the younger constables and walk with him to Robin Hood station and then leave him to walk back whilst I was otherwise engaged.

Robin Hood station was the place of another 'gem' of public relations. I was in the office one day when a frail looking lady dressed in black walked in. She had the appearance of a Dickensian character and asked if she was doing the right thing. Both the office constable and I said whatever her problem was we would deal with it. From her shopping bag she then took an object, placed it on the counter and explained that it had been on her mantle shelf for many years but had decided to get rid of it. The object in question was a World War 2 incendiary bomb. After taking her name and address we shepherded her out of the station and leaving the bomb in situ called for the attendance of explosive experts. When they arrived, it was taken out into the rear garden of the station and blown up. Life is full of surprises.

On another occasion for one of my visits, I was driving into the station car park, slowed appropriately but unfortunately the motorist following me braked too late and collided with the rear of my car causing slight damage. It was an obvious case of careless driving but because my arrival had been noted by 3 or 4 police officers looking out of the window, I decided that there may be a suggestion of bias if they were called as witnesses and the offending motorist appreciated words of advice instead of a summons.

Dealing with tragedy is always a possibility for any police officer and throughout my service I think I have been called to a wide range of incidents which have destroyed individuals and families. A concerned caller informed that she was worried about her neighbour who she hadn't seen for some days. With a constable I went to the house and looking through the kitchen window I saw the lady householder lying on the floor. I broke a window to gain access and saw that the woman's head was on a pillow in the gas oven. We dragged her out and whilst the constable called for an ambulance I endeavoured to keep her alive. After what seemed an eternity I could hear the two-tone siren of the ambulance and the patient was removed to hospital. I felt cheated that my efforts had been in vain when she died two days later.

Christmas is expected to be a time of happiness particularly when families celebrate the festivities together. When we received notice from a hospital in the early hours of Christmas Day asking that we deliver a 'death message' I decided to do it myself anticipating that it would require extra sensitivity. A young husband, father of 2 children had been admitted to hospital the previous evening with an unexpected illness and had died during the night. Following a well tried format I went to the next door neighbour and asked her to anticipate that I may need some assistance. The young mother, now a widow came to the door in her night attire. Behind her I could see a Christmas tree with presents on the floor. There is never an easy way to break such bad news and her distress was apparent. I would never forget that particular Christmas morning.

There can be another twist to tragedies however and again Christmas was the setting for the visit of a police officer bringing news to a destitute family who were so poor they could have stepped out of a Charles Dickens's story. . I was made aware of a family who had cooked a large chicken on Christmas Day, decided they didn't want it and were going to consign it to the dustbin. Horrified I told them I would make sure it could be delivered to suitable recipients. My plan was simple; find a needy family and give them the chicken which was ready for the table. Not so easy. Schools, social security offices and all other points of normal contact were closed. I then had a brain wave and went to a local Roman Catholic Church where I saw the resident priest and explained my problem.

The priest identified a needy family and together we went to the house. That is where the plan started to go wrong. I could only speculate what must have gone through he minds of the mother and father, looking out of the window and watching a police inspector and priest walk up the path. Were we bringing news of a death in the family? Was one of the children in trouble? When they opened the door I reassured them nothing was wrong and asked if they had anything for dinner. They informed me they had some sausages left from the previous day – Christmas Day. When the priest and I gave them the chicken the pleasure of the moment was, again a moment to treasure.

Throughout my active police career I hoped I could always temper enthusiasm to catch criminals with compassion when necessary. Late one winter evening we received a call from a woman with information of child neglect. At the house subject of the complaint we found a girl of about 10 years, her brother aged about 5 and a baby in a pram. There was no heating or lighting in the house, the children were poorly clothed and there was no food in the house. We learned that the father had not been seen for some time and their mother had gone out and not returned. At that time, women police were not included in general duties but were regarded as specialists to deal with matters affecting women and children. I requested the assistance of police woman Irene Philips and without the red tape which would bedevil such decisions in later years, on my own authority, took the children to a place of safety. I was angry that a mother and father could have caused such distress to children but later my attitude changed…

We found the mother who was scarcely out of her teens a poor pathetic woman wandering aimlessly with inadequate clothing against the cold temperature. We learned that her husband was in prison awaiting trial for sexually abusing the 10 year old girl and there was no income for her to pay for the necessities to provide for the children. We made arrangements for her to receive some assistance and re-united her with her children. A few days later my wife suggested that some of our children's unwanted clothing would be useful for this family and I took them to their home.

On return to the police station I received a call from the police woman inspector who was the supervising officer of policewoman Philips. She told me that she was concerned the policewoman was becoming too closely involved with the family which, I explained was embarrassing for me because I had just delivered some baby clothes for the children. After a few moments, the policewoman inspector admitted she herself had sent some cigarettes and other small gifts to the destitute mother. We agreed to say no more about police woman Philips's involvement with the family.

As an inspector, whilst my supervising responsibilities were not reduced, administrative work increased leaving less time to patrol the streets but it was still possible to follow my enthusiasm to catch criminals. Covering two police stations and an area of several square miles, a car was essential for my duties and sometimes I took a constable with me. On one occasion, with a constable I was sitting in my unmarked police car on a pub car park watching the world go past when details of a stolen car were broadcast over our radio. Minutes later the car was driven past and we followed. I was not trained as a pursuit driver and my car carried no indication that it was a police vehicle. Eventually the suspect car stopped, the driver and passenger were apprehended and another young constable's 'street credibility' with his colleagues was increased a notch or two.

I frequently adopted a policy of patrolling in a police van with one of my sergeants driving and 3 or 4 of the less experienced officers. The intention was to increase the confidence of the constables and one way to do so was to visit pubs after official closing time. Whilst I would give words of advice or warning to the licensee for serving after hours, the sergeant and constable would move amongst the customers encouraging them, to drink up and leave. We seldom experienced trouble and it gave the constables a good grounding in talking to members of the public getting used to exercising their authority with the assurance that the sergeant and inspector were close at hand.

I was still very active in my athletic interests and one night was able to put it to good use. As we turned into a side street we saw two men rifling a parked car but they ran off as we approached. We gave chase and I followed one of the suspects. When he threw away items which he had stolen I retrieved them and continued running after him knowing that I could probably out-run him. I didn't try to catch him, waiting until he would be out of breath. Unexpectedly he ran into a night club with me close behind. The patrons of the club witnessed what one of them later described as a Keystone Cop chase as I arrested my car thief.

For me it was just another incident, another felon arrested but the following night I was summoned to the office of my Chief Superintendent John Smith. With a stern expression he informed me that a serious complaint had been made against me. I had never had a complaint registered previously and I was bewildered as to what I had done. With what appeared to be suppressed anger, the Chief Superintendent told me that the night club owner had complained I had raided his club with other police officers, with no warrant, disrupted his business and molested his clients.

My discomfort was apparent and my superior containing his bottled up mirth no longer burst into laughter and said that the night club owner had been highly amused about the incident and described it as the best entertainment at the club for a long time. He even suggested that we should do a repeat performance. It was obvious that my boss was well pleased and when I paraded my Relief later that night, he accompanied me and congratulated everyone on their outstanding work during their period of night duty which had resulted in a large number of arrests for serous crime.

Every police station has its regular 'odd characters' many of them harmless, some seeking to cause trouble. Sparkhill police station was no exception and one of ours was Mr. Johnson who lived at 29 Poplar Road, a name and address firmly implanted in my memory. Mr. Johnson's complaint was that his house was frequently burgled and the police failed to deal with the matter. Because of the frequency of his complaints and there being no evidence of a burglary, I decided to deal with him the next time he reported that his house had been broken into. I went to his home and found that his front door, in additions to the usual locks, was also fitted with a padlock. He explained that when he left the house, he always made sure that the padlock was left in a particular fashion but when he returned, it was not as he had left it. That was his evidence of unlawful entry.

I felt sorry for Mr. Johnson who obviously suffered from delusions and spent some time with him explaining that he had nothing to worry about but if it ever happened that someone had actually broken into his house we would deal with it. I felt pleased that I had dealt with the problem satisfactorily but the next day I read in the station occurrence book that he had again complained that his house had been burgled and he knew who was responsible – Inspector Stowe! The record made in the book could have had serious consequence for me but fortunately my Chief Superintendent saw it for what is was and there were no repercussions.

One day I was on duty when two young boys were taken into the station accused of theft. The story outlined to me was that a bus conductress, following her normal practice had placed bags of coins in her cash box which she secreted in the supposedly secure place on the bus. The two boys had taken some of the bags of coins but they were seen by the conductress who detained them and called the police. The boys were about 9 or 10 years old, the money had been recovered and I considered it appropriate to adopt a lenient approach.

The boys were accompanied by their mothers and in my admonishment; I told them that "in the olden days, thieves may have had their hands cut off." The one mother, without saying a word, lifted her child's hand to show that he had no fingers, a victim of the thalidomide tragedies. I took her to one side and made my profuse apologies which she accepted. How are the mighty fallen!

On another occasion when administering an official caution to a young boy, he reached across my desk, picked up a heavy ebony ruler and hit me on the head. Only my authoritative image was injured but I made it quite clear to him and his parent the possible consequences of similar future transgressions.

Although there was always a duty night time CID officer available to whom serious crimes should have been reported, he would have been responsible for a whole division with about 15 – 16 stations to cover and would have been hard pressed to deal with all reported crimes. Consequently one night when a report was received that a young woman had been raped, I decided to supervise the enquiry myself.

The nature of the allegation was that a young 16 year old girl had visited a disco with a strict understanding from her mother that she must be home by 10.30pm. It was the one night of the week when she was permitted to go out unaccompanied.

The disco was in the city centre and during the evening she met a man who was friendly towards her. When she realised that it was time to leave so that she could catch her bus home, he offered to take her in his car if she would stay a little longer and she agreed.

When they did leave, she realised that he was travelling in the opposite direction to where she lived but he reassured her by explaining that he needed petrol. When he eventually stopped in an estate of multiple tower blocks of flats he said he had left his wallet in his flat and rather than sit in the car waiting for him, she could go with him to the flat.

Too late, in the flat, the girl realised how naïve she had been and was subjected to an assault which resulted in the allegation of rape. The offender appeared to have some concern for her and drove her to a few yards from her home, then gave her 10 shillings to compensate for her dress which had been torn in the assault.

It was nearly 1.00am when I was informed and together with a police woman I collected the girl from her home. Unfortunately I realised that the police woman was not very experienced and had never before dealt with a similar allegation. After she had interviewed the girl I was informed that there was no evidence of a rape having been committed.

I was anxious to trace the offender but the information available to locate the scene of the crime was very limited. The victim only had a vague idea of the route travelled and could only say that it was in an estate with many blocks of high rise flats; that they had used a lift to one of the upper floors and that inside the flat near the door was a table on which she had left a glass half full of water.

Eventually after gentle encouragement she identified the estate which was on the opposite side of the city to where she lived. It was in fact a disused airfield where I had been stationed when serving in the Royal Air Force – Castle Bromwich which now consisted of tower blocks of flats. Which particular block was not clear but she was certain that we were in the right location. There was no alternative but to enter each block separately, travel to each floor and look through the letter box of every door to identify the room she had described. My actions would at least have caused curiosity or even suspicion if the residents had seen me.

By 7.00am I was becoming tired and frustrated but when we entered the lift of one of the blocks of flats, the girl became excited and pointed to a cigarette packet on the floor. "This is it," she explained, "I remember that cigarette packet." It was only a small point but absolutely crucial and I continued peering through letter boxes with renewed determination. Eventually when I looked through one letter box, on a table in the hall was a glass half full of water.

A sleepy young man opened the door after my unceremonious banging and ignoring his protestations of innocence, he was arrested, cautioned and taken to the police station whilst I collected supporting evidence from his flat including the glass on which the girl's finger prints were clearly visible.

Subsequent medical examination revealed that the girl had been subjected to a brutal anal penetration and subsequently the offender was sent to prison for four years.

House Fires

The policing arrangements at Sparkhill, in common with other areas had 4 inspectors one for each Relief which usually consisted of 3 sergeants and perhaps 15 – 16 constables. The shift pattern was such that we worked one week of night duty every four weeks. It seemed to me that every time it was my turn for night duty, we dealt with a house fire. Of course the responsibility to deal with the fires always remained that of the fire officers but such occurrences may involve criminal acts – arson or murder, there may be road closures to implement, arrangements to be made for homeless occupants and many other issues requiring police attention.

One such fire resulted in the death of a young man who appeared to have become disorientated in the smoke and tried to escape from the bedroom through a wardrobe door rather than the door of the bedroom. Another fatality was recorded when an elderly couple fell asleep in their arm chairs in front of the television. One of them had been smoking and the lighted cigarette had dropped onto the upholstery and the fire ensued.

Even with fires, there can be occasions that with almost black humour there is a lighter side to the story. In the small hours of the morning a fire was discovered in the bedroom of a lodging house where almost all the rooms were independently occupied. We ensured the safe evacuation of everyone but could not account for the person who had occupied the room which was the seat of the fire. Our enquiries established that it was a man who needed crutches to walk. An hour or so later a man answering the description was found sheltering in a doorway about a mile away. He admitted he was the missing person and explained that he had been smoking in bed which had caught fire and he had left the house. We asked him if he had warned the other occupants and his reply was quite amazing; "They don't talk to me so why should I talk to them?"

On another occasion, not on night duty but late turn, a young mother was doing the family ironing, dinner was cooking in the oven but the idyllic family scene was disrupted when their baby started choking, apparently having swallowed a foreign object. Panic ensued; she and her husband dashed to their car to take the baby to hospital; they drove off although the husband was only a provisional licence holder; a short way down the road they collided with a police car; the mother realised she had left the iron on the ironing table and total tragedy loomed. However police officers can have an understanding streak and everything was resolved. They performed first aid and relieved the baby's distress then took baby and mother back to the flat where they lived while the husband sorted out his driving problems with another officer.

On their return, the ironing board was smouldering and perhaps about to ignite but sadly the dinner in the oven was beyond redemption. It was a near thing but another house fire was averted and with regard to all the circumstances no further action was necessary.

The Changing Face of Policing

1967 was the year when traditional policing changed for ever. Until then members of the public had been familiar with police officers walking the beat, available to give advice or deal with incidents and from their very presence bring about an atmosphere of law regularity. In 1967 a nationwide change took place with the introduction of the unit beat policing system. The theory was that a team of officers, one for each 8 hour tour of duty with one on rest day, would use a car to patrol their designated area; performing foot patrol in vulnerable areas then driving to another area for more foot patrol. Human nature dictated that the theory was defective and officers quickly ignored the expectation to carry out foot patrols and remained in their vehicles throughout their tour of duty only leaving them when dealing with specific incidents.

The cars were first introduced in the Lancashire police area and were a distinctive black and white, giving rise to the colloquial name 'Panda cars'

One consequence was that the skill developed by engaging persons in casual conversation on the street and using their acquired experience to detect wrong-doers was lost. If a suspect was observed and justified questioning, immediately the police officer stopped his car and approached a person, a confrontational situation was likely to develop which could easily escalate to a serious level. Skill in talking to members of the public cannot be learned in books but can only result from individuals' techniques.

The first day of the new system, Birmingham Police had large numbers of the new 'panda car' vehicles at holding areas ready for the signal to drive into their respective divisions throughout the city. It was a Saturday morning and ironically some young men on the Sparkhill sub-division decided to arrange a spoof abduction of one of their pals who was part of the agreement. The young man was walking along the pavement when a van pulled up alongside him and several men brandishing pick axe handles bundled him into their van and drove off. The intention was to demonstrate that ordinary people would not react to witnessing what appeared to be a violent incident.

Unfortunately for them, Sparkhill residents did re-act and several 999 calls were received as the procession of the new panda cars was arriving in the area. Within minutes the abductors' van was surrounded by several panda cars and rather than deal with them for wasting police time we considered it had been useful practice for the implementation of the new policing system.

A Change from Operational Policing

Although I was always confident of my own ability, confidence can sometimes be seen by others as arrogance and although I always tried to carry out my duties competently and with confidence, I never considered that I was arrogant – I hope not. Consequently my attitude to my duties led to confrontation with a local politician. He was the chairman of the Watch Committee, Councillor Charles Collett, a pompous man always seeking publicity who lived in a large house at the junction of two roads in the affluent part of Sparkhill. On more than one occasion he complained about a car parked on the wide pavement outside his house causing obstruction. One day he visited the station to complain about the car and I explained to him that merely because the car was on the pavement that would not justify taking action against the owner. His complaint and my response were correctly recorded in the station occurrence book.

The following day when I paraded for duty and read the occurrence book I saw that he had made a further visit and demanded a note be made in the book the nature of which impinged on my competence and demanding that something be done to deal with the owner of the car on the pavement. Perhaps it may have been prudent to take a more cautious approach but I went to his house and confronted him. I explained again the limitations to pursue a prosecution against the car driver and told him that if he had any complaint about me to make it to my superior officers, not to my subordinates.

It could have been co-incidence but later that day I received a call from my Chief Superintendent who told me a vacancy had occurred at the Birmingham Police Training Centre, Tally Ho and thought I was the right person to fill it. The posting was to be taken up with immediate effect and I didn't argue because it was obvious a decision had been made, I enjoyed instructor's duties and the hours I would be working were regular with no shift work.

Tally Ho was not only the Birmingham Police training centre but also provided sporting facilities where I had competed in inter divisional athletic competitions

Chapter 9. Family Life and Holidays

Even though my promotion had increased our income, we still had little spare cash and lavish holidays were beyond our reach but fortunately the children were too young to realise that they may have been missing the normal holiday attractions other children enjoyed.

The policeman neighbour and his wife who had facilitated the adoption of our children owned a small caravan which was in a field at Hope Bowdler, a small village in Shropshire and although we only used it for a week or so, the farmer who owned the field was very friendly and we enjoyed seeing his dogs working with the sheep. One of his dogs was elderly and no longer able to work but he would lie at the gate to the yard, occasionally visiting the hen coops where he would steal an egg as a little snack. It was the first time our little dachshunds had met sheep and were not at all comfortable when we woke one morning and found the field full of sheep.

Another budget holiday was taken in a cottage in the mid Wales town of Presteign which was owned by one of Ann's relatives. We had no transport of our own but were fortunate to borrow father in law's Austin A35 car.

Pear Tree Cottage was an experience! It had no running water necessitating regular visits to the village pump 100 yards away; no sanitary system other than a chemical toilet which had to be emptied in a field opposite and limited cooking facilities. Although the town was very small being the County Town it was entitled to hold its own Court of Assize or to use its correct terminology, Her Majesty's Court of Oyer, Terminer and General Gaol Delivery. I was particularly interested when I realised that we were able to witness the pomp and ceremony of judges in full wigs and robes each carrying a traditional nosegay, processing into the court buildings.

When out walking one day I also saw for the first and only time in my life, a mole burrowing away in the hedgerow.

Other holidays were spent in rented cottages in Barmouth, North Wales, Leeston in Suffolk, Beer in Devon and perhaps the most memorable, Dartmouth. Although in every one of those locations, entertainment for the children was minimal they were of such an age that they would not have realised other children of their peer group from more affluent families would have experienced more exotic vacations. Unfortunately the truth was we could not afford greater expense.

Our house was approximately 6 miles from Sparkhill police station and when I served there as an inspector I would run to and from work using the distance as a useful training exercise. The practice almost caused serious medical problems when I developed sciatica in my right leg. I found that although I could run, I experienced intense pain and discomfort in walking, sitting or driving a car. When eventually I capitulated to my wife's insistence and visited my doctor he pointedly told me that it was running which caused the problem and I must rest.

I recall one day in the canteen at the police station a cartoon appeared, drawn by one of the sergeants who often displayed his artistic skills. The picture depicted a very bean-stick figure in running shorts and vest with an inspector's uniform on a hook behind him, alongside the very rotund figure of the 'F' division football coach, PC Lloyd with a caption "And I say, "Running does something for a fellow." The originator of the sketch was worried I might take exception to the portrayal but someone else pointed out that when you are caricaturised, you have arrived! The original of the cartoon remained in my possession as a cherished memento.

After the gift of the little Morris 8 car and a later change to the Vauxhall Velox, our finances would not support continued ownership of such a luxury and for a period of time we were without our own transport other than the BSA 250c motor cycle we had owned before the children joined us. But Ann urged me to buy another car. I agreed on one condition, that she learned to drive. It would be an understatement to say that she was reluctant, even to the point that I completed her application for her driving licence which eventually she agreed to sign.

Ann's father owned a Hillman Imp car, a tiny compact vehicle which in due course he sold to me for a price within my capabilities. By that time, Ann had a driving licence and after a few preliminary lessons to familiarise her with the controls, we set off one Sunday afternoon to my sister's home in Sutton Coldfield about 12 miles away, a journey which took us through the heart of Birmingham. We didn't collide with anyone or thing, observed all the restrictions of traffic signs and arrived at our destination with no mishap.

After her first experience, Ann became very competent, passing her test at the third attempt and thereafter driving became second nature to her.

Following the Special Course - University

It had always been acknowledged that the outstanding students completing the Special Course should receive some extra credit but it was not decided until after the third course had been completed how it should be achieved. The 3 outstanding students from the 1st, 2nd and 3rd courses would all be given university scholarships to further their potential in the Police Service. I was not one of those 3 from the first course but considered that if promotion to the highest ranks would favour those with degrees, I would join them. Whether this attitude of mind reflected my determination or conceit is for others to assess.

I was accepted by the University of London as an external student to undertake a 5 year course leading to a Bachelor of Law (LL.B) degree. I agreed with Ann that with our young children, I would endeavour to undertake my studies without interfering with family life. I registered for a correspondence course and night school classes anticipating that it would require at least 18 hours study each week (3 hours for each of 6 days) and whenever possible I would carry out my studies after the children had gone to bed. On my rest days when posted to work early turn, 6.00am – 2.00pm I would still get up at 5.0am and do my studies before the family got up.

The structure of the 5 year course was to take an intermediate examination after 2 years and the final examination in 2 parts, the first after 1 or 2 years with the second part after 2 or 1 year. In addition to the necessary text books I purchased I made extensive use of the city library sometimes borrowing as many as 9 or 10 books contemporaneously. Although the normal limit was 3 books per borrower, I used tickets in my wife's name and also my neighbours, with their approval of course.

To prepare for the intermediate examination I was required to study The English Legal System, Tort, Contract and Roman Law. Out of the four, I anticipated great difficulties with Roman Law, never having studied Latin at school and resorted to learning by heart many of the Roman Law principles. Gradually I became increasingly fascinated and appreciated that although our legal system was different, many aspects of our law could be traced to Roman law origins.

At the night school classes studying the English Legal System I was joined by another police officer, Superintendent Geoff Floy whom I had worked alongside when he was an inspector. Other students in the class were from established legal backgrounds, magistrates' clerks, solicitors etc but at the end of the course, Geoff and I were the only ones who achieved a pass mark.

I had always endeavoured to prepare for examinations by total commitment to the necessary studies but the association of other students is always beneficial. Consequently when I had the opportunity to attend Leeds University for a two weeks course, I readily accepted. I recall that on the day I left Birmingham my family accompanied me to the railway station where I boarded a steam engine train; which for many years was the last occasion when I experienced such a journey.

Studying had become a way of life if not an obsession and I would use the time travelling on buses, and waiting for buses to cram more information and understanding until after 2 years, the crucial testing time arrived – the Intermediate examinations.

There were probably 100 persons in the examination room and our answer papers would be identified only by a dedicated examination number. I felt reasonably confident, satisfied that I had prepared as well as I could have done. Obviously other examinees were not so confident and within minutes of the instruction to turn over our question papers, several left the room leaving their answer papers blank. The exams were taken over 2 consecutive days with 4 papers each of 3 hours duration. After 12 hours during which all the cramming for the exams was drained from me, I left the examination room to return home. Such was the mental effort of the exams that when I left I was quite oblivious to everything and had no more understanding of where I was nor what I was doing than a robot would have had. I 'came to' about 45 minutes later walking towards my home and 3 miles from the examination room. I was mentally exhausted.

Results of the examination were to be published at the University of London showing only the examination number of successful examinees. Full details would be sent by post at a later date. On the day of publication, Ann and I travelled to London anxious to learn whether 2 years of study had been worthwhile. Lists of successful candidates' examination numbers were displayed in glass fronted notice boards arranged on the pavement in front of Senate House at the University with students gathered round the boards of their respective faculties. Some students were shouting and embracing in excitement as they saw that they had passed whilst others sat on the kerb completely despondent. Being a mature student and accompanied by my wife I hope I appeared to be under more emotional control but when we saw my examination number included in the passes, we were as excited as anyone else.

Returning to Birmingham, the pressure was about to commence again with other subjects to be studied; evidence, land law, criminal law, equity, constitutional law and domestic law, some of which were compulsory whilst others were by choice from many specific subjects. I decided that I would sit part 1 of the Final examination 2 years later, intending to take part 2 after a further 12 months.

My studies continued and it was now more or less a settled way of life but when I took the part 1 of the Final examination I was less confident of my achievement. And I was far less enthusiastic to travel to London for the results. However, with Ann's insistence we did so and again, I was very relieved to see that I had passed.

Whilst continuing the studies I had not forgotten my Chief Constable's advice and was constantly scouring advertisements for appointment to other Forces. My first 'success' was to the Bath & Somerset Force where I was short-listed with 5 other candidates one of whom was a detective inspector with whom I had worked on 'F' division. Full of confidence, I was disappointed when he was selected over the other 5 and I was annoyed that when we returned to Birmingham he changed his mind and withdrew. Other short lists for me included Glamorgan Police, Essex, Gloucestershire, Derbyshire and the Metropolitan Police. For that particular interview I was travelling to London by train and the person sitting opposite seemed strangely familiar. Eventually my curiosity urged me to ask if he was Dr Ramsey, Archbishop of Canterbury. It was and we had an absorbing conversation for the rest of the journey. I hope I didn't bore him because I found the encounter to be very interesting.

I was becoming frustrated by the repeated rejections and when I answered an advertisement for the Wiltshire Constabulary I travelled to Devizes accompanied by my father-in-law to give me some moral support. It was also a day out for him in the pleasant countryside. On interviews for other Forces I had always attended the Force headquarters with the other interviewees. At Devizes, I was the only one and I presumed other applicants were to attend at different times. The interviewing panel included the Chief Constable, Mr. George Glendinning, an ex-Metropolitan police officer and Assistant Chief Constable Mr. Tanswell who I later found had a terrifying reputation for discipline and procedure.

A few days later I received notification that the post of chief inspector was offered to me and I was required to notify my acceptance. It was July 1969 and to celebrate my birthday we were about to start a completely new experience in our lives.

Chapter 10. Chief Inspector, Warminster Sub-Division

Transferring to the Wiltshire Constabulary was more than a change of rank and location, it was a totally different lifestyle with every aspect taking on an exciting element of exploration. The Constabulary was run on a very tight budgetary control with no excess expenditure tolerated. There was no uniform available for me when I took up my post and my initial duties were undertaken in plain clothes which caused problems from time to time for the first few days.

We were housed in accommodation which was part of the police station with a door into my office leading from the hallway of the house. There was no central heating but open fires where we could burn coal or more frequently, logs. It was a large draughty house, difficult to warm adequately particularly in the winter leading my superintendent, Eric Clark to comment that I should open the fridge door to raise the temperature in the house.

Whilst it was convenient to have my office more or less part of the house, to the children it may have been regarded as just another room. One day when I was in my office discussing a particular matter with one of the town's doctors, Denise bounded into the office shouting "Daddy come quick, Lloyd's being sick."

Warminster, where we would live for the next 3 years, at that time was a small market town with a population of about 10,000 having its own court sitting once a week under the supervision of the senior magistrate Mr. Elgar, a retired barrister and a man who could readily be described as 'a character'. My duties would include the preparation and prosecution of all routine court cases.

The small village of Tisbury which was in my jurisdiction also held a court periodically and the magistrate was Mr. George Lush who also acted as Her Majesty's Coroner for the area. I was to become well acquainted with Mr. Lush when all too often it was necessary for me to convene coroner's inquests.

Warminster was also noted as a military town, having the School of Infantry and a resident Battalion based at Battlesbury Barracks. Located on Salisbury Plain, in my area of responsibility, was Imber village which had been subject to mass evacuation of the residents during the Second World War to allow its use for military training. The village residents had apparently been given an assurance that they would be permitted to return when the war ended but it never happened and the Military retained it for training purposes.

I knew of course that Salisbury Plain is identified for its archaeological significance, most noted being Stonehenge but until I arrived in Warminster I had not appreciated its significance in the study of unidentified flying objects – UFOs. Warminster attracted visitors from all points of the compass for the possibility of seeing for themselves one of these strange objects from outer space. Very shortly after my arrival I became acquainted with a local newspaper reporter, Arthur Shuttlewood who had written several books on the phenomena and was totally convinced of their existence. I featured in one of his books following a casual meeting with him and a local resident in the main street one evening. The local man was explaining to Arthur his experience of seeing a UFO and the sighting was given credibility in one of Arthur's books by quoting "and this was said in the presence of police Chief Inspector Stowe!"

Did I ever see a UFO myself? Yes and no. On one occasion having attended a Mess dinner at Battlesbsury Barracks, Ann and I were driving home in the small hours of the morning when we saw a strange mass of light, its intensity pulsating from dim to a brightness. We stopped the car and for several minutes wondered at the strangeness and possible identification of a UFO. Eventually our reasoning decided that the light was a full moon with early morning mist drifting across our line of sight. It was not a UFO.

On another occasion on a moonless night I went to a location known as Cradle Hill which boasted the most frequent sightings of UFOs. In the sky I could see the outline of mysterious objects whose shapes were changing as I watched. As I drew closer to the hill I found that youngsters on motor cycles were riding up and down the hill and their headlights were shining through branches of the trees creating images on the clouds. Definitely not UFOs!

Whether UFOs existed or not is a matter of personal opinion but it is significant that Warminster was very near to Boscombe Down where many secret Government experiments were conducted but never publicly acknowledged. That could possibly explain many of the mysterious sightings.

The sub-division had a geographical area of approximately 400 square miles with 8 village police stations and was one of 3 sub-divisions within the Salisbury division which was under the supervision of a chief superintendent and a superintendent as his deputy. Once a month a divisional meeting was held with all chief inspectors from the other sub-divisions present.

The village of Tisbury had a police sergeant supervising 2 constables and 2 other constables a few miles away at Mere on the Dorset border. Sergeant Bill King was the only authority in the area acknowledged by the villagers. If a licencee required an extension of hours or if permission was required to close the roads for the annual village carnival, it was to Sergeant King that application was made. Sub-divisional chief inspectors, divisional chief superintendents, even county chief constables were regarded as of no consequence in matters of village life.

On my first visit to Tisbury police station, I was appalled to find that having 2 cells in the police station, one was used as a repository for bicycles and other miscellaneous property whilst the other was used as a storage place for Sergeant King's dahlia tubers. The posters on the notice boards were years out of date and the general appearance was that this station would be a target for my modernising plans. However, I was cautious. I realised that this interloper from the city with grandiose ideas could alienate the officers who had worked in the area for many years, knew the locals and were accepted by the villagers as being synonymous with law and order.

My caution was justified and I quickly learned to respect his experience which helped me to avoid pitfalls which could otherwise have undermined my authority. Tisbury was close to the stately home of the Lord Lieutenant of the county Lord Margadale whose annual garden party was due to be held shortly after I arrived in Warminster. Sergeant King asked me if I would like to attend and in due course I received a gold edged invitation card for Ann and me. On the day of the garden party, mixing with members of the aristocracy, I saw my chief superintendent who asked me rather tersely how I had managed to receive an invitation and when I told him it was because of Sergeant King's influence, he admitted that he also owed his own invitation to the sergeant. When, out of curiosity and interest I attended the Boxing Day hunt, Sergeant King was to be seen handing out the traditional stirrup cup to the huntsmen and women.

We didn't realise it at the time but the arrival of a new chief inspector in the town was newsworthy for the local newspaper and the public at large. One of the first realisations was when my wife went to the dry cleaners to collect garments she had deposited a few days earlier and expressed surprise that the shop keeper knew her by name. The explanation was "Well you are the new chief inspector's wife." Similarly, with Lord Bath as a near neighbour at Longleat, I was very worried when a small van arrived one day with a gift of venison from Lord Bath. I refused the offer but the driver warned me Lord Bath would be very disappointed that I had declined his gift. I asked for advice from my chief superintendent at Salisbury and the answer was quite simple. I was to select the best joint for the chief superintendent, have what I wanted for myself and distribute the remaining joints to the sergeants and constables.

It was only 2 or 3 years previously that Lord Bath had brought lions to Longleat and although the reaction of Wiltshire residents had varied from curiosity to hostility, the venture had proved successful and became increasingly popular. The attractions at the safari park were continually expanding, sometimes with unexpected consequences. One morning, a local tradesman came to the station to report a rather unusual accident when he had been delivering to Longleat. As was his normal practice he was driving down a little used lane at the rear of the estate when he collided with a hippopotamus. A quick telephone call to Longleat revealed that they had bought two of the animals for the lake and had underestimated their ability to find a way out of their enclosure. Fortunately they were at liberty for a relatively short period of time and the tradesman probably earned himself many free pints in the pub recounting his experience.

40 years or so later on a television wildlife programme based at Longleat the man who had been involved in the collision was interviewed and recounted the experience. I felt a sense of personal vindication because having recounted the story many times myself, I am sure my listeners may have been sceptical at the authenticity of my story.

There were other gifts from the gentry which initially tested my principles. Pheasant shoots are an established part of rural life and in my sub-division during the appropriate season they were frequent and popular. Some of the constables were permitted to earn a little extra money by acting as beaters for the shoots. On more than one occasion I would find a brace of pheasants on my back door step; I never discovered the identity of any donor and if I asked questions I would always be reassured that it was quite normal.

Geest Industries had a large warehouse in Warminster and it was not unusual to have a large stem of bananas delivered to the station intended for the staff. In other circumstances such gifts could have been construed as gratuities intended to influence the impartiality of the police but I became satisfied that acceptance was part of the integration process into rural life.

Included in the police station complex was the sub-divisional social club having a bar, a 'fruit machine' and snooker table. It was popular with the regular police officers, special constables who provided a valuable supplement to our limited manpower and other approved members at least one of whom was a local magistrate. Particularly on Saturday evenings the club was always well patronised and to enhance the cordial atmosphere, Ann adopted the practice of providing cheese and onion rolls which proved immensely popular and allowed us to mix without the constraints of rank difference.

One aspect of my new duties which was strange to me was that my station was only open from 8.00am until midnight with the constable on night duty patrolling the street and periodically visiting the station to make contact with Salisbury. As was the common practice at the time, he would use his pocket book to record where he was every hour during his tour of duty.

One night when my family and I were asleep in bed, I was awakened by a banging on my front door and saw a uniformed policeman. The reason for getting me out of bed and the story which unfolded was as follows:

He and his colleague on motor patrol had seen a car parked in a lay-by. In the car was a young woman who, when questioned admitted she had stolen the car from her boy friend and from the glove compartment took an engagement ring which she said resulted from their broken engagement after a row. They were faced with a dilemma because without a policewoman, they were reluctant to take any positive action with her. The short term solution was for one police officer to take the woman in his car with his colleague driving the stolen car following the police car with headlights on to refute any later allegations of impropriety.

They arrived at my house with the intention of calling for a policewoman from Salisbury, 20 miles away, in order that the woman could be searched then taken to the cells at Salisbury. Ann and I had quickly learned from our short time in a county Force that the policeman's wife often undertook police work when necessary and she having decided to get up and make cups of tea offered to search the suspect and accompany her to Salisbury. Before she did so however, I decided to question the suspect. She sat opposite me, her short skirt exposing most of her thighs and grubby finger nails arousing a suspicion in my mind. I leaned forward, yanked off the wig and found we were then talking to a young male soldier who had gone absent without leave from his base at Lichfield in Staffordshire. We often wondered how the incident would have developed if I had allowed my wife to carry out her intention to search.

The particular lay-by which brought about this incident was also the scene of a more tragic event. One morning I was called to the lay-by where the body of a young male person had been found under a plastic sheet. What appeared initially to be possibly a murder evolved into the conclusion that it was an unfortunate accident. The young man had been hitch-hiking and decided to rest in the lay-by and went to sleep with the plastic sheet as some sort of protection. Unknown to him, indeed unknown to anyone, he chose a spot over a gas main which had sustained a leak and from which gas was escaping. Normally it would have gone unnoticed but gradually a fatal pocket of gas was contained under the plastic and he died from gas poisoning.

A similar incident was reported when it appeared that the pavement in the main street was on fire. The Fire Brigade attended and when I arrived, their officer in charge did not seem to be particularly perturbed because the source of the flames, which were not excessive, originated in the same gas main which ran under the lay-by. He explained that while the gas burned, there was little danger until the leak could be sealed. The same phenomena occurs in oil refineries when surplus gas is burned off. The experience made me question in my own mind the story of Moses and the burning bush; was there a gas leak from a subterranean oil field?

Of necessity I was expected to be involved in many enquiries which would normally have been carried out by subordinate ranks but I only had 4 sergeants and no inspector and I considered that it was quite proper to carry out such duties particularly if there were likely to be serious consequences. One such occasion arose when a car was found in a forest glade with a hose pipe connected to the exhaust. Inside were two bodies, a man and a woman. By co-incidence a police officer from another area had been reported missing and there was suspicion that he may have been the male person.

I attended the scene and decided to call for a second opinion from the Force detective chief superintendent. We were reasonably satisfied it was a suicide pact but his particular interest was directed to the state of the bodies. He considered himself something of a crime novelist and saw the opportunity to include in his next book some of the features. He noted that the smoke from the exhaust fumes had deposited soot on all of the exposed body hairs covering arms and legs giving them a surreal appearance. He thought that quite unusual and very interesting.

It was not the only occasion when I was called upon to investigate a disappearance. One day I was in my office and one of my sergeants informed me that a resident from a local village wanted to see me. He was shown in and he explained that his wife had gone missing. I asked why he had insisted on making the report to me when any of the police staff could have taken the details. He seemed to prevaricate and when I pressed for more information he admitted that he knew where his wife had gone. The matter was becoming more irritating for me because if he knew where she had gone, she couldn't be considered as a missing person but then he dropped the bombshell. His wife had run away with the village based policeman; one of my constables. It didn't take long to trace the couple and eventually matrimonial stability was restored for both families. Sadly it was not the only time when I was involved with the officer's family life because a few months later he was tragically involved in a road traffic accident and his child died when she was thrown through the windscreen of his car.

A Visit from the Assistant Chief Constable

We had moved from Birmingham to my new appointment half way through the 12 months devoted to study for part 2 of the law degree final examination. I realised that to settle into my new role with the pressures it would involve would leave insufficient opportunity to study for the exam. I decided that instead of taking it in 1970 I would postpone my attempt for 12 months.

Very shortly after my arrival I received a visit from one of the Assistant Chief Constables, Mr. Jones. We walked together down the main street whilst he discussed with me the duties I would be expected to undertake and also used the opportunity to learn more about me. He was interested in my intentions for a law degree and when I informed him of my intention to postpone the examination for 12 months, he made it quite clear to me that was not acceptable and I was to take the exam when I had originally intended.

I increased my study efforts and on several occasions Ann would come to my office at 1.00am or 2.00am to find me asleep at my desk, head on the open books and notes I had been making. Eventually I did take the exam but the complexities of Land Law, Equity and Jurisprudence undermined my morale.

I had travelled to London for the Intermediate examination results with an open mind; for part 1 of the final I had been apprehensive but for the part 2 of the final examinations I was convinced I had failed to achieve the required standard and refused to go to London. However Ann was persistent and once again we found ourselves at the front of Senate House with large number of students looking for their own results. We found the appropriate glass fronted notice board and anxiously scanned the lists of successful students. No where could I see my number. I had not passed. In those few minutes, the disappointment of five years study was overwhelming and my hopes and aspirations were dashed. I was so despondent I hadn't realised that Ann had moved away from me but a few minutes later in great excitement she propelled me to another board which did include my number. I had passed with honours! In the space of a few minutes, total despair had been replaced by exuberance beyond my wildest expectations.

In August 1970 we made yet another journey to London but this time there was no reluctance. We were to attend the Royal Albert Hall for the presentation of my degree by the Chancellor of the University of London, Her Majesty Queen Elizabeth the Queen Mother. Thereafter, when appropriate I could include the letters LL.B (Hons) after my name. On my next appearance as prosecutor in the magistrates' court, the clerk to the court Mr. Fred Knight announced to the magistrates and everyone assembled the details of my success. Once more the local newspaper considered it sufficiently newsworthy to feature me in its columns.

I had formed a close association with the court officers and also the solicitors who frequently appeared for the defence when I was prosecuting. Many of the cases before the court were routine, mainly motoring offences and only occasionally was there something out of the ordinary. One such case was that of a young soldier at the School of Infantry who had bought a car to enable him to travel to his home in the West Country at the weekend. The vehicle was not in good mechanical condition and travelling on the A303 which crosses Salisbury Plain, the engine died. That was his first misfortune. The A303 can be a desolate road and it would be everyone's nightmare to breakdown there but the soldier was in luck. He was able to coast into a lay-by where there was some heavy plant machinery which had been left for use by road repairers. One of the items of machinery was a caterpillar tractor with a bulldozer type blade and although he had never driven such a vehicle he reasoned that if he could use it to push his car to the top of an incline, he could freewheel down the other side and hope to start the engine by a 'jump start'.

Unfortunately after raising the blade and moving up to his car, he lowered the blade which by his mis-judgement landed on top of his car. That was his second misfortune and the third misfortune occurred when a passing police patrol spotted what was happening and arrested him for taking a vehicle without the owner's consent. When the details were related to me it was difficult not think of it as a Fred Karno sketch and when I presented the case to the magistrates, it was very difficult to do so with a straight face. The magistrates were not so composed and could scarcely stifle their amusement. Having considered that the soldier had suffered sufficiently, they imposed a token penalty.

The Terrible Toll of the A36

The A36 trunk road ran through my sub-division carrying traffic between Bristol and Southampton. A single undivided carriageway winding through the country-side it was the scene of many road traffic accidents. The first in which I became involved was a collision between a petrol tanker and a coach full of elderly passengers outside Knook army camp. It was prior to the issue of my uniform and it was embarrassing trying to direct operations when no one, including the police officers at the scene, recognised me as the officer in charge. Fortunately no one was seriously injured and the immediate proximity of the army camp allowed us to move the passengers to a place of safety and provide temporary storage space for the damaged vehicles.

Because it was a major trunk road, any road traffic affecting the free flow of traffic could have serious consequences. Diversions could not easily be implemented because the surrounding villages could not tolerate heavy goods vehicles and any other alternatives would involve many miles on alternative routes. Consequently it was always a priority to restore normal conditions as soon as possible. There were occasions however when it was difficult to do so and enquiries to investigate the accident had to take priority.

I was sitting down to my breakfast one day when traffic officers asked me to attend the scene of an accident. A motorist had collided with a heavy goods vehicle and his car had burst into fire. The charred body was still trapped in the car when I arrived with the road completely blocked. Physical identification was impossible but in his pocket we found a yale door key. Enquiries of the vehicle licensing department revealed an address and whilst the driver was removed to the mortuary I went to the house and established that the door key was one for the front door. Doctor Kennard was the police pathologist with whom I became very friendly over the next few years and he performed an autopsy revealing contents in the stomach confirmed to be the same as the breakfast consumed by the deceased which helped to confirm his identity.

Although basically a relatively quiet market town Warminster's association with the military did bring some unique problems which impacted on my police supervisory responsibilities. Battlesbury Barracks was a base for tanks and other armoured vehicles just outside the town boundary. The low loaders on which the tanks were transported were towed by massive tractor units weighing in excess of 10 tons and they were a frequent sight on the A36. One of the towing units had become defective and was to be taken from Battlesbury

Barracks to another army base at Bovington, Dorset. The intention was to tow it with another towing unit secured by a tow bar with a single securing point on the towing unit and two points on the disabled casualty vehicle. The vehicles proceeded at a slow speed without untoward incident but after about 3 miles, approaching the village of Codford St. Peter, down a slight incline, the disabled vehicle broke loose and careered across the road. The person in the driving seat had no control because with no engine, there were no brakes and no powered steering.

Travelling in the opposite direction was an animal transporter vehicle carrying about 100 sheep. The driver of that vehicle had no chance to avoid a head-on collision and was killed instantly. The sheep on the upper deck of the vehicle were catapulted through the front of the vehicle, several of them being killed and many suffering broken legs. The military vehicle slewed across the grass verge and came to rest in a field 5 – 6 feet below the level of the road.

After several hours during which the animal transporter was removed, the sheep slaughtered and taken away, there remained the problem to recover the disabled military vehicle. A 3rd tractor unit fitted with a steel hawser winch was backed up to the field and connected to the casualty vehicle. Slowly the slack was taken up and the casualty winched towards the road level. It had almost reached safety when the hawser snapped and whipped across the road which fortunately we had closed to pedestrians and vehicles as the casualty trundled back into the field. The process had to be repeated, this time successfully.

If that accident was one of the worst with which I had to deal, 8 people killed in one afternoon was another reminder of the dangers of the A36 and other roads in the area. One sunny afternoon in August 1970 one of my sergeants was at the scene of a double fatality on the A350 3 miles south of Warminster when another emergency call was received reporting an accident on the A36 at an accident black-spot near the village of Norton Bavant. The constable who answered the call asked for urgent assistance and I attended and found a scene which could only be described as carnage. It was at a point where the road turned at right angles across the railway line and then another right angle turn onto the other side of the railway line. It was known locally as Skew Bridge. The accident shocked the town and evoked country-wide sympathy.

A family of 7 from Crawley had been to Longleat and were on their way home in a car but at Skew Bridge collided head-on with a lorry loaded with aggregate. Out of the 7, mother, father, two children and two grandparents were killed instantly and the 7th, a teenage girl was unconscious. She was taken to Frenchay hospital in Bristol and remained in a coma for several months. A pet poodle in the car was not physically injured but was very stressed and was put to sleep.

The funerals for the 6 persons killed were held at Christchurch, Warminster and it seemed that the whole town turned out to pay homage. The church was full for the service conducted by the vicar, The Rev RA Ford assisted by the vicar of Warminster, The Rev AT Johnson.

In reporting details of the accident, the Crawley local newspaper, quoting the brother in law of the mother and father who had been killed paid tribute as follows: "The police in

Warminster and especially the chief inspector in charge, to our minds went far beyond the call of duty in giving us every consideration and help when they had many complications to deal with."

Though the accident was a terrible tragedy, there was a very touching end to the story. The teen aged girl recovered and returned to the town with her uncle to whom had fallen the responsibility for funeral arrangements to publicly thank the town folk.

Not all domestic upheavals are the result of road traffic accidents but can be equally catastrophic. Shortly before midnight one misty November evening I answered the door to the vicar of a local church (Christchurch). He was accompanied by an elderly gentleman. The problem which they recounted was that the man's elderly wife was missing from home. They were a retired couple who had identified Warminster as the ideal location to live out their retirement years. It was Saturday evening and they had watched television together until she left the room, he, thinking that she was going to bed. Shortly afterwards he followed but she was not in the bedroom and the front door of their bungalow was ajar. She was not anywhere in the garden or nearby road and in a panic he had gone to the vicarage which was nearby.

After some discussion the vicar brought him to me. By the time I had heard the details, I had just one constable reporting for night duty and we both set out to look for the missing woman. It may be seen as a sad reflection on society as a whole that reports of missing persons may ultimately reveal something more distressing and our enquiries in the following days included a thorough search of the house and garden, house to house enquiries and press publicity. Although the couple had lived in their house for over 6 months, not one of the neighbours could remember ever seeing them and no information was forthcoming.

We widened our search including the use of police dogs and after 7 days we found her body huddled in a small copse 200 – 300 yards from her house. The conclusion was that for some reason she had wandered out of the house with no protective clothing, had become disorientated and laid down where she died of exposure.

There was a positive result from the incident because at that time my wife, Ann, as a member of the WRVS had formed a luncheon club in Warminster where elderly persons could go for fellowship and pursue their hobbies. She encouraged the widowed man to join and the result was the development of his own circle of friends to support him in his loneliness.

Her experience with the luncheon club justified an appointment in due course as a county organiser for the WRVS. Even though she had been reluctant to learn to drive, she made good use of her newly acquired skills.

Although not on the A36 there was one other road traffic accident which was particularly significant for me. Late one evening I was informed that a serious accident had taken place on the A350 about 2 miles south of Warminster. It was at a spot where the road dipped into a sharp bend. I attended and found that a Range Rover had overturned and the sole occupant, a woman dressed in a fur coat had been killed. We arranged for her to be taken to a nearby hospital where there was a mortuary and when we stripped the body I found inside one of the sleeves a half smoked cigarette. The conclusion I drew was that she had been smoking and perhaps smoke had gone into her eyes causing her to lose control and the cigarette had dropped into the wide opening of the sleeve.

Enquiries were made and we established that she was the wife of the owner of a horse racing yard near Newbury. I would not normally have used the telephone to notify a relative of a fatal accident but because it was after midnight did so on this occasion. I was surprised that the husband was totally dismissive of his wife's misfortune and when other facts came to light, his attitude was more understandable. Apparently she had gone to Bristol for some reason. On the way back she had stopped at a café and unexpectedly met one of her husband's stable lads. After some conversation they went their own ways. There was no suggestion that he had been with her at the time of the accident and one could only speculate as to why by co-incidence they had met at the rendezvous.

New Experiences

Having the School of Infantry as my near neighbours, it was inevitable that I would form a close association with many of the military officers and Ann and I were invited to many of their social events. We were treated as equivalents in their mess and shared in many of their activities. One day I was invited to be an observer at a Firepower demonstration in which tanks and heavy artillery were deployed on the ranges located all over Salisbury Plain. As part of the demonstration I was offered the role as tank commander in one of the Centurion Tanks.

I was kitted out with appropriate protective clothing including helmet and headphones. My call sign was Alpha One and as we moved in convoy across the plain I received a call through the headphone "Alpha One – fire" which left me bewildered and on a second more frantic call I turned to look at the tanks following ours and saw that our tank was actually on fire. The tracks of the tank had collected dry grass which had eventually been wedged near the hot engine covering and ignited. We stopped and the fire was quickly doused by the crew and no lasting harm was done.

An incident involving a less potent weapon occurred one day which in different circumstances would have been regarded as a 'domestic disturbance'. The resident of a bungalow resided opposite a small holding, the owner of which sited a disused railway truck on the edge of his land opposite and about 20 yards from the front door of the bungalow. There had been disputes between the two men for several weeks but reached a climax when the owner of the bungalow confronted he other man with a shotgun and fired at him, peppering the railway truck with shot. The police were called and I was requested to take charge.

In later years when Health and Safety considerations often restricted police action or risk assessment would have dictated that I call for "back up", my sergeant and 2 constables kept a respectful distance, whilst I, being rather more confident, or stupid, went to the bungalow, and rang the bell. The door was opened by the owner and I informed him of the allegation which had been made. He paused for a moment then reached behind the door and I then found myself facing a man with a double barrelled shotgun. What could have become potentially dangerous for my personal safety, became a non-event when he handed the gun to me and he was arrested whilst we made further enquiries. The history of the dispute suggested that the owner of the bungalow was more sinned against than sinning and proceedings resulted for only minor offences.

My transfer from a city police force to a county area made me realise very quickly the degree of authority and responsibility for the individual officers of whatever rank. In the city, a constable would always have superior ranks or specialised departments to direct or assist enquiries of whatever nature. In the rural environment of the county, a constable would frequently be called to serious incidents where he would deal with the incident using his local knowledge, experience and initiative. The probability was that any possible assistance from other police officers would be many miles away. Particularly at night when off duty, an officer could receive a call at his home and he would be expected to respond.

Similarly, in the city, for a chief inspector there would be restrictions on the level of his authority. As the officer in charge of the sub division, I was expected to take decisions commensurate with my rank. I attended road traffic consultation meetings and when the Military required that the main road be closed to allow the occasional Beating the Retreat ceremonies, the approval was within my remit.

I considered that I had a comprehensive knowledge of road traffic law and having become concerned that the yellow line markings in the town had become badly worn I insisted that they be re-instated in accordance with legal requirements. After numerous requests, eventually, one Sunday morning when there was very little traffic, the work was undertaken. Unfortunately, wherever there was a hint of yellow lines, the workmen had laid double yellow lines indicating a complete prohibition on waiting.

The highways engineer was not well pleased when I asked for dotted yellow lines or single yellow lines be restored to replace the illegal double lines.

Even though I had received basic instruction at recruit training concerning diseases of animals, as a city police officer I had not been involved in enforcing that legislation. Now, as the officer in charge of a rural area it was necessary to revise my understanding of the laws to ensure that movement of animals and restricted areas were undertaken strictly in accordance with Regulations.

Another aspect of rural life was the village fêtes in which the village residents competed with each other for the most spectacular event. Road closures such as were required caused very little inconvenience to other traffic and were usually policed by special constables. The chief inspector, being the local "police Chief" was expected to put in an appearance at the fêtes and I was always pleased to do so, sometimes accompanied by Ann.

Other functions at which it was expected that the chief inspector would attend were the many formal dinners hosted by The Chamber of Trade, Round Table, Licenced Victuallers, the Fire Brigade in addition of course to the Military invitations. Not only were my professional horizons widened as the result of my transfer to the Wiltshire Constabulary but Ann and I enjoyed social activities the nature of which we could never have dreamed had we stayed in Birmingham.

We Would Like You to Join Rotary

One day in 1971, two men walked into my office who were to change the course of my life so dramatically that I could never have anticipated the consequences. The two were prominent business men in the town and the purpose of their visit was summed up in a simple statement, "We would like you to join Rotary". Jack Harraway was the owner of a garden centre and Maurice Main the owner of a bakery business. I hadn't known them previously but their friendship continued long after I moved from Warminster.

Like so many non-Rotarians I knew nothing about the Organisation other than there was some presumption of integrity associated with being a Rotarian and they involved themselves in community service. I was taken aback by their unexpected invitation perhaps not quite dumbfounded but certainly I felt very honoured (and so I should be because Rotary is a very honoured and honourable Organisation).

I quickly became involved in the activities of the Rotary Club and realised that life as a Rotarian opened doors to friendships and experiences world-wide. Having joined Rotary we realised our social life became even more extended with new experiences. On one occasion the Rotarians decided to organise a treasure hunt which would require the participants to drive their cars over a prescribed route trying to identify the various clues which would lead to the next check point. Ann and I were invited to join the organisers at dinner one evening and we were so impressed by the impressive display of Royal Doulton table ware that we resolved we would have similar plates when we could afford it. Piece by piece over many years we achieved that ambition.

One benefit of Rotary membership is that it entitles the member to automatic access to every other Rotary club in the world and visiting other clubs is encouraged whenever possible. One of my first opportunities was a few weeks after I was accepted as a Rotarian and we went on holiday to Dartmouth. We rented an apartment for one week and the day before we were due to leave I went to the local Rotary Club for lunch. During the meal one of their members asked me if I had ever been mackerel fishing and when I replied that I hadn't, he invited me to join him in his boat but I explained we were due to leave the following morning. He insisted by saying that we could go that afternoon and still somewhat reluctant, I told him that Ann was waiting for me at our lodgings. My new friend persisted and I collected Ann and the children for our fishing trip.

I learned that catching mackerel is surprisingly easy and with a length of trailing line on which we had tied hooks concealed by strips of tinfoil we quickly caught a dozen fish. Unfortunately our excitement was tempered by Ann suffering sickness and when we returned to firm ground, she vowed never to repeat a fishing trip.

Bereavement

Anyone who has owned a pet, particularly if such a pet was taken into family life as a surrogate child, will understand the sadness when the pet dies. We loved our two little dachshunds and in the late evenings when the children were asleep in bed, Ann and I would sit each side of the fireplace, Mitzi would go to Ann whilst Amanda came to me. For a few minutes they would sit on our laps exuding the smell of warm toast, typical of their breed sharing our own special time of relaxation.

On one of the occasions when I had attended the divisional meeting at Salisbury, returning in the late evening, the dogs were upstairs but when they heard me, Amanda bounded down the stairs in her usual excitement, leaping the last 3 or 4 stairs in one jump. There was nothing particularly unusual in that but later when they came to us for their cuddle, Amanda whined for me to pick her up onto my lap whereas normally she would be stretching up expecting me to give just a little assistance. During the next few days it became apparent that she was suffering from some serious physical limitation in her movements. We went to a veterinary surgeon in Frome who diagnosed damage to the vertebrae in her neck, something to which dachshunds are prone. Although we returned home with her the condition deteriorated and eventually after another visit to the vet we retuned alone.

Mitzi was now the sole pet in the house but it seemed only weeks later that she developed some form of diabetes which caused an insatiable need to drink whenever and wherever she could from puddles, drains and anywhere she could find water. Ann took her to the vet and when I looked out of my office window and saw her walking alone back to the house, trailing the dog's lead I realised I would never see Mitzi again.

Although we had no dogs of our own, close neighbours, Maureen and Steve Ashton were breeders of basset hounds at any time having between 20 – 30 in their kennels. Although we were never tempted to own a basset, Maureen and Steve became firm friends and we spent many happy hours with them including one afternoon when we joined them with other enthusiasts hunting with the hounds. That was a completely different experience to riding to hounds dressed in scarlet coats. We followed on foot in Wellington boots and parka jackets through fields and hedgerows. There was no suggestion of chasing foxes and even when they picked up the scent of a hare or rabbit they became very excited and seemed incapable of actually following the scent.

Not Such a Quiet Backwater

I had formed a close association with many of the officers at the School of Infantry but I had not met the new Commandant who had taken up post until one quiet Sunday afternoon. Brigadier Frank Kitson had recently been the Officer Commanding British Forces in Northern Ireland and was an acknowledged expert on counter terrorism visited me at my home. We sat in my living room and he explained that one of his subalterns had received information that the Brigadier was to be assassinated and he thought he should inform the civilian police. I realised that such a possibility was something which necessitated advice from other quarters. My chief superintendent was unavailable but when I contacted his deputy, he also considered it to be too important for him and sought advice from higher authority.

Although I had received the visit from the Brigadier in the early afternoon, by 5.00pm his house had an armed guard and he himself was taken from the police station back to his home in an army convoy even though when he had arrived he had done so unaccompanied, relaxed and to all intents and purposes, making a social call. I never saw him again because shortly afterwards I was informed he was making a lecture tour in Australia.

Another incident which could have had more serious consequences concerned a registered firearms dealer who lived in one of our villages. We knew that he also had business premises in London and there was a suspicion he was not as thorough as was legally required documenting the movement of firearms between the two sets of premises. I had also received information that he was storing large quantities of machine guns. This was at a time when 'the troubles' in Northern Ireland were resulting in armed conflict between the IRA and Loyalists.

The divisional superintendent and I obtained search warrants to be executed at his home address and because we anticipated he would have large numbers of firearms, military personnel were requested to assist. Mr. Dinely, the firearms dealer was also the acknowledged source of World War 2 military vehicles and armour which were used in films and known to be a difficult person to deal with. To my surprise he admitted me to his house without argument and when I informed him of the purpose of our visit he gave his full co-operation.

In a barn with doors secured by a flimsy padlock were wooden crates packed with hundreds of machine guns, so many that eight 3 ton trucks from the School of Infantry were required to take them away to be catalogued. Checking the guns against the registration documents lasted several days and it was found that they were legitimately in his possession. However, the security of the weapons prior to our intervention was grossly inadequate and when they were returned to him they were taken to more suitable premises. The political instability in Northern Ireland together with the threat to Brigadier Kitson brought home to us that even in a sleepy village in Wiltshire there could be the possibility of terrorist activity.

Renewing Acquaintances

One of my colleagues from the Special Course was David Read from the Hastings Borough Police Force who had been appointed commandant of a regional police training centre near Exeter. I was pleased but surprised when I received an invitation from him to become a visiting lecturer at the centre. Not only was I able to renew my acquaintance with him but on occasions I was able to take my children with me for a day out and give them the opportunity to swim in the centre's indoor swimming pool.

Chapter 11. New Fields

In the summer of 1972 several changes took place in Wiltshire Constabulary. A superintendent in the Swindon division retired and in a small police force having only 7 – 8 officers of that rank there was a vacancy to be filled. I was informed that I was to move from Warminster to Swindon and although I would not have presumed to be in line for promotion I wondered if the move would prove advantageous. In the event I was to undertake the duties as deputy to the superintendent sub-divisional commander.

Whereas Warminster in its totally rural setting had been like chalk and cheese in comparison to Birmingham, Swindon was very much an urban conurbation very similar to Birmingham with its reliance on heavy industry, crime ridden housing estates and traffic congestion. Although the railway industry on which the town had built its reputation was in decline, there remained some significant reminders of its past. I was keen to familiarise myself with the area and one of my constables took me to what appeared to be a derelict wasteland which was in fact where steam engines had discharged clinker from their fire boxes over many years.

What I saw resembled a scene from a science fiction setting. The area was protected by a security fence but I could see large holes in the ground many issuing smoke and steam. In some of the holes, red hot ashes were still smouldering even though there had been no recent dumping of waste materials. In spite of the security arrangements in place, the potential for some serious accident was very real and I was relieved that a few months later the site was completely cleared and rendered safe.

Whilst in the rural area I had been well used to police control of shotguns, I didn't expect to have enquiries associated with them in the urban area of Swindon. It was ironic therefore that soon after my arrival, one day before setting out for my office, I was called to a house near to where we lived. It was an incident the like of which I had never previously experienced. A man had committed suicide by placing the barrel of a shotgun in his mouth and pulling the trigger. I had become used to violent death and mutilation of bodies but the effect of a shotgun blast in that instance is best left to the imagination rather than graphic description.

Swindon boasted a second division football team which necessitated a large influx of police officers from other divisions for their home matches. With a total constabulary establishment of approximately 900 and 100 or more required for the matches, it was a major logistic exercise on those occasions to draft in officers from the rural areas. Warminster officers would require to leave their own police stations at 8.00am or 9.00am to parade in Swindon for deployment to the match. On these occasions, Wiltshire was denuded of officers who should have been performing duties in their own areas. For all of the home matches, I was the senior officer on duty whilst my superintendent and the divisional chief superintendent were more likely to be in the directors' box watching the match. Although we occasionally experienced crowd control problems, generally the matches were reasonably trouble free.

The County Ground where Swindon played their matches could be approached from several directions with 5 major routes converging onto a traffic roundabout complex which accounted for much of our traffic flow problems. The Road Research Laboratory was commissioned to design an alternative road lay-out to improve traffic flow and reduce congestion. Having recently completed a short traffic management course I was directed to liaise with representatives from the laboratory.

The first action was to remove the large traffic island and replace it with a pattern of moveable rubber kerbs forming a centre island and a small mini island at each of the 5 inter-sections. In the centre of the new traffic island was a double decker bus on which the laboratory officials and I observed the traffic flow. At each of the 5 points where the roads converged onto the island a police constable was posted. When the laboratory official blew a referee type whistle the police officers would stop the traffic; when the whistle blew again the traffic would be allowed to flow and measured by the official with a stop watch. Again the whistle would blow and the traffic stopped then allowed to flow again. After each measured flow of traffic, the officials would alter the pattern of the islands and measure another flow.

The experiments continued for several days until they were satisfied they had the best lay-out. And the temporary islands became permanent to measure the long term effect. One revolutionary aspect of the experiment was that traffic approaching the junction could choose to travel clock-wise or anti-clockwise through the configuration. It took several weeks for the Swindon residents to familiarise themselves with the new traffic management scheme although visitors would remain confused for years afterwards. The location quickly became known as the magic roundabout but in spite of scepticism from many quarters, the improvement was obvious.

The site of the magic roundabout was also the location of the town fire station. The town Road Safety Officer without any consultation as should have been expected authorised a traffic calming feature – a speed bump, to be laid across the road outside the fire station. On a day shortly afterwards, a female employee at the fire station rode her pedal cycle out of the station, turned left onto the road at the point where the speed bump was located, lost control and fell under a lorry. She was killed and although the subsequent inquest recorded a verdict of accidental death, it was significant that the speed bump was removed soon after the accident.

There are occasions when ordinary everyday routine matters have developments which are unexpected. One of my responsibilities as a senior supervising officer was to make annual assessment reports on my subordinates. One young detective constable Anthony Burden impressed me with his ability and when completing his report I suggested that he had the capability of senior rank. I was pleased when many years later I discovered that he had been appointed chief constable of the South Wales Police and later, he appeared in the New Year's Honours having received a Knighthood. His achievements gave me great pleasure. Many years later attending a Requiem Mass in Westminster Cathedral, both of us in uniform we recognised each other and without any embarrassment, embraced, perhaps with curious stares from other police officers present.

Another Detective in the Family

Shortly after our arrival in Swindon, Ann made a momentous decision; she took employment with Sainsbury's supermarket as a store detective. She had no previous experience in that field but after suitable training became totally committed to her new profession. Varying her duties between Wantage, Bath, Newbury and Swindon not only did she develop a natural flair for her duties resulting in detaining many shoplifters, her natural aptitude never deserted her. There were many occasions when I was shopping with her and she would spot a suspect taking goods without offering payment and on occasions it was possible for her to draw the attention of a store's supervisor to the miscreant. She continued in her duties for 3 years but though she was competent and successful, not all shoplifting cases are open and shut, black or white.

One person detained by the store's managers as the result of her observations was identified as a man whose professional status was such that he probably had no need to pilfer but his actions would doubtlessly lead to his ruination. It was obvious that such a high profile suspect would contest the evidence and make counter allegations. Enquiries which unjustifiably impugned her character and integrity caused much personal anguish and it proved to be her final case. Although the decision was Ann's, I was relieved because violence from shoplifters is not uncommon and although she always erred on the side of caution when detaining suspects there was always a risk which could not have been pre-determined.

Swindon Viewpoint

Whilst in Swindon I made the acquaintance of Mr. Richard Dunn. He worked in the television industry and launched a local TV programme called Swindon Viewpoint. As the name suggests it was devoted to items of local interest and he made a suggestion that we could include a police input.

The approval of the chief constable was requested and he was only too anxious to explore the possibility of police/public relations using the medium of television coverage. It was agreed that I would be the liaison officer with the television crew.

The broad intention of the programme was of the 'fly on the wall' principle where the police would be filmed undertaking their normal duties and the film later edited to highlight the more interesting aspects. The area selected for filming was the Pinehurst estate which had a high crime rate and a population in general, not particularly supportive of the police. However, the local beat 'bobby' Police Constable 77 Wally Cuss was a competent, respected, no nonsense officer regarded by many of the residents as friendly and often turned to him for advice and assistance.

.Our patrol areas were identified by code names and '1 Bravo' was the identification for police constable Cuss. I was given the responsibility to prepare a script to include the officer dealing with a variety of every day incidents but included an unexpected addition. A distraught householder reported to him that her valuable dog had gone missing. Perhaps more as a public relations exercise than an expectation to recover the dog, he contacted divisional headquarters. Much to his surprise and the relief of the dog owner, the dog had been handed in and to complete the fortunate result, the television crew was on hand to record the re-union of dog and owner. It was an interesting experience to participate in the programme but was my one and only excursion into television production.

A Remarkable Lady

Whilst working in Warminster I had knowledge of a constable who had died leaving his widow to continue the restoration of a cottage they had purchased. She in turn was friendly with a lady living in the Swindon area, Mrs. Sadie Price. Mrs. Price had visited another friend dying of cancer in Princess Margaret Hospital Swindon. A few days previously she had seen a television programme about a new scanning machine which would detect cancer in its early stages. When her friend died a few days later she asked why the hospital had not used a scanning machine and when she was informed that they did not possess one because they were too expensive, she announced that she would raise the money to purchase one.

The target sum of money was £20,000 but Sadie greatly saddened by the death of her friend, was obsessed with the challenge she had set herself. The police widow and Sadie set up a committee to raise the money and asked me to assist. Every means of fund raising were explored including a Street Collection, House to House collection, collecting re-cyclable materials and canvassing support from sponsors.

The suppliers of the scanner we wished to purchase were a German firm who notified us that a substantial increase in price was due and also value added tax would be introduced which would increase the cost even further. If we signed a contract the original price quotation would be honoured. We were in a quandary. We had collected slightly less than half the target amount which would have been sufficient for the deposit but by signing would have committed us irrevocably to fulfilling the purchase. We signed.

On October 1974 the Evening Advertiser, Swindon's local newspaper carried a report and photographs showing Sadie formally handing to consultant radiologists the Scintiscanner installed at Princess Margaret Hospital. Her dedication and total commitment to fundraising for the life saving equipment was a triumph for the hospital but sadly affected the harmony of her domestic life. Without doubt she was the driving force for fundraising but I was pleased I had been included in her efforts. Several years later long after I had left the Wiltshire Constabulary I visited Swindon police headquarters. Some of the police staff whom I remembered were still there and one of the constables took me on one side and thanked me for saving his life. I was mystified until he explained that he had received treatment at the hospital including a scan by the Scintiscanner. A cancerous growth which had been detected had been successfully removed. I felt very humble that Sadie's determination had achieved positive results.

Skittles

Swindon police headquarters was an impressive building far removed from the antiquated nature of many other police stations throughout the county. In addition to, what was then, a modern communications centre, adequate cells, and car parking facilities was a feature peculiar to Swindon. In the basement there was a skittle alley. Skittles in the West Country was a popular recreation, played mainly but not exclusively in pubs. Whereas other pubs may have had their darts tournaments, domino competitions or even shove halfpenny, the passions generated by skittles was common place in many West Country pubs. Although I was surprised to find the alley in the police headquarters, never having played before I quickly became as enthusiastic as other competitors.

There was a league table which included teams from the senior officers (The Executive Eagles) in which I competed; the inspectors (the Bath Stars); the sergeants (The Zebras); the traffic wardens (The Yellow Perils) and the policewomen's team, 'The Policemen's Playthings', a name which would certainly raise questions of political correctness in later years. Rank had no bearing in the league games and teams of whatever composition had only one thought – to win and I think it fair to say that win or lose, there was never any resentment. Many large business organisations may employ schemes to encourage team building but my experience of our skittle matches certainly proved that there was no more successful way to bond with work colleagues.

Family Development

Whilst I was establishing my professional credentials and Ann followed her store detective commitments, our children Lloyd and Denise were also developing their own particular interests. Lloyd proved his capabilities in the school football team and prepared himself to fulfil an ambition first voiced when we lived in Warminster. Even in later years I did not understand what had influenced him to express a desire, in fact an obsession, to join the Royal Navy. My Service background was in the Royal Air Force and we had lived in a military area but at the age of 9 he was totally focused on his intended career.

In Swindon there was a Sea Cadet Corps which enabled him to experience some of the attributes of a naval career and make him more determined to achieve his objective. Joining the Sea Cadets would also influence my future life in ways I could not have envisaged at that time.

Whilst Lloyd was focused on his future intentions, Denise tended to, figuratively speaking, nibble at many recreational interests but allowed her undoubted ability in many of them to remain under developed. She tried ballet dancing, athletics, swimming, tennis, gymnastics all of which suggested she had latent talent but music seemed to hold her interest more than any other of her recreational activities. As with many other children, her first musical skills were learned on the recorder but then she showed an interest in the violin. To encourage her with both instruments I gave myself a crash course to familiarise myself with the required techniques.

For her violin tuition we were fortunate to make contact with a tutor who had moved away from London to the less frenetic existence in a village on the outskirts of Swindon. He and his wife lived in a cottage and had committed themselves to a life of self sufficiency. In their garage they had 2 deep freezers well stocked with provisions; she prepared and cooked all their meals including bread; they kept chickens to provide eggs and she shopped once or twice a month to stock up for the subsequent weeks. They had no television and a neighbour passed on to them the daily newspapers when they had read them. The music teacher and his wife were the most generous, warm hearted couple we had ever met and when they invited us to tea one day, it was a meal to remember. We sat outside and enjoyed fresh boiled eggs with home made bread followed by home made jam. The cottage in which they lived faced directly onto a lane and twice a day when the cows from a nearby field were taken for milking, the animals would peer through the windows into the living room and the whole atmosphere was one of idyllic bliss.

We were amused when they told the story of their son who was an accomplished musician and played with a youth orchestra. One year shortly before Christmas he was on the continent and telephoned his parents to the effect he would like to come home for Christmas and could he bring some friends. They assured him they would be pleased to see him but when he arrived with half the orchestra they were just more than a little surprised. For that Christmas they had young musicians, male and female sleeping in every available space and the one bathroom in the house had a notice in several languages directing when it was to be used by the boys and girls. During the days of Christmas they visited other villages and farms giving impromptu concerts and according to the parents it was the most wonderful Christmas ever.

In such a warm family environment and with a superb teacher, Denise certainly learned the basic skills of playing the violin.

Although in Warminster we had not settled very well into Church life, having been disappointed with the Methodist and Baptists, in Swindon, we became members of the Bath Road Methodist Church, partially influenced by neighbours Betty and Arthur Walters who lived opposite our house. They were probably the first people to welcome us to our new home and the friendship which developed was to last for many years even after we moved away. At the church I joined the choir and Ann became involved in other Church activities. It might be fair to assume that our children were not so enthusiastic even to the point of supplementing their pocket money with the coins given to them for the Church offerings at Sunday morning worship.

A Return to the Police College

Having successfully completed the Special Course and subsequent promotions, I was anxious to develop my potential as far as possible. The Intermediate Command Course at the Police College was a 3 month course designed to groom potential senior ranks in the required skills. I submitted an application but my chief superintendent was reluctant to give his endorsement on the grounds that he could not be expected to lose a chief inspector for 3 months. However he did agree to my attending a selection interview in London and if I was successful, he would put my name forward for the course.

I passed the interview, he kept his promise and in October 1972 I returned to the Police College as a student once again. Having overcome the reluctance of my own superiors I was disappointed that some of the other members on the course who had been sent from large Forces resented the compulsion for their attendance and considered it a waste of time. Fortunately those individuals were in the minority and the remainder including myself and representatives from several overseas police Forces took full advantage of our advanced learning.

I subsequently applied to attend the Senior Command Course which was a recognised stepping stone to higher rank. Again, success on the interviews was to be measured by extended interview technique which were to be held at a hotel in Eastbourne. I was accommodated in a hotel some 200 – 300 yards from the hotel at which the interviews were held. On the day I was required to present myself to the selection panel there was a strong wind blowing and it was raining. I arrived for my interview like the proverbial drowned rat feeling dishevelled and unsettled. I did not pass the interview but later developments in my professional career perhaps suggested that I had lost nothing having been rejected by the interview.

My return to duties at Swindon marked the start of increasing frustration. I realised that promotion to higher ranks in the Wiltshire Constabulary was on the principle of 'filling dead men's shoes' and officers having served for the longest period in the Force were likely to be selected rather than others with less service. This policy resulted in a detective chief inspector with 29 years service being promoted to uniform superintendent undertaking duties with which he was unfamiliar. He retired 12 months later having a pension entitlement based on his superintendent's salary. Having only 16 years service I could anticipate many years of stagnation waiting for my turn. Another factor which I had to take into consideration was the attitude of the divisional superintendent – Superintendent Arthur Mayes, who co-incidentally lived a few doors away from our home.

When I returned from the Intermediate Command Course, my chief superintendent was interested to hear that my commitments at the College had been to prepare a treatise on football hooliganism and also one on traffic management. He requested to see them and a few days later a furious superintendent Mayes insisted that any communication between me and the chief superintendent must be channelled through him. It would be fair to say that he had a reputation for verbal aggression and many others also experienced his brusque manner. Perhaps his bark was worse than his bite and those who knew him better than I were more aware of how far they could bait him. There was the occasion when one of the inspectors walked along the corridor passed the open door of his office and was heard to express in obvious annoyance "Jesus Christ.". The inspector dodged back to the open door and said, "You called Sir?"

Whilst my duties did not normally include the investigation of road traffic accidents as had been the case in Warminster, there were some occasions when I was involved. One Saturday afternoon at about 4.45pm an elderly lady was hit by a car and suffered fatal injuries. There was no suggestion of dangerous driving on behalf of the driver but on a straight stretch of road, howbeit in the dusk there seemed no reason for the woman not to have been seen. I asked for any record of previous accidents on the road and was interested to find that 3 years previously there had been an accident at exactly the same location, also on a Saturday at the same time of the year and at a similar time of the day. Incredibly it involved the same woman. We established that she had visited a store on the other side of the road to collect a newspaper and always wore dark clothing. We drove along the road at the same time of day and saw that ahead of us the road curved to the right but a building at the apex of the curve was painted black. The result was that for a few seconds any pedestrian crossing the road would become indistinct with the dark background and that had been the fate of this woman on two occasions, the second of which was fatal.

Giving encouragement to young officers should always be a part of a supervising officer's responsibilities whether by the 'carrot or stick' approach. One such constable was given the task to investigate an apparent trivial complaint of ladies' underwear stolen from the washing line. Unfortunately not every police officer would have carried out his duties as tenaciously as he did. He obtained the name of a suspect and went to his house to make his enquiries. Although the young officer had very little experience, he conducted the interview with such determination that the suspect not only admitted the minor offence about which he was questioned but later admitted an offence of attempted rape.

Of course, encouraging young inexperienced officers can result in unexpected consequences if the supervisor's advice is questionable as happened when we were asked to investigate the matter of a lady who had not been seen by friends and neighbours for several days. I dispatched a sergeant and constable to investigate and was horrified when the sergeant later reported that they had broken down the door of the house where the lady lived. His explanation was that they had done so to make sure the lady had not suffered any accident or illness in the house. Unfortunately every internal door had been locked and they had forced open every one. It transpired that the lady was on holiday. On this occasion the sergeant showed a decided lack of common sense.

We ourselves became the victims of crime when Ann received a phone call of an indecent nature. Anyone who has not had a similar experience may not appreciate the distress which can be caused and Ann was very upset. When a further call was received we outlined a strategy. Whenever the phone rang it would be Ann who would answer to give the caller the impression that there was no male person in the house and encourage him to keep talking whilst I would ask the GPO to trace the call. When he did call again Ann said that she would be prepared to meet him at some suitable rendezvous but what she did not appreciate at that time was our daughter overheard the conversation and she became very upset that her mummy was planning to meet another man. My efforts to have the call traced were frustrated because the telephone operator could not understand the significance of my request.

When a further call was received it was obviously from a call box and when the caller's money ran out, Ann asked him for the number and she would ring back. He gave the number and when Ann rang, a female answered. Ann said she expected a male person to answer and the woman told her a young boy had just left the phone box as she waited to use it. She gave a detailed description and one of my constables was able to identify the suspect as the son of a divorced woman who kept a small grocery shop. The telephone calls we had received were always at a time when we could assume the shop was closed for business and decided if the boy was the caller, he was doing so without his mother's knowledge when the shop was closed.

Our mysterious caller had always identified himself as "Master Bates". We made a telephone call to the shop and when a male voice answered we asked if he was "Master Bates". The irate answer indicated that he was not but our enquiries revealed that divorced mother had just re-married and had been away on honeymoon. The male person who answered was her new husband and the woman's son had had the run of the shop allowing him to make the calls. He was prosecuted and given a stern warning by the court.

Mother and father circa 1930

With sisters Vi, Pat and brother Alf recently
returned from Military Service

With Vi, Lily and Pat following the award of the MBE 1987

George Dixon Grammar School August 1946   **Déjà vu. Rotary fancy dress party 1990**

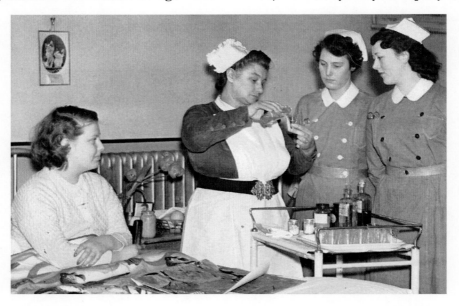

Student Nurse Ann Madden (2nd from right) Yardley Green Hospital 1954

On leave from RAF, West Kirby 1953

RAF Police training, RAF Netheravon

Preparing for church prisoner escort, RAF Steamer Point

Outside Detention Barracks, RAF Steamer Point

August 1954, we announce our engagement

Wedding day 23rd February.
The Salvation Army Band played 'Here Comes the Bride' on the railway station platform

Ann with babies Denise and Lloyd

After five years of study I obtained my Batchelor of Laws degree whilst
Chief Inspectorat Warminster. August 1970

President of the Police Superintendent's Association of England and Wales 1987/1988

Awarded the MBE. Truly a day to remember, December 1987

Commissioner's Representative in Hamburg 1989.
Left to right, Constable John Barney, DAC David Maynell and Karoline

In Hamburg market place with officers from Belgium, USA and Switzerland

Retirement July 1990. With Sir Peter Imbert and Lady Iris

My colleagues presented me with a ceremonial sword and Ann received a huge bouquet

Hosting our Rotarian friends from Norrkopping did not go quite according to plan!

**The ambulance and mini bus purchased whilst I was Chairman
of the Chingford Association for the Physically Handicapped**

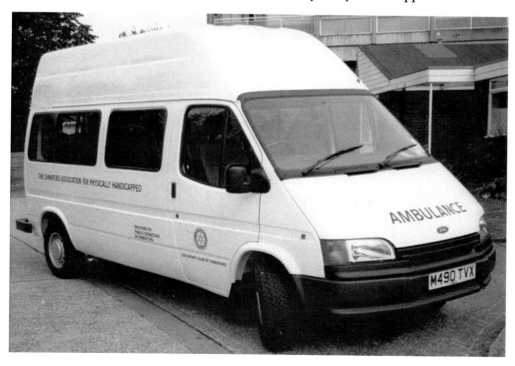

A grant from the Jack Petchy Foundation assisted in the purchase of a mini bus for the Waltham Forest Sea Cadets Unit. A similar vehicle was purchased for the Clapton & Hackney Sea Cadet Unit whilst I was acting Chairman

A memorable day on the Orient Express special excursion

On 23rd February 2007

Leslie and Ann Stowe

Will celebrate their

Golden Wedding Anniversary

You are invited to their OPEN HOUSE on Saturday 3rd March –
call in and stay as briefly or as long as you like between 6.30pm
and 10.0pm – drinks with cold and hot buffet

*(No presents thank you but if you wish, make a donation to RNLI, a
collecting box will be available at the house)*

For catering purposes, if you intend to come, could you please let us know

We cruised to Norway with Saga Holidays to admire the attractions

Whilst I was not able to join an athletic club in our new home on occasions I did enjoy a solitary long distance run. The Ridgeway is an ancient footpath running down the spine of England and passing Devizes and Swindon. A charity walk had been organised for some purpose and I had been asked to take part. It wasn't practical for me to walk from Swindon to Devizes with the other walkers but I agreed to run from Devizes to Swindon. Someone had tipped off the Press and my picture appeared in the Evening Advertiser with an accompanying story. Apparently it was unheard of for chief inspectors of police to appear in running kit.

I had joined the Rotary Club, we were active members of the Church, had good neighbours and a wide circle of friends but professionally I was worried that I was getting into a rut. I knew that if I wanted further advancement it would involve a move to another Force. The Metropolitan Police had recently re-introduced the rank of superintendent and advertised vacancies. There were probably several hundred chief inspectors in that Force who would be in line for the posts and I did not hold out too much hope but I answered the advertisement and was pleasantly surprised to be called for interview. New Scotland Yard has a special aura and although it was not my first visit there, I was nonetheless a little nervous.

The Commissioner, Sir Robert Mark chaired the interview panel and afterwards, together with other applicants I waited for further instructions. When I returned to Swindon I broke the news to Ann that I had been offered a post as superintendent in the largest police Force in the country. I could scarcely believe what had happened. Although Police Regulations had recently been altered to allow inspectors and chief inspectors to claim overtime payments, the Wiltshire Deputy Chief Constable had informed every one of those ranks that he did not expect any claims to be made. Consequently from the basic salary of a chief inspector I would be entitled to the pay of a London superintendent, London weighting, London allowance and in addition a general pay rise was imminently due. My salary was effectively doubled by the transfer.

Prior to our departure from Swindon I decided to change our car. It sometimes happened that military personnel who were serving in the area and posted overseas would be looking for a quick sale of their motor vehicle and I had the opportunity to purchase a Vauxhall Viva car at a reasonable price. It was certainly more suited to our growing family requirements than our Morris 1100 which had served us well for three or four years. However having moved to London and visiting Ann's parents in Birmingham one day, the car could have been involved in a catastrophic accident.

When driving down a dark street in Birmingham we encountered a stretch of road where resurfacing was taking place. With no warning we hit a ridge in the road where the surface was approximately 2" higher than that on which we were travelling. There was no immediate effect but driving down the M1 I was conscious of a regular thump, thump, thump. When I arrived home and took the car for servicing, we realised the cause of the noise we had heard. Both front tyres had fractured across the width and we could have experienced a blow out at any time. The potential consequences did not bear consideration.

Chapter 12. The Start of a New Life - London

I was due to take up my appointment on 1st July 1975 and 2 or 3 weeks before, I was required to attend New Scotland Yard to complete various administrative details. Having no idea of the true size and complexity of the Force, a chief inspector, Bob Peedle was detailed to act as my mentor and guide visiting uniform stores and to view the house which was one of two options for me to consider. The house was located in Chingford, on the north east side of London at the edge of Epping Forest. From the house I could see the trees of the forest barely 100 yards away and decided it was the house for us. It was one of 4 brand new terrace houses and it transpired that although my house was the only one which was a police owned house, my next door neighbour was a police constable who owned his own house.

I was permitted to take up occupancy a few days prior to my effective transfer to the Metropolitan Police in order to take measurements for carpets and curtains. In the late evening we decided to try and find somewhere where we could have a meal and eventually found ourselves in a road where there were many shops one of which was a fish and chip shop. Having made our purchase we then realised with some apprehension that we did not know how to find our house again. I knew that our address was in a small group of houses newly constructed and probably unknown to people living in the area. I tentatively asked in the shop if anyone could give us directions back home and by a strange co-incidence the person standing next to me offered to take us because he actually lived in an adjoining house. How lucky can that be?

The house had no carpets or curtains and a little preliminary work was necessary before we actually made our departure from Swindon. We were allowed access in the week prior to transfer and having written to the President of the Rotary Club of Chingford informing them of my wish to join them, I was pleasantly surprised when, busy fitting a hall carpet, Peter Bloor, the Rotary Club President appeared at my door and gave me valued assistance. One of the aspects of Rotary Fellowship is that at any time it is possible to meet friends who were previously unknown. Peter and his wife Joy were to remain close friends for many years to come and my introduction to the other Rotarians was to have a great influence on our lives.

One example of the world-wide influence of Rotary friendship was made manifest to me in an unusual way. When we lived in Swindon, our son Lloyd had been receiving a course of dental treatment to correct some defect in his teeth's alignment. Because of our transfer to London he would be unable to complete the treatment but his dentist gave me the name of another dentist in Chingford who could complete the treatment. To make contact with the new dentist was not a priority for me. However when I made my first visit to the Rotary Club I found myself sitting next to the dental surgeon who had been recommended to me – Don Soul who was also a Rotarian. A strange co-incidence.

When we had lived in Swindon a not uncommon incident would be when a bullock or other animal escaped from the abattoir resulting in an operation to isolate the animal and call up a police marksman to effect its dispatch. Such occurrences would always merit a photograph and a few inches of column in the local newspaper. Imagine our concern when a day or so after we arrived in Chingford to find not one but probably a dozen bovine creatures meandering down the road near to where we now lived. It was obvious to me that some careless person had left open the gate of a field somewhere and unless they were recaptured they were likely to cause mayhem. Fortunately I spoke to our neighbours and learned that in Epping Forest, grazing rights dating back to the Middle Ages allowed cattle to roam throughout the area of the forest which included where we lived. In some ways it allowed us to escape from the frenzy of modern life to see half a dozen cows chewing the cud as they lay on a traffic island or wander down the road creating a better traffic calming facility than any number of speed bumps.

Ann was not ashamed to admit that she was terrified of cows and one quiet Sunday afternoon we saw 4 or 5 animals outside our house in the cul-de-sac where we lived. We thought it was just another example of these inoffensive beasts adding their own air of tranquility until our neighbours called on us to help drive the animals away. They explained that if they rubbed against our cars as they would rub against trees, there was likelihood that they would damage the cars. Several of us cautiously directed the animals to a path alongside our house towards the trees of the forest. They caused no problem and Ann felt very pleased with herself until we went for a walk a few minutes later. We went down the same path taken by the animals and 50 yards further on where it joined the road was one of the bullocks apparently waiting for us with the widest spread of horns I had ever seen. Ann's composure disintegrated and we delayed our walk until the coast was clear.

One of my tasks was to make arrangements for my children's schooling and travelling on a bus to the appropriate offices I passed Walthamstow Greyhound Racing track. Emblazoned over the front entrance were the words "Welcome to the Stow" which I thought to be going just a little overboard to make us feel at home.

Barely half a mile from our new home was the Waltham Forest Sea Cadets' Unit – TS Acorn and it proved to be an unexpected bonus for Lloyd who joined their ranks without delay. Neither of us realised the implications for my future involvement with the Sea Cadets when he joined but it would to be a very influential factor in my life for many years in the future.

Denise was anxious to continue her violin tuition and it was a coincidence that one evening we heard the sound of a violin coming from a nearby house. We made enquiries and found that the person playing was actually a qualified teacher and we were able to make arrangements for her to give lessons to Denise.

Barkingside

My first posting was to the Barkingside sub-division as deputy to the chief superintendent Bert Berry MM who was approaching the end of his service and suggested that I should accept full responsibility for running the division whilst he could spend more time on his other pursuits but would be available if I needed him. As with my move from Birmingham to Wiltshire which needed many adjustments to a different culture and way of life, so the change from Wiltshire to the Metropolis also demanded a new appreciation of policing attitudes and commitments.

Shortly after my arrival and before I actually commenced my duties at Barkingside, the Commander of the area, Commander Colin Hewitt arranged for a luncheon reception in order that his senior officers could meet the new superintendent. I knew that the Met was a large Force but was surprised that the gathering of 4 – 5 chief superintendents, a similar number of superintendents and chief inspectors more or less equated with the senior officer ranks in the whole of Wiltshire Constabulary. In that Force, Colin Hewitt's equivalent rank would have been the Assistant Chief Constable a man regarded as only one step down from God but here in the Metropolitan Police first names were the order of the day in a very relaxed atmosphere. I was encouraged to see there were 7 other persons in the room, including the Commander, wearing Rotary badges and immediately I felt that I was among friends. Many years afterwards I learned that members of the Rotary Club of Barkingside had assumed the new superintendent would obviously join their club and found it difficult to understand when it was learned I had become a member of the Chingford club.

Although my service in the Met commenced on 1st July I was not due to start my duties as deputy to the chief superintendent until 1st September when his serving deputy, superintendent Stephenson was due to retire. Those 2 months proved invaluable to familiarise myself with the area in which I would be working including the police stations at Woodford, Chigwell, Loughton and Debden for which I would have a responsibility as well as Barkingside. There were other important duties carried out from Barkingside which included the armed escort of cash from the Bank of England as appropriate. The local magistrates' courts, coroner's court, firearms training centre and helicopter base at Lippets Hill were all centres of police activities which justified visits. In addition I had virtually 2 months grace to learn a little more about Force policy and their bible, 'General Orders'.

In the Birmingham Force there had always been a strong emphasis on discipline and in Wiltshire the most stringent restrictions were imposed on Force expenditure, in the Met, these two factors seemed to be relegated to minor considerations.

My office at Barkingside was on the second floor accessed by a staircase leading from the rear of the building. On the first floor was the station canteen and one morning I noticed several constables having refreshments even though it could not have been their allocated refreshment time. I went to the main office and asked the station sergeant to tell me how many men he had out on the streets. He reached for the duty sheet but I insisted he tell me how many were on the street. He couldn't. I then asked him how many were in the canteen. Again he could not tell me. I made it quite clear to him that officers who wanted or needed to be in the station should only be there with his approval. If they weren't they would be liable to disciplinary proceedings for neglect of duty. I left him to deal with the issue in his own way but I never had need to make a similar observation after that.

Although the incident in itself was comparatively trivial, during the whole of my time in the Force, I found it to be typical of the casual attitude of some officers to their duties. Many years later after I had retired from the police Service, I was approached by a man who said "You don't recognise me do you sir?" It was the same sergeant, also retired, who admitted that I had frightened him to death but had taken my advice to heart and thereafter adopted a more positive approach to his supervisory duties.

There seemed to be little overall restriction on expenditure and when I moved in, the stores liaison officer suggested I should have all new furniture in my office which was totally unnecessary. In later years I realised that most senior officers taking up new posts would expect new furnishings and décor. Claims for overtime working were manipulated to the full even though there was never any suggestion of fraudulent claims.

September, when I took up my post, was also the time when the Area cross country race would be held and a notice appeared in the canteen which invited intending competitors to add their name to the list which I noted included such unlikely participants as Mickey Mouse and Father Christmas. It may have been presumed that when my name appeared it was the result of some person playing a prank on the new superintendent. However, came the day of the race, I appeared in running kit, enjoyed the race and finished 3rd with the comment from one of the Barkingside officers "Blimey Guv, you aren't supposed to win!" Our team won the trophy for the event much to the disgust of the commander of the adjacent division whose team had been the firm favourites to win.

Having made my debut in the athletic field I was persuaded by one of my sergeants, Lawrie Durrant to join his running club the Orion Harriers. Not only did I make new friends but I also found that I renewed acquaintances with athletes against whom I had competed when I served in the Birmingham Force.

In my own way I felt I was settling in but soon realised that the monolithic Metropolitan Police organisation had its own restrictive practices. One of the first incidents in which I became involved was a little out of the ordinary in the built up area of Barkingside. 5 horses including a donkey were found wandering in the High Street. It so happened that I was on duty at the time when the animals were 'arrested' and having served in a rural area dealing with all aspects of the law in connection with animals, I was confident on the appropriate action to take. I arranged for them to be taken to a 'greenyard' and endorsed the report with a recommendation that after the minimum period they should be sold if the owner had not been traced.

Whereas in Wiltshire I had made such decisions and dealt with any necessary court procedures, in the Metropolitan Police a veritable army of solicitors were employed to make such decisions and police superintendents were not expected to encroach on their domain. My recommendations were not accepted and various directives were received from them until after 3 months they directed a course of action identical to that which I had originally recommended but in the meantime we had incurred expenses of over £13,000 in greenyard fees.

If I was not entirely satisfied with the professionalism of the Barkingside police officers I could not fault them on their involvement in social activities. There was unquestionable enthusiasm for their sub-divisional football team and I even found myself making up the numbers for one match when they would have otherwise fielded a team of 10 instead of 11 men. Within days of taking up my post I learned that a sub-divisional dinner/dance was due to take place and found that Ann and I were seated at the top table alongside the Deputy Assistant Commissioner, John Crisp and his wife, he having the equivalent rank of a Chief Constable. He was the officer in overall command of 3 Area, which included our sub-division.

During the evening he invited Ann and me to his home for dinner some time and assuming that he was just making polite conversation was very surprised a few days later to receive a telephone call asking me to agree a day and date. Obviously there was a very much more relaxed attitude to rank differences than I had previously experienced. I considered John Crisp to have all the attributes of a gentleman and that was not the last time we were entertained in his home.

Feeling more relaxed about the difference in rank we invited John and his wife to our home for dinner and then at the New Year we received an invitation to a New Year's party at his home. During the evening his wife said to Ann, referring to me, "When you've finished with him, I'll have him." Shortly afterwards there was an embarrassing report in the tabloid newspapers that she had left her husband in favour of a deaconess from a local Church. It made us wonder about the remark made to Ann.

Bert Berry was as good as his word and allowed me a free reign in running the sub-division. After visiting the local swimming baths he would arrive in the office at about 10,00am for a briefing on current events. When he was satisfied, he was likely to disappear more or less for the rest of the day but he was always available for advice when necessary. I was grateful to Bert for his philosophy because I was able to establish my credentials and justify my appointment. There were many chief inspectors who would have expected that they, not interlopers from outside Forces should have been promoted.

In my previous Forces I had taken little interest in Police Federation matters but when it was announced that the Area Superintendents' Association Branch meeting was to be held, I attended. I had no previous experience in this field of police activities but when nominations were invited for the Branch Secretary's role, my name was proposed, someone seconded the proposal and I was elected. My predecessor immediately left the table where he was sitting with all relevant papers, congratulated me on my appointment and so began my involvement with police politics.

On occasions I was required to stand in for the senior officers at the adjacent sub-divisions and the investigation of complaints against police officers which allowed me to gain a wider knowledge of the area in which I lived and worked. Visiting so many stations I formed friendships with many of my fellow senior officers including chief superintendent Ron Burnhams. He was the secretary of the Metropolitan Police Male Voice Choir and association with Ron would form a strong influence on my life and future activities.

We had never owned any of the houses in which we had lived and although happy with the accommodation provided on transfer to London we were anxious to buy our own. We were still without any substantial funds but when we found a house which we considered suitable, we cashed in insurance policies and from various sources scraped together the necessary money for a deposit. At that time police officers were entitled to rent allowance and it was obvious that it would have been foolhardy not to have committed ourselves to home ownership. We decided that we would remain in the Chingford area and eventually identified a house with vacant possession which would be our home for many years to come.

City Road

Up and down the City road, in and out of the Eagle.
That's the way the money goes — Pop goes the weasel.

A few words from an old nursery rhyme which have nothing to do with policing but I was interested to find that my new place of employment – City Road police station was next door to the Eagle pub which had gained notoriety from the nursery rhyme. 'Pop' refers to 'pawning' (something with which I was only too familiar in my childhood) whilst 'weasel' is derived from Cockney slang 'Weasel and stoat' meaning 'coat.

The New Year of 1977 was also the new posting for me when I transferred to City Road police station on G division as deputy to a woman chief superintendent Jessie Moss. Jessie had a pleasant personality but I was of the opinion that she had been promoted beyond her competence probably as the result of sex equality policies. It seemed the usual practice for chief superintendents was to wear plain clothes in preference to uniform. One morning she arrived at the station and as was usual, started checking the station books when the station sergeant asked as politely as possible "Excuse me madam but who are you?" When I learned of this embarrassing incident I felt somewhat vindicated that I always reported for duty in uniform.

There were adequate canteen facilities at the station but my chief superintendent always excused herself at lunch time and would take what I considered to be an inordinately long refreshment break. The reason emerged one day when one of the constables mentioned that he had seen her with her man friend in the nearby park. Although she was unmarried and much older than I was, it seemed that romance was in the air and in fact she married her paramour a few weeks prior to my posting to another station.

One of our public houses, The Horns, was a continual source of concern, flouting the licensing laws, suspected drug dealing and also a favoured meeting place for CID officers. Several attempts had been made to deal with the irregularities and it was suspected that some police officers who used the pub were compromising the efforts of the uniform officers' operations. We decided that enough was enough and arrangements were made to deal with the problem. I arranged for 2 constables from another area to work in plain clothes in the pub to gather evidence of the offences we suspected were being committed. On the evening of the intended raid, we held a briefing inferring that the intended pub was on another division. Once outside the station with the police officers in their vehicles, we gave details of the actual location which maintained the surprise factor. The subsequent raid and successful prosecution served as a warning to other licenced premises. I felt that at last I was becoming fully integrated into the Metropolitan Police.

The Hackney and Stoke Newington areas were not the most pleasant in which police officers were expected to work and the public attitude ranged from being unco-operative to outright hostility. I had many complaints against the police to investigate and whilst some may have raised suspicions of questionable police conduct, many were the normal process for accused persons to refute the allegations against them. One such case concerned a man named Watkins who alleged that he had been subjected to an unprovoked assault by a police officer in a pub. My investigations included interviews with everyone who had been in the public house at the time of the alleged assault. The allegation was that Watkins had been hit in the face by a police officer in plain clothes. The police officer's explanation was that Watkins had caused a disturbance, picked up a glass to strike him and the officer struck first in self defence.

To identify the customers of a pub at a specific time several months after the alleged assault seemed to be an impossible task. However, the pub was the home pub of the British darts champion, Eric Bristow who was playing in a crucial match. Everyone I spoke to remembered the occasion because the disturbance created by Watkins had caused their champion to wait until Watkins was removed. What I could not do was identify any person who had seen the police office strike Watkins until I spoke to the bar tender. He admitted he had witnessed the incident and said Watkins had deserved it. I concluded that all of the customers, who must have seen what happened, were trying to protect the police officer.

Watkins was charged with assaulting a police officer, convicted and sent to prison. As a result of the many unfounded allegations he had made, many hours of police time had been wasted and I visited him in Wormwood Scrubs prison. He adopted a cocky attitude until I told him that he was to be prosecuted for wasting police time and cautioned him. He did not make any immediate reply but a pool of urine slowly spread on the floor where he sat opposite me in the prison interview room and I considered that was some indication he acknowledge his guilt...

The police Commander in charge of the division was Geoffrey McLean but because I didn't fit into the stereotype senior officer of the Metropolitan Police, we did not always see eye to eye. In fact it would be accurate to say that the atmosphere when we were in discussion usually was tense.

All superintendents and chief superintendents were required to work a roster as Late Duty Senior Officer until 1.00am or 2.00am with the expectation that if a serious incident occurred there would be a senior officer quickly available to take charge and determine a course of action. One night a fire occurred at a café and being on duty, I attended and waited until the fire brigade officers had completed their work. It was established that the internal floors had collapsed into the cellar of the building but suspicion as to the cause of the fire was increased when a nearby resident told us there had been an explosion. Later investigation by the fire officers indicated it was probably a petrol bomb which had been used.

Although the CID officers were not particularly interested I was anxious to trace the person or persons who would normally have lived in the premises and I decided that the debris in the cellar should be removed with the assistance of officers from the Special Patrol Group. It was long tedious work but eventually my suspicions were confirmed when a body was uncovered and the incident became a murder enquiry for the CID to pursue.

As a senior officer I would not normally be expected to patrol the streets but I took every opportunity to do so particularly when acting as Late Duty Senior Officer. One night I was in the back of a police car with two constables one of whom was a woman, not many months out of training. I chatted with them and asked the woman if she had ever had an arrest. She said she had and when I asked for details she told me that they had been following a car when the passenger had fired a gun at them. She seemed to regard it as something which was quite normal and it made me realise that even if some officers were not as smart as I would have liked, there were many who carried out their duties effectively and conscientiously.

There were occasions when my professional principles obviously clashed with those of my peers. Nearing Christmas time one of the chief inspectors asked me for a donation of £10 towards the station's Christmas party. Apparently the usual practice was for the senior officers to provide a fund to buy drinks for the rank and file. I had always maintained an intolerance of officers drinking on duty and certainly not in the police station. When I voiced my views it was obvious that I was not the most popular member of the supervisory ranks. I pointed our that Christmas office parties were prone to cause trouble but the party went ahead. It transpired that one of the invited persons was the licencee of a local pub and after leaving the station he was arrested for drunk driving. The local Press enjoyed the chance to high-light the fact that his condition was the result of his close friendship with the police.

The City Road police officers were also enthusiastic in their social activities and a formal dinner had been arranged with suitable entertainment. Although smoking was socially acceptable at that time it was obvious that some smokers lacked the etiquette to avoid annoyance to non-smokers. The seating arrangement placed me next to one of the chief inspectors and when we were eating our main course, he had a lighted cigarette in his hand which was cupped under his chin whilst he was talking to me. A length of ash dropped onto my meal and although he apologised and tried to brush it off, the enjoyment of the evening was spoiled and it seemed to me another aspect of standards not expected of senior ranks.

Whilst I was serving at City Road I met one of those men for whom any words of admiration seem inadequate. He was Captain Joe Burlison of the Salvation Army and was the officer in charge of one of the Army's Social Centres in Hoxton. Joe was an ex-miner, a diving expert and was always on stand-by for any calls to respond to world wide emergencies. We became firm friends and I found his knowledge of the area and the people living there to be invaluable. He used to operate a 'soup run' for destitute persons in the city centre and accompanying him occasionally gave me an insight to some of the problems of the homeless. Unfortunately he died prematurely from a cancer related illness but his biography 'No Peak too High' is a lasting memorial to a remarkable man.

Not forgetting my athletic interests, on occasions I would run the 8 miles to work and because it was a normal activity, did not attach too much significance to my training runs. However, it is not always apparent what impression is created in other people's minds and 35 years later whilst sitting in a hospital waiting room, I was approached by an elderly gentleman who addressed me by name. I had to admit that I did not recognise him until he identified himself as having served under my supervision at City Road where I was known as the governor who runs to work in his shorts. Some notoriety!

City Road Police station was the base for a number of police horses and it was common knowledge that manure from the stables found its way to police officers' gardens and probably allotments. No one raised any objection to this little "perk" until one morning when the detective chief superintendent required to use his unmarked police car and realised that during the previous night duty, someone had used it to transport sacks of manure. The smell in the car persisted for some days and the detective chief superintendent was not best pleased. As far as I recall, the culprit was never identified.

Also within the responsibility of City Road was Old Street Magistrates Court which included a firing range used by police officers for further training in the use of firearms. Although my supervisory duties did not require me to take an active rôle, more or less out of curiosity I did visit from time to time.

The largest street carnival in Europe takes place on the last weekend in August in the streets of Notting Hill. Although the carnival was firmly established and gave great pleasure to thousands of people, it also provided the opportunities for criminal activities. In its early years police were subjected to outbreaks of disorder at the carnivals and resorted to using dustbin lids to protect themselves from missiles. In subsequent years police training had introduced riot shields to be used to ward off bricks, bottles and fire bombs.

My first deployment was whilst I was at City Road and at that time the number of police on duty ran into thousands. It was for me, the only time when, in a group of officers I was subjected to a petrol bomb assault. Fortunately no one was injured and on the following two occasions when I was required at Notting Hill I was responsible for reserves of police available but held in an area well away from the carnival itself.

Rochester Row

The time came to move on and in 1979 I was posted to the central 'A' division at Rochester Row police station. This was a Victorian style building having a large Mounted Branch complement and included in the horses stabled there was Burmese, the Queen's mount for official occasions especially the Trooping the Colour ceremonies. The horse was greatly admired by regular staff and visitors but had an irritating habit of biting off tunic buttons of anyone standing too close.

In addition to the offices and cells in normal use, the station complex also included disused buildings not suitable for regular use but which served as storage areas.

Police duties in the central area included the need to police large demonstrations and public order events requiring the deployment of large numbers of officers, many of whom would be drafted in from other divisions. Some of the police operations were to control violent outbreaks of disorder as with the Brixton riots whilst others were expected to be more civilised such as the New Year's Eve celebrations in Trafalgar Square and Parliament Square.

I realised that some of the operations were planned with a hard fist approach expecting the police on the ground to give no quarter to overcome the disorder rather than a more subtle approach but as a superintendent and a comparative newcomer to the Met my views counted for little. Lack of clear objectives and briefing resulted in inefficiency by the officers in their duties. When an intruder broke into the Queen's bedroom the police response was to flood the area with additional constables many of whom had not been adequately briefed as to the responsibilities expected of them. One year when on duty in Trafalgar Square I asked one constable what his duties were and he told me he was posted to Piccadilly Circus but found it more interesting to come down to 'The Square'. I left him in no doubt that unless he returned there promptly he would face disciplinary proceedings for neglect of duty.

Because Rochester Row had suitable accommodation it was selected as the temporary alternative to the maximum security police station at Paddington whilst that was undergoing a programme of upgrading. The block of disused cells was renovated but strict instructions were issued that it was intended and only to be used for persons arrested for terrorist offences. For several weeks it was maintained, cleaned daily without any persons being detained until 30th April 1980.

On that day, the Iranian Embassy in Knightsbridge was guarded by a solitary armed officer from the Royalty and Protection Group, police constable Trevor Lock. At 11.30am the embassy was attacked by a group of fanatics who forced entry and took everyone hostage, including Trevor Lock. A massive police operation ensued to contain the scene and effect the rescue of the hostages. From that moment, Rochester Row police station assumed an atmosphere of tense anticipation with the knowledge that the terrorists would be taken there when they were arrested. All normal activity at the station seemed to be on hold waiting for the prisoners to arrive.

The hours became days and on the fifth day at about 6.00pm I informed the staff that nothing seemed imminent and I intended to go home. As I walked into my house I saw on the television the dramatic action of the SAS making an assault on the embassy. Although I returned to the station immediately it served no purpose because no prisoners were taken and the terrorists ended up in the mortuary. The hostages were released unharmed.

Although opportunities to perform operational duties were limited as a sub-divisional commander I always took advantage when I was duty senior officer to join the crew of a police car and be on hand with them to answer calls. I never ceased to be impressed by the skills of the drivers who could travel safely at high speed, anticipating gaps in the traffic to arrive at the scene of the emergency. I also walked the beat with some of the junior officers which allowed me to more fully assess their abilities and effectiveness.

It was also possible, if not a requirement to direct enquiries myself from my desk. One Christmas morning although I was not expected to be on duty, I visited the police station shortly after a fatal non-stop accident at about 7.00am on Lambeth Bridge had been reported. By co-incidence the accident had been witnessed by one of the station cleaning staff when on his way to the station. He described the offending vehicle as having a black woman passenger in the front seat. Inspector Robert Davies (later to become Assistant Chief Constable in Thames Valley Police) and I discussed the possibilities of tracing the driver and decided that a black woman at 7.00am on Christmas morning was possibly employed as a cleaner at a hospital. There was no suggestion of racial prejudice or stereotyping but in 1980 it was a reasonable conclusion. Enquiries were made at local hospitals and the woman was identified but details of the non-stop accident were not cleared up immediately. It transpired that a vehicle in front of the one in which she had been travelling collided with the pedestrian and her driver had been too close to avoid striking the body lying in the road. No charges were brought against her driver.

Although I was reasonably happy at Rochester Row, one Friday afternoon I received a message that I was to telephone Deputy Assistant Commissioner Geoffrey McLean, the officer who had been my Commander at City Road and with whom I had had a strained relationship. He had subsequently been promoted and was now the deputy to one of the Assistant Commissioners, Wilf Gibson at New Scotland Yard. I made the call and Mr. Mclean said "What do you think of the idea?" I replied perhaps naively that I knew nothing about it and his next comment was totally unexpected "I want you to come and work for me." I asked when and he said "Next Monday." I suggested that I would need a little time to clear my desk and it was agreed that I would start the following week.

New Scotland Yard

When I reported to Mr. Mclean I found that my duties would have a wide remit. I was to be staff officer to the Assistant Commissioner and Mr. Mclean with additional responsibilities for the Obscene Publication Branch which was under the day to day supervision of chief inspector Peter Kruger and also the small section responsible for investigations for illegal immigrants and enforced repatriations. That small section was to create political and administrative issues which would return to me long after I retired from the police Service.

One of my principal duties was to monitor the Force overtime which was of continual concern to the Commissioner and Receiver who was responsible for the Force finance control. The manipulation of Police Regulations to make claims for overtime payments was endemic throughout the Federation ranks and meticulous records were maintained for every individual officer's payments. Every week, the Assistant Commissioner was required to report to the Commissioner the state of the overtime claims and explain what measures he had taken to reduce claims which may have been considered excessive. The Commissioner at that time was Sir David McNee and my office being directly opposite the lift which brought him to his office, he would call in to receive a briefing from me on the overtime. He would then go to his own office, summon the Assistant Commissioner with the knowledge that he was already in possession of the information he would expect in answer to his questions.

Although I was identified as the officer in charge of the Obscene Publications Branch, I had little involvement in the day to day operations although for the experience I did accompany the officers occasionally when they executed search warrants. There was little glamour in searching for and seizing property which may eventually be used as evidence in prosecutions. Several tons of books, magazines and videos may have been seized which would all required to be viewed to determine whether it was suitable to place before the court. This was not pornography of the girlie magazines but depravity of a nature beyond the imagination of the lay man. The officers themselves became inured to the effect and they cultivated an ability to fast forward a video and only stop it when something specific caught their attention. In the viewing room there were 8 – 10 viewing screens showing videos simultaneously but the one which would attract close attention would be the one showing the current test match or perhaps Wimbledon tennis championships.

One aspect of their work which was particularly worrying became obvious from the nature of some of the videos which they viewed involving children. They uncovered evidence of a communication network among paedophiles which they identified as PIE – Paedophile Information Exchange. One worrying aspect was that the tentacles of this network appear to reach into all levels of society. It would be fair to say that their revelations were met with some degree of scepticism by ranks higher than mine but in later years child protection policies would result in a massive commitment to tackle the problem.

The other section for which I had a specific responsibility was the group of officers investigating illegal immigration and the removal of such persons often accompanying them to their intended destination under an 'escorted repatriation' policy. Whilst much of their work was routine there were potential pitfalls. Corruption and bribery were endemic in some of the countries to which illegal immigrants were repatriated and the highest integrity was expected of the officers. I was never made aware of any incident where their standards were compromised but the risk was always a possibility. Shortly after my involvement with the section, my line manager Commander and I decided that there should be a change of personnel by rotation with a period of 3 years as the optimum length they should serve before being replaced. The decision was not completely arbitrary because there was an increasing awareness in the Metropolitan Police that any suggestion of nepotism should be avoided and vacancies for specialised posts should be openly advertised. The decision to change the officers was not popular in their small group but it was appropriate to balance their experience against the possible advantages of introducing new personnel with new ideas.

As would be expected, there were occasions when the officers experienced various levels of resistance when effecting a removal necessitating the use of implements of restraint. They were also liable to suffer personal injury including bites and following concerns expressed by the officers I issued an instruction that only under extreme circumstances could gags be used. It was many years later after I had retired that a fatality occurred when a lady named Joy Gardiner, subject of a removal order died in police custody. The four officers effecting the removal had used mechanical restraints and also tape to gag her mouth. Unfortunately she suffocated and the officers were charged with manslaughter. I was called to give evidence at the Central Criminal Court to give evidence of the instruction I had issued. Although the officers were acquitted my evidence before Mr. Justice Mantel was nerve wracking and something I could never have anticipated 10 years previously when the instruction was given.

It was my duties with these officers that brought me in close association with officers from the Immigration and Nationality Service. The officer in operational command was Colin Manchip and together we drafted a policy which would be accepted for large scale operations to detect and arrest illegal immigrants. Press publicity alleged 'fishing trips' where police and immigration officers would raid premises primarily staffed by persons of ethnic origin with the expectation that some illegals would be discovered. The policy we drafted had to be approved by the Home Office and required that subsequent raids were properly researched with all available records checked before a raid took place. We realised that however carefully we dealt with the issue of illegal immigrants it would always be a very sensitive area of policing and many years later would spawn a huge Government

Department charged with securing the country's borders. An example perhaps of 'from little acorns, oak trees grow'.

Although my duties at The Yard were varied and interesting I was anxious not to be overlooked for promotion and was disappointed that my first application for a chief superintendent's 'Board' was rejected. I made application for a vacancy as Assistant Chief Constable in the West Mercia Constabulary but that was also unsuccessful. However my second application for a promotion Board was successful and in 1981 I was promoted to the rank of chief superintendent. Mr. McLean, my boss quipped that if anything went wrong in the Obscene Publications Branch it was better to blame a chief superintendent than a superintendent.

The IRA Bombings

My years at 'The Yard' co-incided with the time of developing political unrest in Northern Ireland and incidents of IRA activity in mainland Britain. On 26th October 1981 one of the Metropolitan Police civilian explosives experts, Kenneth Howorth attended a Wimpy Burger bar in Oxford Street where a suspect package had been discovered. Unfortunately whilst attempting to defuse the bomb, it exploded and he was killed. He was later awarded a posthumous George Medal for bravery.

It became my responsibility to make arrangements for Kenneth Howorth's funeral and because of the political sensitivity and propaganda implications, a high level of security was essential. With the agreement of Military senior officers, arrangements were made for the funeral service to be conducted in the chapel of Chelsea Barracks which were permanently under heavy guard. It was important that everything that could be done should be done to pay tribute to a brave employee of the Metropolitan Police and any reasonable request by the family should be agreed. Accordingly I was authorised to approve necessary expenses which would be paid by the Force. On the day of the funeral, in addition to the hearse, there were 10 following cars for the mourners. The route would take the cortège from the family home in Buckinghamshire to the chapel and as was the normal practice, the funeral director made an assessment of the duration of the journey. Fate dictated that there was very little traffic congestion on the way into central London and the cortège arrived much too early for the Service. The consequence was that for 20 – 25 minutes the funeral procession wound its way round the streets of Chelsea in order to drive into the barracks at the appointed time.

On December 17th 1983 central London was busy with Christmas shopping crowds when a coded IRA message was received by the Samaritans who passed it to the police warning of a car bomb outside Harrod's store in Knightsbridge. The suspect car was identified and as police officers arrived the bomb detonated killing 3 police officers and 3 civilians with many more persons injured including one police officer who lost both legs. Again it could have been considered a propaganda coup for the IRA and from the highest level directives were received for a high profile memorial service for the 6 persons killed. It fell to the Assistant Commissioner, my boss to ensure that appropriate arrangements were made for the Service which was to be held in Westminster Abbey. With a small committee I was given responsibility for the actual detail. The guest list of invited persons included representatives of Royalty, politicians, local government as well as families of the bereaved.

On the day of the Service, nothing could be left to chance; no mistakes could be made and I went to the Abbey in good time to be on hand for last minute queries and to welcome guests. One of the guests was a man who as speaker of the House of Commons, George Thomas had been one of my heroes and had been elevated to the Peerage as Viscount Tonypandy. As he walked through the doors of the Abbey I greeted him and said rather cautiously, "How do I address you?" "How about George?" he replied.

In my office I had left a policewoman to deal with any last minute calls which may have had any bearing on the Service arrangements and she had asked my permission to join me at the Abbey when no further calls were likely. I agreed and when she left the office, she ran the 400 – 500 yards from my office arriving breathless and face flushed from the constriction of her uniform collar. As she stood in front of me she fainted and in my effort to prevent her falling I grasped her shoulders but was unable to stop her slowly collapsing backwards with me on top of her. Fortunately no members of the press were close by otherwise a photograph of a uniformed police chief superintendent lying on top of a policewoman at the Memorial Service could have made front page headlines.

The funerals of the victims of the bombing had taken place some weeks earlier, that of the 3 police officers at the Chelsea Parish Church of St Luke's, at which the police choir were on duty; one of a journalist in the Church of St Brides, Fleet Street and one in Barrow-in-Furness, Cumbria where, together with a Deputy Assistant Commissioner I represented the Metropolitan Police. The sixth person was a citizen of the United States where his memorial was held.

There were other occasions when the Force was expected to be formally represented and following the murder of two police officers a few days apart in June 1982 in North Yorkshire I was deputed to attend a Memorial Service in York Minster. It was the first time I had visited the Minster and looking at the small railway network and cranes being used for renovation work, I stood in awe paying silent tribute to architects and builders whose skills hundreds of years ago without the use of modern engineering equipment brought about the construction of this magnificent building. Because I was an invited guest, a seat had been reserved for me but I found that it was occupied by someone else. Rather than make an issue I opted to sit in any available seat and found one without any difficulty. As I sat down, the person in the next seat said, "Hello Sir." I found that I was sitting next to a police officer who had been one of my probationary constables – PC Pickering when I had been an inspector in the Birmingham City Police some 15 years previously. As some would say, "It's a small world."

 One fascinating aspect of my duties at this time was to receive reports which recommended appropriate awards for acts of bravery by both police and civilians. It was my responsibility to read the reports which had been submitted, summarise them and pass them to a committee headed by the Assistant Commissioner who would them make a recommendation to the Home Office or other Organisation, which included the Royal Humane Society for whatever award seemed appropriate. I never ceased to be amazed at the incidents of bravery displayed almost every day in London, not only by police officers but also by members of the public. Any one of those reports could have formed a script for a television series were it not for the fact that they were confidential. However the details of some of those reports were so amazing that they should have received more publicity.

Police had received information that a bank raid would take place at a bank in Edgware Road and plain clothes officers had premises under observation. When the attack took place, the officers pounced but were unable to prevent the suspects running away. A passing motor cyclist saw what was happening and gave chase on his motorcycle. When they ran up a narrow passageway, he left his motor cycle and ran after them. One of the robbers turned and fired a gun at him. The bullet hit his crash helmet, travelled round the inside and lodged in the other side. By some peculiar act of fate he was unhurt but his brave actions justified a bravery award.

On the night that Kenneth Howorth was killed by an IRA bomb in Oxford Street, a coded message was received that there was a second bomb in a department store a few hundred yards away. Another explosives expert, Peter Gurney went to the store and knowing that a few minutes previously his colleague had been killed and that he himself was at risk, he safely defused the device. For that selfless act of bravery he was awarded a second George Medal, having previously received a similar award for another act of bravery.

The Royal Humane Society regularly received recommendations for bravery where saving life was involved. One such report concerned a light aircraft which crashed into the sea a few hundred yards from the beach. Fortunately it was witnessed by a man in a sailing boat who was able to make his way to where the plane had disappeared beneath the surface. He dived and brought one of the plane's occupants to the surface then dived again and saved a second person. When the report was considered by the Royal Humane Society he was awarded a Bronze Medal and although he was reluctant for any ceremony, he was presented with the medal at London's County Hall. Shortly afterwards I received a request from the RHS to recover the medal because he should have been awarded a Silver medal rather than the less significant Bronze. I contacted the recipient of the award who was adamant that he would not agree to a second presentation and he met me at New Scotland Yard where we exchanged the medals with no more formality than a greeting and handshake.

I received numerous reports where someone had stopped breathing and mouth to mouth resuscitation had been successfully performed. April 1st was approaching and my staff and I decided to play an April fool's prank on the Royal Humane Society. The Bible story in 1st book of Kings contains the account of Elijah using a form of resuscitation on a small boy who was apparently dead. We concocted a report together with witness statements recommending Mr. Elijah for a resuscitation award and submitted it to the RHS. In actual fact our 'prank' backfired as we discovered later. The adjudicating committee sat on 1st April and it was not until our report was under consideration that it was realised it was a spoof. However they entered into the spirit and sent the report back to me asking to make arrangements for Mr. Elijah to visit their headquarters to be presented with an award. We left it there, honours even and no one taking umbrage.

Chapter 13. The Police Superintendents' Association

From my initiation when serving at Barkingside I had been continually involved in representation duties for the Police Superintendents' Association. As a Branch representative I was a member of the District Executive and one of the 'perks' was that every year the Police Superintendents' Association of England and Wales were allocated 2 tickets for one of the Buckingham Palace Garden Parties. Invitations for those occasions were regarded as a great privilege when high ranking military officers, church dignitaries and representatives from every avenue of public life would mingle on the lawns of Buckingham Palace hoping that out of the 3,000 – 4,000 persons that they would have a few moments to remember when they spoke to members of the Royal Family.

My name was drawn out of the hat at the time when memories of the intruder into the Queen's bedroom were still newsworthy. One of my contemporaries at New Scotland Yard was a Deputy Assistant Commissioner who was never reluctant to express his true feelings. He was due to go to the garden party on the same day as Ann and I and when I asked if he intended to go in uniform or plain clothes to avoid embarrassing comments about the intruder, his reply was unequivocal and positive. We both proudly wore our uniforms but we didn't have opportunity to speak to the Queen.

The secretary of 'E' District of the Superintendents' Association which included the Metropolitan and City of London Police Forces was chief superintendent Ken Rivers. He was very experienced but was due for retirement. He had held the post for several years and was respected by his peers and senior officers. I was asked if I would be prepared to take on his duties and I accepted the invitation for my nomination to be submitted to the Executive Committee. I knew that if I was appointed to the post, further promotion was unlikely but considered the new challenge to be the better option. In fact I had submitted an application to the Essex Police for a vacancy as Assistant Chief Constable and although having received a favourable reply, withdrew the application.

My election as District Secretary was more or less a formality with none of the other members of the Executive Committee wishing to contest the nomination. They were all in posts which suited them either as sub-divisional commanders or operational CID officers. Although I was nominally a member of D Department (Personnel) with a Commander as my line manager, in effect I was a free agent undertaking my duties as necessary. Together with the District Chairman Ben Pountain, and the Police Federation representatives, I attended meetings with the Commissioner and his Policy Committee and had unrestricted access to the Assistant Commissioners as necessary. Ben and I were also members of the National Executive of the Police Superintendents' Association of England and Wales meeting with Royal Ulster Constabulary and Scottish Superintendents' representatives. We also represented the Staff Side on the Police Negotiating Board and Policy Advisory Committee. In short it was the most fulfilling job I had ever had in the Police Service.

Throughout our married life I had never encouraged nor dissuaded Ann to take paid employment perhaps having a chauvinistic view that it was my responsibility to provide for my wife and family. However, she was a trained nurse and always sought opportunities to make use of her skills. She had worked at a hospital in Birmingham in Warminster and two hospitals when we moved to London. However, when I accepted the appointment with the Police Superintendents' Association, we both knew that my duties would take me to all parts of the United Kingdom, being away from home for several days at a time and to enable her to travel with me she decided to retire.

Although I had gained in experience from the time I had become involved in the Superintendents' Association matters, the new appointment was much more demanding including the closer relationship with the Commissioner. In October 1985 a series of incidents occurred in the Broadwater Farm Estate of Tottenham the consequences of which were to have a dramatic effect on policing policies and practices. The estate was a huge concrete housing area consisting of flats, shops and community buildings on several levels joined by passages and link-ways at every level. It had the reputation of lawlessness and it was an area in which police officers were regarded with suspicion and hostility. In fact in a national survey it had been identified as the worst place in Britain to live.

On 5th October a black youth, Floyd Jarrett was arrested for allegedly driving a car with a false vehicle excise disc and when 4 police officers went to search his home, his mother, Cynthia Jarrett died of a heart attack. It was the spark which ignited the hostility into a riot situation and several police officers were injured in separate incidents. At about 9.30pm buildings were set on fire and the fire officers and police who were trying to protect them were all subjected to attack. A full scale riot developed and police constable Keith Blakelock was hacked to death with machetes.

The following morning the Police Federation representatives demanded a meeting with the Commissioner to record their anger at the situation which led to the murder and were very vociferous in their condemnation of the leadership or lack of it displayed by senior officers. As the Secretary of the superintendents I was present at the meeting and although embarrassed by the criticism of my colleagues, was totally sympathetic with the criticism that we had been unprepared and officers inadequately trained to deal with such incidents. The political fallout was exacerbated by subsequent arrests of persons alleged to have committed the murder and other serious offences and continued for several years. Within the Force, the resulting self analysis resulted in a wide range of improvements in training and control of serious disorder by senior officers.

Although the Police Federation representatives had expressed their views without reservation the relationship with them was not personally hostile and in the future years we always worked in harmony with the common objective of representing our members' interests as effectively as possible.

Representatives of the Association of Chief Police Officers (ACPO), the Police Federation and Superintendents' Association constituted the Staff side in meetings with the Official Side in the Police Negotiating Board and Police Advisory Board. It was obvious from some of the consultations and committee meetings that the discussions between the two sides were merely window dressing and decisions had already been made. One of the best examples was when we were invited to discuss the possible formation of the Crown Prosecution Service which we were certain had already been agreed and no reservations expressed by the Staff Side would have any effect. The arguments in support of a Crown Prosecution system were that it would remove from the police the involvement of presenting cases at court; it would act as a safeguard against police using dubious methods to obtain evidence and it would save money. Subsequent experience of the effectiveness of the CPS suggested that it did not achieve all of the ambitious targets which were expected and the sheer bureaucracy which developed sometimes caused disquiet for the general public that the new arrangements did not always result in justice. This is not to deny that some benefits did result by the transition of work to the CPS but many police officers remained unconvinced.

The nature of Staff Side representation invariably drew us more closely into contact with Government Ministers , Local Government officials and Chief Officers of Police throughout the United Kingdom resulting in genuine friendships formed which would never otherwise have developed. However in official meetings strict protocol was always observed with no suggestion ever made of impropriety.

The duties of representation had a wide ranging remit and it was inevitable that there were political implications. In 1984 the Government was on collision course with the miners resulting in a massive police deployment at collieries where serious disorder was frequently observed. Police Officers of the Federated ranks were on duty for periods far in excess of the normal 8 hour span for which they were generously compensated by overtime payments. The superintendent ranks were not eligible to claim overtime payments and the longer the disputes continued, the greater resentment was expressed by some of the officers who we of the Superintendent's Association represented. They were working similar hours to their subordinates and housed in equally unfavourable accommodation with no extra compensation. In delicate negotiations, pay rises far beyond the norm were achieved and served in some way to redress the grievances.

Pay was not the only factor in which political differences were aired. Prison overcrowding was an issue which caused many problems not only for the prison staff but also for the police. It became a practice for prisoners on remand to be detained in many police stations which had cell facilities. However there is a vast difference in holding a prisoner temporarily for a few hours in a police cell awaiting a court appearance and detaining a prisoner for 7 days or more awaiting a further appearance. The situation deteriorated over a period of many months with increasing financial cost to the police service with police officers undertaking duties for which they had never been trained. Several meetings were held with Home Office officials including the Home Secretary of the day, The Rt. Hon Leon Britton who gave various insincere promises that the matter would be resolved.

Not only did arrangements continue without improvement but a prison officers' strike ensued resulting in police officers being deployed inside Wandsworth prison. I visited the prison to make my own assessment of the increased pressures on the officers and although I learned nothing of value I was entitled in future to claim that I had 'done time' in Wandsworth in addition to several other prisons which I had visited from time to time in connection with my duties.

The miners' strike disorders and the Broadwater Farm Estate riots following on after other serious riot situations centred on Brixton together with the annual Notting Hill Carnivals all served to bring the control of public disorder to a high level of importance. Bricks and bottles thrown at the police later became supplemented with petrol bombs and police training was constantly under review to effectively address the matter. As a representative of the superintendents it was appropriate and necessary to keep abreast of developments even though I was no longer engaged in operational duties. However, at a mock up urban street area used for riot training I took the opportunity in a training session to be kitted out with protective clothing and be on the receiving end of missiles including petrol bombs. On another occasion together with Federation representatives I was invited to witness the use of water cannon as used by continental Police Forces and to a lesser extent the RUC. After trials it was considered that the use of water cannon in the Metropolitan Police District to suppress violent disorder was impractical, ineffective and the trials were discontinued.

Although my post was identified within the Personnel Branch of the Metropolitan Police I was in fact a free agent and I was never expected to notify my superior officers when I was away from London on Association duties. There was slight downside to the arrangement however in that I was not entitled to secretarial assistance but if the need was such, I could have typing etc undertaken by my Commander's staff. The practical result of this arrangement was that I did 90% of my secretarial requirements myself.

A few months after my appointment the Superintendents' Association decided to take the plunge and move into their own building. For many years they had occupied accommodation at one of the South London Police Stations but the cramped conditions were neither conducive to administrative efficiency nor suitable for a professional body. The London representatives of the Police Federation had impressive accommodation and the National representatives had a large headquarters in Surbiton. With many thousands of members, all paying compulsory contributions, the Federation were much wealthier than the Superintendents' Association with their few hundred members paying voluntary contributions. Consequently it was with a degree of trepidation and moral courage that they finally acquired a headquarters building suitable for their status and although smaller, in comparison with the Federation headquarters, it was adequate.

The premises selected were located in Pangbourne, Berkshire, part of a police station which had become redundant. After considerable renovation and alterations, a formal opening was conducted by the Rt Hon William Whitelaw. One piece of furniture which was necessary was a conference table capable of seating 18 – 20 persons and I was fortunate to learn that the catering Department of the Metropolitan Police had such a table surplus to requirements and after some delicate negotiations, not only was it donated free of charge but the necessary transport arrangements cost the Association nothing.

My duties required that I attend conferences throughout Great Britain as far apart as Edinburgh, Belfast, Swansea and of course, London. The annual conferences of the Association were held alternately in Torquay and Harrogate. For all of these conferences, Ann accompanied me and a great rapport and genuine friendship developed with representatives and their wives from the other Districts. Those meetings were always an opportunity for the men to wear formal evening suits with the ladies dressed in their finery.

Whilst the purpose of the frequent conferences was to discuss and occasionally resolve matters affecting our members, there were many occasion when the formality was overtaken by less serious matters. On one such occasion we were hosting a banquet in Surrey where our guests included the Chief Constable and the Chief Officer of the County

Council whose wife was sitting next to me. During our meal the conversation ranged over several subjects including a mention of the Police Choir until at one point she said something to me which I didn't quite hear. I asked her to repeat her comment and she said "Are you a music lover?" I replied "I thought you said "Are you an amusing lover?" I thought it was a little private joke between the two of us and I didn't realise she had told her husband. When he was invited to make a reply to our toast "To our guests" he could not resist the opportunity to inform everyone present much to my embarrassment.

When we held one of our meetings in Belfast we left the hotel en route to catch our flight back to London when I realised I had left my treasured gold pocket watch in the hotel's safe. There was no time to return and collect it but one of the RUC officers assured me the problem could be resolved. A police motorcyclist was dispatched back to the hotel; I made a telephone call to the management giving permission for the watch to be handed to the officer and he raced back to Aldergrove airport with the watch. Unfortunately we had taken off a few minutes before his arrival but all was not lost. My colleagues from the Northern Ireland Superintendents' Association who had accompanied us to the airport handed the watch to a crew member of an aircraft due to leave for Heathrow. He in turn handed it to a Metropolitan Special Branch officer who kept it in safe custody for a few days until I could meet up with him. The whole operation could perhaps be an example of the old boys' network syndrome.

Although Ann accompanied me for most of these the formal dinners, sometimes a problem was created for her. At this time she had a severe dietary problem being both coeliac and having a lactose intolerance. On occasions this required some variation to the menu to accommodate her. As a token show of appreciation to the catering staff I would pen little poems for their entertainment. However, it became known among my conference colleagues that some of the menu items would not suit her eating requirements and there would be friendly rivalry to sit next to her in the hope that she would pass some tasty morsels to them.

The catering manager at New Scotland Yard was particularly attentive and always remembered that she would need a little variation in the prepared menu. At one dinner the Commissioner, Sir Peter Imbert (later Lord Imbert) was sitting next to me when for our dessert Ann was served a large amount of fruit salad instead of whatever calorie rich alternative was served to every one else. Ann turned to the person next to her and commented that there was too much fruit salad for her to eat and spooned some of it onto his plate. The Commissioner leaned across me and asked her if he could also have some. This little gesture typified Sir Peter's friendly nature and in spite of the difference in our ranks I like to think of him and his wife, Lady Iris as personal friends.

In 1987 my colleagues elected me to be their President and I had the honour to take the platform at our conference in Harrogate with the Home Secretary The Rt. Hon Douglas Hurd as our principal guest and were accommodated in The Swan Hotel. At an informal dinner the night before the main conference presentation, knowing that Douglas Hurd had recently re-married and had a small child, during casual conversation he mentioned that because he was away from home so frequently he made a point of making telephone calls to make sure all was well at home. Ann in her forthright manner asked if he had made a call that evening and when he admitted that he had not she replied "Well you'd better go and do it." Bearing in mind she was speaking to one of the most politically powerful men in the country he took the admonishment without comment and made the telephone call.

Sometime later whilst he was still Home Secretary he hosted a conference in 10 Downing Street where we discussed various aspects of crime prevention and buffet refreshments were provided. Although she had not been in the discussion group I saw Margaret Thatcher quietly enter the room and whilst everyone else seemed more interested in their canapés and wine I went to her and told her that if I returned home and told my wife I had been missed the opportunity to speak to the Prime Minister, I would be admonished. We shook hands or to be more precise, we held hands whilst we chatted for a few minutes and although she may have been known in political circles as the Iron Lady, I found her to be gentle in her manner and very pleasant in our conversation.

As the representative of the London Superintendent ranks I was included in the official list of invited guests to some of the functions organised within the Metropolitan Police. These events included the annual horse show at Imber Court and the annual dog show. The usual procedure was that I would receive an invitation to attend on either the Friday or Saturday of the week of the event and one year we were notified that Her Majesty the Queen would attend on the Friday. I asked Ann which day she would prefer and casually mentioned that the Queen would be present on the Friday. She agreed that day would be our choice. On the day whilst we were in the VIP enclosure she whispered to me that the lady in front of us looked very much like the Queen and when I assured her that it was she admitted that she thought I had been joking when I said she would be present.

It was at that time I thought we had overcome Ann's fear of horses, something which had concerned her since early childhood. I had a discussion with the senior officer of the Mounted Branch who assured her that her fears were unjustified. He took us to one of the stables where a mare in foal was awaiting the arrival of her offspring. The officer explained that she was a very gentle animal and after much persuasion, Ann finally overcame her phobia and stroked the animal. With her new confidence we went the following week for the dog show and saw the officer from the Mounted Branch. In casual conversation he told us that the mare which Ann had so bravely stroked had actually bitten someone the following day. Ann's fear of horses immediately returned.

Buckingham Palace

Having received the notification of my award of the MBE, or to be precise, to become a Member of the Most Excellent Order of the British Empire, Ann and I were determined to say nothing to anyone until we saw it in print. We deliberated for days as to where we were likely to obtain a newspaper as soon as they were on the streets. We thought that perhaps Piccadilly Circus was the most likely. However, when I mentioned the problem to one of my Superintendent colleagues in London he suggested I make a telephone call to one of his friends at the Telegraph printing premises on the Isle of Dogs.

Not knowing personally the individual concerned, I made the call and was asked to be at the premises at 9.00pm on the day of the printing. We duly arrived and asked for the contact person only to be informed that he was the General Manager and he was not available but he had directed his night duty manager to receive us, take us on a tour of the premises and watch the newspapers being printed. I was taken aback by this generous arrangement and explained that my intention had only been to obtain a copy as soon as they were available. We were asked why it was so important and Ann said that we knew a friend was to be included in the Birthday Honours and we wanted to make sure before extending congratulations.

Our enthusiasm and barely controlled excitement was tempered when he suggested that with national elections having taken place two days earlier publication of the Birthdays Honours may be held over. However, we were not to be disappointed and at one stage of the newspaper production a document like a huge photographic negative was transmitted from premises in Fleet Street into the room where we were. Our newly found friend placed it on a lighted screen so that we could read it and when Ann saw my name, she threw her arms round me and gave me a kiss.

We were then taken to the printing presses and the first newspaper off the press was given to us together with several other copies and later, we were given the actual metal printing sheets when they were removed from the printing rollers as a memento of our visit. It was well after mid-night and too late to disturb Denise but I phoned Lloyd and told him of the publication. He then told his partner Josephine, "My dad's got the MBE; I'm too posh for you so push off." They never married but continued life together with their son Benjamin graduating from University of Canterbury and daughter Georgia progressing satisfactorily through senior school. Publication of the newspaper resulted in many cards and expressions of congratulations being received and my photograph with biography appearing in the local Press.

Whilst I was very pleased to receive the award I was still a little bewildered as to why I had received the honour which may have been as the result of my involvement in community affairs or perhaps because I had been the National President of the Police Superintendents' Association, but there must have been many other persons with similar credentials who were not recognised. I felt pleased that every one of the groups with which I was associated said "OUR Les has got the MBE" which suggested that THEY all shared the honour.

Of course having had the award publicised, there was still a further wait to receive the medal and it was to be another 6 months before I received an invitation to go to Buckingham Palace to be presented to Her Majesty Queen Elizabeth. One of the Deputy Assistant Commissioners insisted that I use his official car to travel to the palace and on the day, Ann in a superb outfit accompanied me to 'Buck House'. The fact that we were caught in traffic congestion made me worry that we would be late but we did arrive in time.

Ann was taken off in one direction to a seat in the Grand Ballroom whilst I was directed to The Long Gallery, which as the name suggests was a long room with many pictures on the walls where I found myself amongst about 200 other persons to be presented to the Queen

The formal procedure was explained to us and we would be taken 10 – 12 at a time to doors which led into the ballroom where the presentations were to be made. From that point we would be called individually to a point in front of the Queen, turn to face her; a slight bow and then one pace forward to stand directly in front of her. She would shake our hand, attach the award to our jacket on a little clip which we had previously fixed in place.

The Queen may say a few words to us, we would step back, another slight bow, turn away from the direction in which we had approached and leave the room. As the number of persons in The Long Gallery slowly took their turn I, and a young Women's Royal Air Force Officer began to wonder if we had been forgotten but eventually we were called.

When it was my turn to make my entrance, on the stage, stood the Queen flanked by several 'Beef Eaters'; a band was playing quietly in a gallery above the Queen and a gentleman in formal courtier's attire stood holding a velvet cushion on which rested my medal. I made my bow, stepped forward and took her hand and she then placed the medal on my jacket. She asked me where I worked and told her we were near neighbours because my office was just a few hundred yards away in Buckingham Gate. I then turned and left the room and was somewhat surprised when another courtier removed my medal and placed it into a box which he then handed to me. Once outside in the open air we posed for an official photograph in the palace courtyard and then walked across to a grassed area outside the palace where a police photographer took many more photographs with the palace in the background.

The day of the presentation ceremony coincided with one of the Superintendents' Association meetings which was to take place in a hotel in Sloane Square. I had arranged with my son and daughter with their respective partners to join us for lunch. As I stood at the hotel entrance in my police uniform, an American tourist obviously mistook me for the porter and asked me to take her luggage to her room. How are the mighty fallen! From an audience with the Head of State to hotel porter all within an hour or so.

It was a wonderful day and one which we are never likely to forget.

Hamburg 1989

One day I was summoned to the office of the Commissioner, Sir Peter Imbert who asked me if I could speak German. Because the police choir had made several trips to Germany I had learned sufficient to hold a conversation in their language. He explained that it was 800 years since the port of Hamburg had been established and it was also 175 years since the Hamburg Police had been formed. There were to be celebrations and he had been invited to go. Unfortunately other duties would prevent him accepting the invitation and he wanted a representative of ACPO (The Association of Chief Police Officers); a representative of the Superintendents' Association and a representative of the Police Federation to go in his place. There was no question that I would not accept and soon found myself in the company of Deputy Assistant Commissioner David Meynell and Police Constable John Barney.

Consequently on Tuesday 6th June 1989 I drove to Harwich where my car was parked in police headquarters and I met my two travelling companions as we made our way to the DFDS ferry SS Hamburg and then to our respective cabins. Unknown to us officers from Special Branch had informed the captain of the vessel that VIP police officers would be on board but we only learned of this when a message was broadcast over the tannoy "Would the occupier of cabin 347 please report to the Purser's office?" The occupier of cabin 347 was David Meynell and the result was that we had all been invited to the Captain's cabin and formally welcomed aboard by Captain Günther Kullack . When we were nearing our point of disembarkation we were invited to the bridge as the ferry eased down the river Elbe into the port of Hamburg.

Our escort and constant companion for the duration of our visit was Inspector Karoline Starkgraff who was awaiting our arrival with a Mercedes limousine driven by Gerhard and we were taken to our accommodation in the Bundeswehr akademie. We later dined in the Friesenkeller restaurant with about a dozen police officers and afterwards went to a 'keller' (pub) which was dimly lit and had antique musical instruments, old manuscripts and pictures of composers on the walls. In the pub there was a very friendly atmosphere but I quickly learned a little matter of protocol. On the bar were several bowls of 'monkey nuts' and I carefully placed the empty shells on the counter only to be told that it was expected that we drop them on the floor where it was easier to sweep them up.

The following morning after breakfast we were collected by Karoline and Gerhard and taken to the office of the Police President Dirk Reimers where we had coffee together with other police officers from Switzerland, Belgium and New York who were also guests invited to the celebrations. We visited the Command and Control Centre and the Public Relations Branch. After lunch we visited the Ambulance Control and Fire Brigade Headquarters where I was encouraged to climb the 100 foot turntable fire escape giving me a wonderful view of Hamburg. Our non-stop itinerary continued with a visit to the to the River Police (Wasserpolizei) for an hour or so on the river. In the evening after dining in a floating restaurant we were escorted down the Reeperbähn which is the notorious 'Red Light district' and much to my amazement we met the Salvation Army holding an open air service.

Day 3 of our visit allowed a visit to the central division of the Hamburg police and escorted by a local officer, we walked the beat through the city wearing our uniforms with a visit to the Rathause and then lunch at police headquarters where we exchanged gifts with our hosts. After lunch we were photographed in the Gänsemarkt (market place) by more Press agencies then I had ever previously experienced. The local residents and visitors were treated to the unusual sight of their local Hanseatic City police officers dressed in historic police uniforms accompanied by 2 police officers from Switzerland, one from New York and of course the Metropolitan Police. Pictures and articles about the event appeared in many of the newspapers. Later we visited the Bereitshaftpolizei (riot police) looked at their vehicles and travelled in one of their APCs (armoured personnel carriers). Later we were invited to a barbecue which they had arranged and rounded off the evening by visiting another keller packed with patrons enjoying roast pig washed down with beer brewed on the premises. Needless to say we indulged in the food and drink.

Karoline lived with her mother Helga in a flat in Hamburg and invited the three of us to take breakfast with them on the day in which we were to visit the 'Open Day', part of the overall celebrations. It was a fascinating experience which, much to our surprise featured a pipe festival (bag-pipes) including Highland Games and where we met the Deputy Provost of Glasgow. What had been a full day of activities was by no means over for us because the late evening was the occasion of a magnificent Ball with something like 1,100 other guests. It was 2.00am before we returned to our lodgings.

On the Sunday of our visit we again took breakfast with Karoline and Helga in their home after which Karoline, David and I went to the English church nearby. Helga had packed a picnic lunch for us which we shared on the bank of the Alster canal before making our way to the helicopter unit for a flight over the city. The day was completed when we attended a farewell dinner hosted by the Burgermeister and again we exchanged gifts with our hosts. During the meal, David, John and I discussed the protocol that we should make an expression of our thanks speaking in German. Because I was the only one of us who had sufficient linguistic skill I volunteered. I carried with me a set of 'crib' cards on which were written various phrases of a general nature and when strung together could create a credible speech. I received polite acknowledgement of my efforts and thought no more about it until the next day.

We had decided that as some token of our appreciation we would take Karoline, Helga and our driver Gerhard for lunch and had booked places at a well known restaurant. When we sat down I received a rather frosty acknowledgement from Helga which perplexed me because for the whole week of our visit she had accepted us almost as family members. I learned a little later that because we had depended on Karoline to act as our interpreter without ever speaking in German myself she was a little resentful that she had struggled with her limited knowledge of English whilst I had not been equally considerate. As we commenced our meal she told me that if I wanted to speak to her I must speak in German. However we all enjoyed the meal and David bought champagne for us to toast our hosts.

We had a little time for shopping before we prepared to depart and I went to a large departmental store intending to buy a gift for Ann. Intent on using my limited knowledge of the language, before I entered I carefully rehearsed what I intended to say; "I want to buy a present for my wife. I come from London and speak very little German. If you speak slowly I will understand." The smartly dressed manager listened to me, did not reply immediately then snapping his fingers in the air he called in English "Fraulein; this gentleman wants to buy a present for his wife." He then smiled and escorted me to where the female shop assistant was waiting to serve me.

Encouraged by my success I visited a shop selling porcelain and china. In the window I saw a wall plate which commemorated the 800th anniversary of the founding of the port of Hamburg. I decided it would be suitable to add to our home and entered the shop, using my carefully rehearsed speech. The lady in the shop laughed good humouredly and said "It's alright. I'm English. I moved here from Surrey." If nothing else I felt more confident speaking in the native language.

We returned to our lodging accommodation to pack ready for our return home and then in the evening accepted an invitation from the Police President to join him at his home for a meal with his wife, Martha and family. In common with many German homes, the house included a basement where we adjourned after the meal, partook of drinks with an occasional game of darts until 2.00am

The final day of our visit took us to the Kriminalpolizei and in the company of officers from the Bundesgrenzschult (Border Police) we visited the border with East Germany and made our way to Bremerhaven to board the ferry for our home journey. On the quay as we pulled away we could see Karoline and Gerhard waving to us and when we returned to our cabins we indulged ourselves with a lovely chocolate cake baked for us by Karoline.

For nearly 2 weeks we had been entertained as VIPs, had made many new friends and I concluded the most rewarding experience of my police career. Immediately after our return, David was awarded an OBE in the Queen's Birthday Honours.

My friendship with Karoline and Helga continued for many years and there were frequent occasions when we visited each other.

Approaching Retirement

The conditions of service in the Metropolitan Police required that chief superintendents were obliged to retire at the age of 55 whereas every other Force in the country allowed service until 60 years. This anomaly had resulted from a pre-war agreement with the Commissioner Lord Trenchard who had instituted a fast promotion scheme for outstanding young officers but to avoid a 'log jam' in the senior ranks, it was agreed that to maintain the chances for promotion, superintendent and chief superintendents must retire comparatively early in service..

On my return from the visit to Hamburg I was in my last year of active service and had to think of retirement. I feel sure that had I not approached the commander of the Personnel Branch and asked that a replacement for my post be identified, no one would have questioned if I had continued well beyond my 55th birthday. Although making this move there was no intention at all that I would 'wind down' and intended to continue my Association work until the very last moment. The conferences and committee work continued as hectic as ever and I was away from my office more than I was in residence. One particular committee on which I represented my colleagues was a Sex and Race Equality committee at New Scotland Yard.

A proposal had been made that when female police officers working in central London became pregnant, they should be posted to the outer divisions to protect them from undue potentially violent situations. My colleagues were strongly opposed to the suggestion on the grounds that all divisions were likely to face serious public disorder and it would have been impractical to police the outer divisions with an imbalance of pregnant police officers. Rather crudely some of the divisional commanders pointed out that a kick in a sensitive area of the male body was just as painful in Waltham Abbey as in Westminster.

When I made my contribution to the committee's deliberations the female 'Chair' took exception to my comments and much to my surprise, the minutes of the meeting were produced within 24 hours, omitting my expressed views and were passed to the Assistant Commissioner who approved them and then the committee was disbanded. It was reformed shortly afterwards under a different name without a representation from the Superintendents. I considered it merely a show of pique but the point had been made and the proposal was never implemented.

My successor was identified as chief superintendent Vernon Jones who was a Country and Western music enthusiast and had created his own image on the division where he worked by dressing in cowboy style clothing and playing his guitar. We worked alongside each other for a few weeks prior to my actual retirement.

As was the practice with many serving officers, a retirement party had been arranged but my independent existence in this respect was somewhat of a disadvantage. Whereas my colleagues in divisional command postings had an administrative staff and subordinate officers to undertake such arrangements as were necessary, I was very much sole administrator and organiser. The date of the party was set for 4th July, one week before my last day of service and it proved to be a poor choice.

On 4th July 1990 Germany was due to play England in a world football competition, a match which would be televised. On the same day there was a conference in London of senior officers from several European countries planning the strategy for a forthcoming meeting of Ministers. 4th July is of course the day on which American Independence is celebrated and some of my invited guests had been invited to the American Embassy. The Queen Mother decided to hold a private party to which the Commissioner, Sir Peter Imbert had been invited. On the evening of the party a train on the District line became disabled in St James's Park tube station, and no trains were passing through. Everything seemed to have conspired against me but 100 guests still attended and the football enthusiasts were able to watch the match on a large TV I had installed in the restaurant.

It was particularly pleasing for me that Sir Peter Imbert took early departure from the Queen Mother's invite and was able to join me and my other guests. As a memento of my service, my colleagues presented me with a ceremonial sword suitably engraved which took place of honour displayed on the wall of my study. Ann received a large bouquet of flowers.

The Door Closes on my Police Career

During the latter months of my representative duties it had been agreed with representatives of ACPO and the Police Federation at national level, after much discussion, that there should be a standard practice throughout all Police Forces that when an officer retired after a full term his Certificate of Service should suitably reflect the achievement. The previous arrangements varied from some Forces holding a presentation ceremony to others where the certificate was sent through the post or internal dispatch. We had faced a similar situation with the presentation of Long Service and Good Conduct medals and had persuaded all Forces to hold presentation ceremonies. It was agreed that the Certificates of Service deserved similar treatment.

When I received my certificate I was not best pleased. It was stamped with a facsimile signature of the Assistant Commissioner Personnel Department; the covering letter sent from the office of the woman who had chaired the Sex and Race Equality meeting was signed 'pp' by a junior clerk; it recorded that I had served in the West Midlands Police (which was formed in 1974 as an amalgamation of several Forces including Birmingham City) and it was sent through the post. I returned the certificate to the female head of the appropriate Branch with a suitable letter outlining my disgust. She sent a letter of apology which she signed herself and arranged for me to have a certificate presented personally by the Assistant Commissioner. I considered her apology a suitable recompense for her attitude in the Sex and Race Equality meeting.

As I approached the compulsory age of retirement I made 3 promises to Ann. 1. I would not take full time employment; 2 We would have at least two months break after I retired before I took any other employment and 3. I would not work in central London. My last day of service in the Metropolitan Police was Friday 12th July and I started a full time new job on Monday 15th July with the General Council of the Bar with offices in Lincoln's Inn, one of the four Inns of Court in central London.

Chapter 14. The Bar Council

The reason for my change of heart and failing to keep my promises was that 2 or 3 weeks before my intended retirement date, I received a phone call from an ex-colleague, Maurice Taylor who had been a commander at Hendon Police Training Centre. He worked with a retired police sergeant, Don Ormisson in the discipline office of the Bar Council dealing with complaints against barristers. He asked if I was interested in a job with them to start immediately. I indicated my interest but insisted my intention to keep to my retirement date.

The reason for his invitation was that they were becoming overwhelmed with complaints involving barristers who would not pay their subscription and it was intended to take full disciplinary action against them but they needed help to clear the backlog. The Chief Executive of the Bar Council was John Mottram CBE who had served in the Royal Marines and reached the rank of major general. He adopted an authoritarian attitude to his responsibilities but was always fair and prepared to discuss matters as appropriate.

The nature of my intended employment did not develop as intended because one of the barristers subject of their investigations and discipline procedure was determined to fight his case to the highest level. The case papers were submitted to the Disciplinary Tribunal headed by a senior judge. He ruled that the Bar Council were acting ultra vires and ruled in favour of the accused. That decision indicated that every other case which was pending would fail and any further action was discontinued. What had initially appeared to be a promising second career for me seemed to have foundered but it was not to be.

The Government of the day were concerned that the Bar operated closed shop practices which prevented qualified barristers following their chosen career. It is a requirement for any barrister, once qualified and 'called to the Bar' to become a pupil in Chambers. Vacancies in Chambers are limited and for many aspirants, they will never manage the first step on the rung.

In a Green Paper, the Government set out the basis of their criticism and it was recommended that a Bar Practising Library be established comparable to those in Scotland and Northern Ireland. Suitable premises were available in The Middle Temple and the intention was for a barristers' clerk to be appointed and set up the Library. The purpose was that newly qualified barristers would have a base from which to work until they were able to find a place in established Chambers.

At that time every set of Chambers would have several clerks many of them working on a commission basis with very lucrative terms of employment. To expect any one of them to give up a secure position for an uncertain future was improbable. I was invited to apply for the position and perhaps for the one and only time I can remember, reference to my Bachelor of Laws qualification was made when John Mottram, the Chief Executive Officer recommended my appointment.

The new venture was sponsored by the four Inns of Court, Inner Temple, Middle Temple, Lincoln's Inn and Gray's Inn together with the General Council of the Bar. I was given complete autonomy in setting up the Library and in addition to a large collection of legal books which unfortunately were not in good condition I made approaches to all major publishers of legal books, some of whom responded with generous donations.

I visited the librarians of the four Inns and also made visits to many of the prominent Chambers where I took advice from the Senior Clerks. I was given a small staff of a Personal Assistant, Edith Ball, a native of El Salvador and two clerks Anthony and Julie but the hoped for influx of trainee barristers did not materialise. Edith and her husband Tony became close friends and with Ann, we were to share many social outings with them and they were also our house guests at Christmas time.

I was allowed a budget for books of £5,000 pa. which I realised would be totally inadequate; in fact one of the Inn's librarians suggested I would need that amount each year to replace books that disappeared.

After a few months it became apparent to me that it was never intended for the Bar Practising Library to succeed and the Bar would maintain its traditions which denied young qualified barristers developing their chosen careers. Instead they would have to seek employment in alternative professions. After 15 months during which time I and my staff had explored every possibility for the Library, it was decided to cut our losses and close. Edith was to return to her previous position with the Bar Council, Julie was offered a post as an assistant to John Mottram's personal assistant, there was no vacancy for Anthony and once again I was unemployed.

The Middle Temple Arbitration Rooms

When the Bar Practising Library project was abandoned the Under Treasurer of the Middle Temple, Retired Vice Admiral Richard Hill suggested to me that I should keep in touch. The Under Treasurer of the Inn is effectively the Chief Executive Officer, The Treasurer being an honorary appointment usually taken by a Judge or senior QC of the Inn.

Within a few weeks of finding myself unemployed, I was invited to discuss with the Under Treasurer the possibility of establishing an arbitration rooms and conference suite in the same premises in which the Bar Practising Library had been based. I was given a completely free hand in setting up and administering the new project which quickly became accepted as a suitable venue for arbitration hearings and conferences.

Although initially I was the only person employed in the Arbitration Rooms, the volume of work necessitated the employment of a deputy or assistant. We advertised and received about 80 replies many of which I was able to discard on an initial 'paper sift' reducing the list to about 20. After a more detailed examination, I drew up a short list of 6 and interviews were arranged at which I was accompanied by my line manager, Mike Spain. We called three of the applicants for a second interview and finally chose Isabel Montes, a 52 year old lady of Spanish origin who had been made redundant by Thompson's, the well known Travel Company.

Although arbitration proceedings depended on arguments by barristers and solicitors with an Arbitrator who may have been a judge or QC, the proceedings were very relaxed and far removed from the normal formalities of court. We would serve tea, coffee and biscuits during their deliberations and have platters of sandwiches delivered for their lunches. On many occasions there were sandwiches left over and I became a popular figure to the homeless people on the Embankment when I distributed the left-overs to them

Most of the arbitrations in the early years were maritime disasters in which vessels may have foundered and been salvaged. The parties to the arbitration may have included claimants for the vessel, the cargo, claims from the salvage company, the port Authority to which the stricken vessel was taken together with any other interested parties.

On one occasion with a maritime arbitration booked in to the rooms I arrived at work to find that outside in the street, a water main had burst and water was gushing down the gutters. The Arbitration Rooms were below ground level and sometimes rather unkindly were referred to as 'the dungeon' or the 'cellar' but I preferred' Lower Ground level. Whatever the description, on this particular occasion I realised that water was gradually seeping into the room and with the arbitration hearing due to commence, it would have been impractical either to cancel or find another venue.

The Arbitrator was rather phlegmatic about the situation and merely advised the two parties to select either the flood side or the lee side to present their case. Of course it was only a temporary solution and for the following days we used huge suction cleaners and heaters in an effort to dry the rooms. Unfortunately the smell resulting from the saturated carpets could not be tolerated and the whole area of carpet tiles had to be replaced.

Ironically, I had recently completed a large jig-saw puzzle of a humorous nature which depicted industrial premises of a somewhat 'Heath-Robinson' nature which had been flooded and the opportunity was too good to resist . I framed the picture, measuring 30" x 20" and hung it on the wall where it remained until we closed down the rooms.

There were also civil engineering disputes which sometimes involved huge development projects. The most memorable one concerned the Menai Straits which separate North Wales from the Isle of Anglesey. The dispute arose from building a six lane motorway under the straits. On one of the riparian banks was an extensive area of housing and it became apparent that some of the buildings were experiencing subsidence. The conclusion was that the tunnelling for the motorway had caused instability in the adjacent land area.

For the purpose of explaining the intricacies of the claims, a huge three-dimension map of the area was displayed in the room. It was probably 12' x 6' and included every tiny detail of the landscape but the map was in two parts, the roads, houses and detail of the surface could be lifted to reveal details of the motorway under the surface.

For over three months the proceedings continued after which further discussions were suspended and although they were continued at a later date, it was at another venue.

Maritime and Civil Engineering cases were not the only ones using the Arbitration Rooms and many medical negligence claims were heard there. One rather unusual one had started in Australia but before its conclusion, the Judge was required to come to England and his whole court including the claimant and respondent continued the hearing in Middle Temple

Arbitration Rooms. It was particularly significant for us because the Judge directed that the transcript of evidence should include his appreciation for the outstanding support they had received from the Arbitration Room staff.

Another arbitration which was unusual concerned Lord Lloyd Webber. Apparently his pop musical 'Jesus Christ Superstar' had been contracted to appear at a venue in Germany. The claim and counter claim alleged that he had invested millions of pounds to prepare it for the German production but when the show was proving to be a bad investment, the Germans withdrew from the contract. Lord Lloyd Webber wanted recompense for the money he had invested whilst the Germans wanted compensation for the money they had spent preparing for a show which they had been led to believe would be immensely profitable. I do not know what the final outcome was but his arrogance and general demeanour made Lord Lloyd Webber one of the most unpleasant persons I had ever met.

There were other uses of the Arbitration Rooms. With the space available it was possible to install a large photo-copying machine which had the capacity to reproduce 60 copies per minute, double sided if so required, collated and stapled together. It was an ideal solution for the immense photo-copying requirements of the Middle Temple and accounted for much of my time when at work.

The supervisory body of the Inn is known as the Parliament which consists of approximately 200 judges or QCs who have been accorded the status of 'Master', a much sought after honour. Meetings of the Parliament occurred about every three months and they all received copies of the items for discussion. Each item on the agenda could be 30 or 40 pages long and if there were 20 agenda items, each of the Masters could expect to have 400 – 500 pages. Multiplied by 200 for each of the Masters and the result was a photo-copying requirement which would take several hours.

Once the papers had been printed, the envelopes had to be 'stuffed' a term which sounds somewhat crude but accepted terminology. Many of the Masters were located in chambers within either Middle or Inner Temple and could be hand delivered but others would be consigned to the normal postal service. Whilst it was not my responsibility to distribute the envelopes it caused no inconvenience to deliver some of them due to the close proximity of the addressees.

There was one particular occasion when the normal smooth procedure was disrupted. I received the documents for photo-copying very late in the week. Parliament was due to meet on the following Tuesday and with the weekend intervening there was a likelihood that the documents would not be distributed in time. It was fortunate that Ann was away from home for a few days which allowed me to work until well past midnight without disrupting my domestic harmony. I managed to deliver the local envelopes, took the others home with me and posted them in my local post office. As far as I know, all papers were duly received before the meeting.

Another regular commitment for photo-copying was in connection with the training courses which were regularly held for newly qualified barristers. The person in charge of the advocacy training programmes with an eminent QC Michael Sherrard (defence Counsel in the notorious James Hanratty A6 murder trial) and his assistant Christa Richmond. They would require large amounts of documents to be reproduced for the advocacy training with mock trials papers – blue for the one side, pink for the other and yellow for the adjudicator. Christa was a frequent visitor and we always entertained her with coffee and biscuits.

Although the Arbitration Rooms only had a permanent staff of two, our cleaning lady, Ellen was very much one of our small family. She was a no-nonsense lady for whom nothing was too much trouble. She was conscientious and lovable, particularly endeared to me because we shared the same birthday. She chatted to me about her family, her dog and her family life and was very distressed when she was forced to take time off because her health started to fail. She was in and out of hospital for the next few months which latterly coincided with my own hospitalisation for my first hip replacement. When I was discharged from hospital I was determined to visit her when again she was in hospital for what would prove the last time.

I travelled on public transport using a walking stick and went to her ward which was on the fourth floor. At the conclusion of my visit, although she was terminally ill she insisted on leaving her bed and accompanying me to the bus stop to make sure I caught my bus safely. I was very fond of Ellen and was privileged when her daughter Sharon invited me to give the eulogy at her funeral.

When I reached the age of 65, I would have been expected to leave my employment but I applied for an extension which was granted. However, one year later the lease of the building in which the Arbitration Rooms were located was due to expire and Middle Temple decided not to renew the lease and the Arbitration Rooms would cease to function. Isabel and I invited all the Middle Temple staff to visit us on 13th July 2001, my birthday, for a coffee morning with cream cakes. After lunch we were Guests of Honour at a speech making ceremony when we were both presented with suitable gifts to acknowledge our length of service. My gift was an original painting depicting Middle Temple Hall viewed across the gardens.

During my employment at Middle Temple I derived enormous job satisfaction and was sad that I had to leave. I was fortunate that the accommodation available allowed me to sleep there on the occasions when tube strikes would have created difficulties for me to travel to work. Instead of leaving home before 7.00am to catch the train at 7.15am, I could have a lie in until about 7.30am because I was already at work! During my years there I counted many judges and barristers amongst my friends. The venture, built on the never-to-succeed project of the Bar Practising Library had started from nothing to a point where we grossed in excess of £100,000 pa.

Middle Temple has its own 'aura' and on the occasions when I returned I always felt that I was still included in the family of the Inn. It has a wonderful history, the dining hall being the location of the first performance of Shakespeare's 'Twelfth Night' and the rooms are extensively used for filming, in particular 'Shakespeare in Love'. Many of the television programmes with a legal theme use the area in which the Inn is located to create the necessary atmosphere.

Her Majesty the Queen Mother was an Honorary Master of the Inn and on one of her annual visits for dinner, I had the pleasure and privilege of a personal introduction.

Even though my duties required that I would be at the Arbitration Rooms for many hours, there were times when there were no bookings giving me time to undertake necessary Rotary and Sea Cadets' work. In addition I had always wanted to write a history of the Police Choir and after three years of research I realised my ambition with 'The London Medley' which outlined the origins and development of the choir together with noteworthy milestones.

When I had retired from the Metropolitan Police I was disappointed, perhaps resentful that Regulations had curtailed a job I enjoyed; eleven years on when I walked out of the Arbitration Rooms for the last time, I was sad and depressed. Never before had I sought medical advice for depression but after a few weeks I did so and the advice of the doctor? Write your biography!

Chapter 15. The Male Voice Choir

Although I ceased to be a serving police officer on 13th July 1990 it was certainly not the end of my police career. When I transferred to the Metropolitan Police in 1975 and posted to Barkingside division, one of my colleagues in the adjacent division was chief superintendent Ron Burnhams. He was the secretary of the Metropolitan Police male Voice Choir and never missed an opportunity to advertise the fact. It was only a matter of weeks before I was persuaded to accompany him to the weekly choir practice which was held in Trenchard House, one of the section houses providing accommodation for single officers.

I had always enjoyed singing but other than the Salvation Army and the church choir in Swindon, I had not participated in choral singing since school days. When I joined, the police choir consisted of 40 – 50 members, serving and retired officers, and a few civilian members of the police but it was a firm policy that we always performed in uniform whereas other male voice choirs tended to wear blazers and flannels.

The musical Director of the choir when I joined was John Watson, an accomplished conductor who insisted on strict discipline when the choir were singing, whether in rehearsals or in public. I was suitably welcomed and allocated to the second tenors section. I soon learned that my ability to read music was shared by perhaps only 10 -12 others and great demands were made on the conductor and accompanist to ensure note and word perfection was achieved for our performances.

At the time of joining the choir the annual police concert to take place at the Royal Festival Hall was a matter of weeks away. The concerts had taken place every year from 1946 and both the Male Voice Choir and the Metropolitan Police Band more or less regarded it as their concert and merely tolerated each other. They vied with each other as to the number of tickets to be allocated and in the earlier days of the concerts, limits of about 400 were imposed to ensure that sufficient were available for the general public.

In addition to the choir and band, the concerts also welcomed many celebrities from the top echelon of the entertainment world as guest artistes. These artistes included the ventriloquist Ray Allen, Sir Harry Secombe, Jimmy Tarbuck, Richard Stilgoe, Tommy Trinder, Roy Castle and many others. The comperes for the shows were equally well known as the guest artistes but in 1968 the presenter of a television police programme – 'Police Five', Shaw Taylor accepted the invitation and continued as such until 1991.

In 1986 the policy at the Festival Hall changed and 'one night stands' were no longer accepted necessitating a change of venue. The Methodist Central Hall was the first option, where, ironically the first of the annual concerts had been held. Although the venue was not really suitable, our guest artiste on that occasion was the multi-talented Roy Castle who made the concert a huge success.

The following year a move to the nearby Queen Elizabeth Conference Centre proved to be a near disaster from an entertainment point because the venue was certainly not suitable for a concert performance. Our guest artiste on that occasion was Anita Harris, a consummate entertainer and in every way a delightful lady. Her husband Mr. Margolis had approached us as an experienced producer and assured the organising committee that he would take on full responsibility for the arrangements. Unfortunately his assurances did not materialise and it fell to members of the concert committee to make frantic efforts to ensure the venue was suitable . The Choir and Metropolitan Police Band together with the guest artiste all performed to the highest standard but overall the concert was not truly successful. In spite of the difficulties, there was one outstanding success. The concert coincided with a fund raising initiative supported throughout the Metropolitan Police for the Great Ormond Street Hospital for Children and a cheque for £275,162 was presented by the Commissioner to the hospital representatives.

In 1990 the Barbican Centre opened its doors for the annual concerts and it remained the venue until 2010 when the Metropolitan Police Annual concerts were discontinued and subsequent concerts were organised by the choir members themselves.

Although the annual concerts were the main feature of the choir's calendar of engagements, every year from when I joined their ranks, the choir undertook 12 - 15 concerts every year as the result of appeals from Churches and other fund raising groups. It is a matter of speculation how many thousands of pounds were raised as a result of those concerts but wherever they sang, the choir always received an enthusiastic welcome and in many instances returned year after year. The fact that the choir members travelled from all points of the compass over the Metropolitan Police area to fulfil those engagements is a tribute to their commitment and dedication.

The visits to Chingford commenced in 1982 continuing every year for over 30 years and with the organisation of the Rotary Club large audiences were guaranteed. Ever popular with the Chingford supporters, the choir always expressed their enthusiasm for that particular venue.

The choir has always maintained a high reputation as police/public ambassadors and in addition to concerts have often been called upon for prestigious public appearances which included celebrations in Hyde Park for the 100th birthday of Her Majesty Queen Elizabeth the Queen Mother and events to celebrate 150 years since the founding of the Metropolitan Police, 160 years since the founding of the Special Constabulary and 200 years since the formation of the River Police. Annual carol services organised by the Christian Police Association and until they were discontinued in 1990, the annual Road Safety Services were regular commitments for the choir.

Baron Imbert of New Romney in the County of Kent, as Sir Peter Imbert had been Commissioner of the Metropolitan Police from 1987 until 1992 during which time he had been a staunch supporter of the choir. Sadly a few years after his retirement he suffered a stroke but even though he was subsequently confined to a wheel chair he continued his enthusiasm for the choir, attending their concerts whenever possible.

On 5th May 2013 he celebrated his 80th birthday at the Metropolitan Police Sports Club, Imber Court and tentatively asked if a few of the choir members would join him and his guests to sing a few songs. When the choir members were informed of his request, there was a unanimous response and every one of them who could attend, did so providing a concert for about 30 minutes to Lord Imbert and his many other guests.

I always regarded it as a pleasure and privilege to sing with the choir, sharing their sincere commitment to the service of the Metropolitan Police and the community at large. Consequently I took exception to an article published in a London evening newspaper which criticised a suggestion to introduce high ranking military officers into the police service to combat alleged corruption and malpractice in the police service. Included in the article was the following paragraph:

"How would chief constables drawn from the army change this state of affairs? Would they unhesitatingly root out and dismiss errant policemen so the evidence the force collects would be untainted? This is that happy land called Cloud Cuckoo Land in which simple schemes change bad into good, dark into light and bent coppers into singing bobbies."

On behalf of the choir I wrote a response as follows:

"An otherwise excellent article (Policing in fantasy land) included a needless and hurtful comparison. If the antithesis of 'bad' and 'dark' are 'good' and 'light', it does not follow that the antithesis of 'bent coppers' is 'singing bobbies'. Ironically when your readers would have been digesting the article, members of the Metropolitan Police Male Voice Choir, having given up their spare time, were singing at a fund raising concert in London. Every one of them, as with hundreds of other police choir members is of the highest integrity and dedicated to the service of the public, not converted 'bent coppers'.

The choir members felt that we had set the record straight.

In 1980 a new Director of Music was appointed, Gerald Pieti who retained the appointment until 2011. During his directorship the choir produced 4 recordings and undertook several tours to the continent. He worked with several accompanists during his tenure including John Davies, a brilliant pianist whose skills enabled him to accompany the choir with or without music and was accomplished in covering mistakes or shortcomings of the singers. Sadly, at an early age, John suffered a fall when leaving rehearsal one evening, suffered a head injury and died leaving a widow and two young daughters.

Foreign Fields – Lübeck

Following the retirement of my friend Chief Superintendent Ron Burnhams, I was the senior rank in the choir and as such was expected to make decisions on behalf of the choir. In 1981 a police choir from Lübeck, Germany visited London and were hoping to identify a British police choir who could participate in an annual choir festival in their home city. We were pleased to accept their invitation and the choir members travelled in two groups, some flew and others who were not keen on flying, went by ferry. This was a new experience for us and following take off, safely on our way, I was very concerned that some of my colleagues started singing. Being the senior officer I was worried that complaints from other passengers may have resulted and asked the stewardess to tell me immediately if that occurred. Not only were there no complaints but when the first song was finished a round of applause indicated that we were in favour and continued with other numbers until we reached our destination.

One of our members commented as we approached Lübeck that the last time he had flown over the city he was a crew member in a Lancaster bomber dropping bombs during the war. If we thought his reminiscing was perhaps inappropriate, a few days later we were enjoying a social evening with our hosts one of whom, unaware of our member's war time experience, told us that he had been in the Luftwaffe shooting down enemy (our) bombers. It was said in a spirit of friendship and war was just a bad memory.

Both groups of choir members, those flying and those travelling by sea, arrived in Hamburg within a short space of time and were greeted by two of their principal hosts Wilfred Brinkmeyer and Gunther Wachholz. A quick tour of Hamburg in a police coach was made prior to the 60 Km journey to Lübeck.

A reception had been arranged for the choir in the restaurant area of the Police Headquarters where their choir members and their wives were waiting to greet us. I could speak no German but one of our non-police travelling companions acting as interpreter prepared for me a speech of sorts in phonetic phrases. When I stood to deliver my greeting, my nerve gave out and I admitted that I was unable to do it. Their police chief officer Norbert Wolf holding comparable rank to mine, speaking in perfect English reassured me that there was no problem as he and many of those present could speak English. I felt somewhat embarrassed and promised myself that if I ever returned to Germany I would learn to speak the language.

Whilst most of our choir members were hosted in the homes of the German choir, our Musical Director Gerald Pieti, myself and one other were accommodated in a hotel where three non-German speaking visitors stayed up until the small hours trying to converse with the hotel proprietor and his staff neither of whom could speak English.

A programme of visits had been arranged for the choir and as guests of the Bundesgrenzschutz (Border Police) we were escorted to the East German border under strict instructions not to give any indication that we would violate the border. It was unnerving to find ourselves less than 100 yards away from East German Border guards, heavily armed and obviously keeping us under surveillance. The extent of the anti-personnel devices included barbed wire fences, land mines, booby traps, dog patrols and watchtowers with more armed guards. We were told that the defences were not primarily intended to prevent intrusion from the West but escape from the East and we saw many tributes to persons who had been shot in their attempts.

Later that day, three of our choir members were urged to don their uniforms and perform traffic control duties in the busy Marktplatz. The local media representatives were pleased to record the occasion for their readers.

In addition to the concert with the Polizei Chor Lübeck another choir from Braunschweig and the Musikkorps der Landespolizei Schleswig-Holstein (Band of the Schleswig-Holstein Police). participated in the three hours festival with the choirs combining to sing Klänger der Freude in German. The Lübeck choir also sang the "Lübecker Marzipan" song to acknowledge that the city was a world famous producer of that delicacy.

As a memento of our visit we were presented with a magnificent brass double headed eagle, a symbol of Schleswig-Holstein area of Germany. With other trophies from our visits, the eagle remained in my possession for safe keeping.

Our visit to Lübeck resulted in their return to London as our guests, and many of the friendships forged on these visits continued for many years. On their return visit, accompanied by their wives, the numbers were far greater than could be accommodated in our own choir members' homes and the Lübeck visitors made arrangements to stay in a hotel located in Russell Square.

We had made arrangements for a concert to be held in Chelsea Town Hall (how we managed to sell sufficient tickets is still a mystery to me) which proved to be very successful. Our visitors were using 3 coaches parked in nearby streets and we devised a plan to take them back to their hotel, a distance of about 5 miles. We decided that each of the three coaches would have one of our members preceding the coach in a car acting as a pilot.

The plan, such as it was did not go as we expected and as the first coach moved off the other two coach drivers, fearing that they would be left behind followed in close convoy. Those of us who should have been acting as pilots followed in one of our cars for a journey back to the hotel which proved to be quite hair-raising. Ignoring red traffic lights and other hindrances, the three coaches kept together as they raced back to the hotel, our leading car driver apparently oblivious to the situation behind him. Fortunately we arrived back at the hotel unscathed and without any reported traffic violations.

Several of our choir members went to the hotel the following morning to say our farewells and gathered on the pavement outside waiting for our visitors to board their coaches, the inevitable happened. Wherever a group of male voice choir enthusiasts stand around in a group, it will not be long before they start singing. We did not realise that three or four floors up in the building where we stood, nurses who had been on night duty were trying to sleep. We did not realise, that is, until someone emptied a bowl of water on the singers below. It was accepted in good humour by those of us who received the water.

We were obviously well received by our German friends in Lübeck and were invited to make a return visit in 1988 when we travelled by ferry. Once again the temptation to start singing proved to be irresistible and in a lounge area, most of the choir assembled and sang their songs. It was after midnight when we decided to finish and go to bed to the disappointment of some of the people listening who urged us to continue. For this visit I was hosted in the home of Norbert Wolf who insisted on showing me off to the townsfolk with both of us driving round in our uniforms. We drank beer in a bar which was completely contrary to my normal practice as a police officer in uniform.

Following the pattern of other visits, an interesting programme had been arranged for us including a visit to the police training school (Landespolizeischule) in the town of Eutin and the riot police headquarters (Bereitschaftpolizeiabteilung) which included impressive demonstrations of water cannon and unarmed combat techniques.

The principal justification for the visit was to partake in the Fruhlinuskonzert where we shared the platform with the Polizerichor Lübeck and the Polizerichor Fulda with additional music items from the Polizeiorchestra Scheswig-Holstein and for days prior to the concert posters were announcing "Ausverkauff" (sold out). In appreciation of the hospitality shown to them our choir included a piece of music "Die Nacht" (The night) which they sang in German. Their fluency may be judged by a comment that we obviously sang in an unfamiliar dialect..

Foreign Fields – Duisburg

In 1983 the Duisburg Police Choir visited London as guests of the International Police Association and the Metropolitan Police choir were invited to join them for a concert in Greenwich Town Hall which resulted in an invitation the following year for us to visit the industrial city of Duisburg in the Rhur valley the following year. Travelling by ferry and coach they arrived to an enthusiastic reception by the Duisburg choir. After a convivial hour or so sampling the local biers, our choir dispersed to the homes of our hosts and I was somewhat amused to find that my host lived in a suburb with the name "Metmann".

I felt much more competent for that visit with my language capabilities and was able to offer our hosts our sincere greetings speaking in their language. An impressive schedule of visits had been arranged including a tour of ATH – the largest steelworks in Europe; a tour of the police headquarters followed by lunch, a coach excursion round the city and a trip round the harbour with the river police demonstrating the use of fire hoses.

We were invited to a reception by the Oberbürgermeister at the Rathause where we gave an impromptu concert for him and then in the main concert hall we were joined by the host choir and the police choir from Bamberg. At a social gathering, gifts were exchanged including one of the much sought after London police helmets and my own head piece was left in their hands as a permanent memento of our visit.

Foreign Fields – Bamberg

It seems that our brand of music suited our German audiences because following the Duisburg visit we were invited to Bamberg, Bavaria in 1987. It is the largest town in the administrative region of Upper Franconia situated on the river Requitz and escaped much of the damage of the war. It was on this visit that I was fortunate to meet several people who would become life-long friends. Together with Gerald Pieti the choir's Musical Director I was hosted by Paul and Theresa Dirauf who had two sons Hilmar and Marius. Paul spoke no English and Theresa only a very limited ability but both sons were quite adept and we had no difficulty at all in maintaining conversation. Our visit was extensively reported in the local Press extolling the quality of our performances and repertoire.

Before partaking in the "Jubilaumskonzert" which celebrated the 40th anniversary of the Bamberg Polizeisangerchor we were taken on a tour of Bavaria under the direction of one of the senior officers of the Border Police, Reinhard Kilan. At the invitation of the Oberbürgermeister we visited Reinhard's home town of Coburg which was on the East German border. The programme prepared for us commenced with a visit to Coburg Castle which houses an impressive art collection. The Eisenburg Palace included the living quarters used by Queen Victoria, married to Prince Albert of Sachsen-Coburg-Gotha.

A civic reception was arranged for the choir in the Municipal building where they were greeted by the Oberbürgermeister Karl-Heinz Höhe and principal guest, His Highness Prince Andreas of Sachsen-Coburg-Gotha as representative of the Aristocratic House. The Oberbürgermeister outlined the 930 years history of the castle and highlighted the connection with the British Monarchy culminating with the marriage of Prince Albert and Queen Victoria.

I was invited to make a response to the welcome and hopefully acquitted myself reasonably after which the choir assembled in the market square in front of a statue memorial to Prince Albert which had been dedicated on completion by Queen Victoria. We attracted a large crown of listeners as we serenaded them with "Take the Sun", "Calm is the Sea", "A'Roving", "The Old Woman" and "Stouthearted Men".

We were shown a film explaining the development historically of the Frontier politics from 1945 onwards featuring barbed wire fences, minefields including automatic shooting and electronic sensors at the crossing activated acoustically and optically. We were then taken to a viewing point at Eisfeld which gave a clear view of the defences and the armed guards patrolling the Border.

Leaving Coburg somewhat bewildered by the stark contrast between West Germany and East German we then visited Rödental as guests at another reception. The Bürgermeister Gerhard Press explained the historical association between his area and the House of Windsor. Prince Albert, Consort to Queen Victoria was born in Rosnau Castle in 1819 and they both visited the castle many times after their marriage. She is reputed to have remarked that had she not been Queen of England she would move to Rosnau. The castle was undertaking a programme of restoration organised by the Prince Albert Society whose patron is Prince Philip.

After an impromptu concert on the steps of the Rathaus we were invited to sing in the chapel where Prince Albert had been christened. We sang "How Great Thou Art" accompanied by the Bürgermeister who proved to be no mean organist. Returning to Bamberg we visited the town of Staffelstein with yet another reception and we indulged in a local tradition of drinking beer from 3 litre pewter flagons and then a short spell in the market place where we entertained the local onlookers.

In all of these visits we received gifts which were usually wall plaques commemorating the particular town. Staffelstein was rather unique in that their wall plaque was made of wax. Most of the trophies were displayed on the walls of my study but that from Staffelstein was treated with extra care to avoid the possibility of it melting.

After the whirlwind tour of Bavaria in which our political, geographical and historical knowledge had been increased we prepared for the purpose of our visit, the Jubilaumskonzert (40th anniversary of the Bamberg Polizeisangerchor). However, earlier in the day we joined a procession of musicians parading through the streets to the market place, preceded by a London black cab.

The concert was an unqualified success and we returned to our beds tired but happy. The following morning almost created a problem. Gerald Pieti and I woke in good time to take breakfast and travel to the ferry for our return to London. Unfortunately our hosts overslept and we had the slight embarrassment of having to wake them but everything turned out well.

In May 1989 we hosted the Bamberg choir for a return visit and arriving at Heathrow airport they were taken in police transport to the Police Social and Athletic Club, Imber Court where they were introduced to their individual hosts. The visitors found it difficult to understand that whereas their choir members all lived within a few minutes of each other, in London, we were faced with a journey of nearly 2 hours from Heathrow to our home and any sight-seeing arrangements similarly involved long journeys.

Ann and I were pleased to accommodate Paul and Hilmar Dirauf as our guests. It formed the basis of a long lasting friendship for us which resulted in many unexpected pleasures in later years. Accompanying the choir was one of their wives, Ruth Schnieder who acted as interpreter when necessary. We also provided accommodation for her and her husband Herbie borrowing the house of a lady neighbour for the purpose whilst she stayed with her daughter in Norwich for a few days.

For their visit we had organised an itinerary of sightseeing and a concert in the Chelsea Parish Church of St Luke in the presence of the Mayor and Mayoress of the Royal Borough of Kingston and Chelsea followed by a reception in the Peelers Restaurant at New Scotland Yard. There was also a less formal concert in Bedford which was twinned with Bamberg. The choir members were anxious to visit nearby Elstow, the birthplace of John Bunyan,

Foreign Fields – Amersfoort

Our reputation obviously had spread beyond Germany and in 1991 the choir received an invitation to go to the Dutch town of Amersfoort as guests of the Amersfoort Big Band to participate with them in a concert. The journey by road nearly ended in disappointment because the coach driver lost his way, and when at a point where we were long overdue, we pulled onto the motorway hard shoulder to make telephone contact with our hosts. Unbeknown to us they were also very concerned and sent out a police patrol vehicle to locate us. Having done so, preceded by the police car with flashing lights and sirens wailing, we raced down the motorway on the hard shoulder probably causing many local persons to wonder what on earth was happening.

In the town hall reception, having learned enough German to hold reasonably conversations, I had taken a crash course in the Dutch to thank our hosts for their hospitality. Not only did we perform in Amersfoort but we travelled to the city of Zutphen where another concert was held.

The following year we invited the Big Band to visit London where they were included in the annual police concert at the Barbican Centre and were enthusiastically received. Their departure the following morning was even more problematic than we had experienced on the occasion of our visit to them. They were due to assemble at Chigwell Police Sports Club for the road journey to Harwich. Unfortunately it was very foggy and the worried coach driver insisted on leaving at the previously agreed time even though some of the Big Band members were missing.

One of our choir members stayed behind for the late comers to travel with him and hopefully join the others at Harwich. An accident occurred on the M25 causing further delay and after frantic phone calls asking for the ferry to delay its sailing time, the Big Band members arrived with barely 10 minutes to board.

Ann and I hosted the band Director of Music Bert Landman and his wife Nettie who had shared their home with us for our visit to Amersfoort.

Foreign Fields – Trier

In the beautiful Mosel valley lies Germany's oldest city – Trier and May 1996 was the last occasion for the choir to travel to the continent travelling by coach having crossed the Channel in 'Le Shuttle' the journey became beset with problems.

The coach driver was not as experienced in continental driving as we had anticipated and having passed through Paris travelling south, we were perplexed to realise shortly afterwards that we were travelling north through Paris again. The intention had been that we would rendezvous at the Luxemburg border with an escort who would escort us to an official reception in Trier. Displaying more confidence in my German vocabulary I made several telephone calls in an attempt to have a message conveyed to our hosts but whether they were successfully delivered I never discovered.

The end of the story was that we arrived after the reception had finished but a convivial evening with our host choir and another from Holland amply made up for our disappointment in arriving late. The concert which was allegedly the purpose of our visit was hugely successful and we shared the honours with the Trier choir, the choir from Holland and two police bands.

Whether or not the true reason for the choir's visit was music or the wine tasting and sightseeing is a matter of conjecture but certainly the opportunity to experience the splendour of Trier's many attractions, the boat trip along the Mosel to Bernkastle and the evening during which the warmth of the summer sun was complemented by the copious varieties of wine to be sampled were endearing memories for us the visitors. Unfortunately we were never in a position to invite their choir for a visit to London.

America – To Be or Not To Be?

Throughout their history the choir have performed at concerts too numerous to count and have attracted a strong following from their many admirers. None was more enthusiastic than an American lady, Nancy Blair. She was a graduate of Oklahoma University where she studied organ and piano and had an impressive background as choir master in several churches in America and Kuala Lumpa when her husband was employed there. She was extremely wealthy and her husband held a senior executive position with an American oil Company. Nancy was totally captivated by our performance at one particular concert and invited us to sing at the American Church in London. The purpose of that request was to gain support from her fellow Americans for her dream – to take our choir on a coast to coast tour of the USA. She was totally confident that she could achieve her goal and approached several potential major sponsors in America to provide the estimated cost of $200,000. If there was any doubt as to her sincerity and capabilities her previous experience in planning a successful similar tour with the boys' choir of St George's Chapel Windsor, was a convincing recommendation, details of which I was able to confirm.

The tour was scheduled for September/October 1992 commencing in Los Angeles, continuing to San Francisco, Ponca City Oklahoma (Nancy's birthplace), Dallas, Houston, Atlanta and Washington DC. We were to be accompanied by Richard Baker who would act as compère and the whole project was one of the most exciting prospects for the choir. Sadly a few weeks before our intended departure, cancer which had been diagnosed 9 years previously seriously affected Nancy's health, she returned to America and died in Houston, February 1997. The tour did not take place.

Massed Choirs

There were many occasions when the choir joined other choirs for massed festivals. In 1987 I was involved in the organisation of a festival at the Royal Albert Hall of massed police Male Voice Choirs. Ironically the performance actually co-incided with my sabbatical from the Metropolitan Police Choir whilst I undertook duties as the President of the Police Superintendents' Association of England and Wales. In fact I was invited to attend as a VIP together with other Staff Association representatives.

Although the concert was as enjoyable as we would have hoped, it was disappointing that there were many empty seats. The reason was that some seats in the Royal Albert Hall are reserved by patrons and are not available for use even if the patron does not use them. We were advised that if we wanted to have a full seating capability there had to be some other attraction over and above the choral content. It was decided to stage a second festival and I arranged with the Metropolitan Police Historical Society to borrow numerous uniforms of police officers since 1900. A commentary was given as each uniform was paraded and a retiring collection was taken for police charities.

Not only did I have the responsibility of returning all the historical uniforms but the collection of coins was taken back to my office where I spent several hours counting, bagging and banking the money.

In 1992 the choir joined many other choirs in an imaginative project to have 10,000 male voices in concert at Cardiff Arms Park. The list of songs to be sung was circulated and fortunately several were already well known to us, requiring minimal preparation. Other items were completely new and some were expected to be sung in the Welsh language. Individual choirs were expected to practice followed by group practices before the final concert in Cardiff Arms Park. On the day, there was not the 10,000 voices which had been the intention but a very creditable 7,000 with Tom Jones as the guest artiste. The response for the event had proved encouraging however and the following year a similar event was arranged and on that occasion with Shirley Bassey as the guest artiste there were 10.000 voices.

The composite massed choirs had by this time taken the name 'The World Choir' and the next project was for the massed choirs to travel to Atlanta, Georgia and perhaps intoxicated by the previous successes, many choirs, including our own made an initial response and paid substantial deposits. However in the subsequent weeks we became uneasy with developments and withdrew, demanding that the money we had paid should be returned. Other choirs also had doubts and withdrew and although the visit went ahead there were less than 900 choir members and the concert was not the success which had been planned.

It seemed that the concerns which led many choirs to withdraw were well founded and the organisers of the World Choir were arrested for fraud and many choirs who had cancelled their involvement, lost the money which they had paid. Although that was the end of the World Choir, there was another massed choir concert referred to as '2,000 in 2000' with the intention to welcome the new millennium with a concert in Manchester of 2,000 voices. That concert was a success

Requiem Mass, Funerals and Memorial Services

Another regular feature of the choir's activities was to participate in the annual Requiem Mass for Deceased Police Officers at Westminster Cathedral. When I first joined the choir these services were very well attended with representatives travelling from several surrounding Police Forces but sadly as the years passed the numbers reduced and congregations declined to a few hundred but always the choir acquitted themselves with dignity even though few of their number were Roman Catholics.

On more occasions than I can remember the choir have been invited to sing at the funerals of officers who died whilst in service or recently deceased police officers and I cannot recall any funeral of a murdered police officer where we did not sing. Added to the many occasions when I was called upon to attend funerals representing the Superintendents' Association I felt both humble and proud to pay my respects to the deceased even though they were personally unknown to me.. There were too many funerals at which the choir participated to record them all but some of the more noteworthy include:

In December 1983 at the Chelsea Parish Church of St Luke, the choir sang at the funeral service of three officers, Police Constable Jane Philippa Arbuthnot, Inspector Stephen John Dodd and Police Sergeant Noel Joseph Lane, who had been killed in an IRA bomb explosion at Harrod's Store in Knightsbridge.

At Salisbury Cathedral in 1984 the choir sang at the funeral of Police Constable Yvonne Fletcher who was shot outside the Libyan People's Bureau and whose murder would have political repercussions for more than a quarter of a century afterwards.

In January 1992 the funeral of Police Sergeant Alan King was held in his local church in Enfield. Alan had been on patrol, alone at midnight in Walthamstow when he stopped to question two persons who gave him cause for suspicion. He was stabbed and died from his injuries. His death was particularly significant for me because when I had served at City Road police station, as was my practice, I had walked the beat with the constables, one of whom had been Alan. In every way he personified what a beat officer should be – well known and respected by the local population, conscientious and a rôle model for his colleagues. On the tenth anniversary of his death, the choir were invited to participate in the memorial service and I considered it to be a privilege when asked to give a eulogy to Alan.

Nostalgia for the choir's activities could not fail to recall a young lady who sang as a soloist with the choir on many occasions. Wendy Bishop was married to Stephen, a police officer but her professional name was Miette Williams. She was a wonderful soprano with a pleasant personality. Sadly she contracted a mysterious illness which paralysed her and for many months she was confined to a hospital bed. Gradually her condition improved and she was able to use a wheelchair, then arm crutches and finally walking sticks. However at the age of 28 she died and her talents were never completely realised. It was an emotional moment for me to read a portion of scripture at her funeral service.

Stephen resigned from the police and with Wendy's mother and father moved away from London. Eventually he entered the Ministry and in 2009 he re-married and I had the privilege of walking his bride down the aisle.

There were other occasions when the choir was invited to participate which had no specific police service element for the deceased. One such occasion followed the tragedy of the Kings Cross Fire in which 31 people died in the underground station. The fire broke out in the early evening on 18th November 1987 and resulted in the deaths of 31 persons. At a Memorial Service a few months later it was the Metropolitan Police Male Voice Choir who were privileged to be invited to participate in the tributes to the victims.

In 2009 at a moving Memorial Service in Grosvenor Square outside the American Embassy the choir joined a solemn gathering to commemorate the terrorist attack in the USA which forever will be known as 9/11. As with all their appearances on such occasions, their singing added to the dignity of the occasion.

Flashmob – The Opera

There were other occasions when the choir were requested to participate in unconventional appearances and surely the best example was 'Flashmob – the opera'. In an age of increasing technology and sophisticated mobile phones, a phenomenon developed of 'Flashmob' activities. The principle was that persons prepared to participate would receive a message on their mobile phones giving a time, date and location. At the appointed time large numbers of persons would arrive, do nothing in particular then gradually disappear. The practice was much in the style of children who would stand on the pavement pointing to the sky and when sufficient numbers of innocent but curious passers by all stood looking to see what had attracted the attention of the children the practical jokers would scamper away. All harmless fun.

Flashmob the opera was a little more complicated. The idea was to create a live performance of a modern day opera on Paddington Railway station and the police choir was invited to participate. The story line was that a young couple were engaged to be married but the prospective groom was an ardent football fan. On the fateful night, the young woman had planned a romantic evening for her fiancé but unfortunately he forgot because he went to see his team play. On the way to the match he and other supporters were confronted by a group of the other team's fans and a riot situation was imminent until the arrival of a contingent of police officers – the Metropolitan Police Male Voice Choir who sang suitable words for the occasion to the music of the aria from the Anvil Chorus.

By this time the disappointed lady had decided to break off the engagement and return to her mother who lived in Swindon, which required her to take a train from Paddington. The storyline unfolded on Paddington station much to the amusement and perhaps bewilderment of the commuters many of whom were on their way home. Huge TV screens were in place to record the young man arriving at the empty flat he had shared with his lady love, finding the discarded engagement ring together a note telling him it was all over and she was going back to mother. We then saw on the TV screen his frantic dash on the tube to get to Paddington whilst he was singing another well known aria again with suitable words for the tragedy which was unfolding.

When he arrived at Paddington, intending rail passengers had obviously decided to stay and watch instead of catching their trains and the audience could be numbered in thousands. The couple were re-united just before she boarded the Swindon train as the station concourse resounded to the magnificent music of Nessun Dorma. As the couple embraced there was a spontaneous outburst of clapping and cheering and presumably they lived happily ever after. The principal singers were all professional opera singers and the careful planning and rehearsing (not involving the public) resulted in a fantastic experience which could simply be described as great fun.

For me personally there were additional difficulties to overcome. Ann and I were with a group of our friends on holiday in Falmouth, Cornwall and the choir were expected to be on the station at 2.15pm I had to leave my hotel very early to catch a shuttle service train to Truro where I caught the Cornish Express arriving in Paddington at 2.10pm The live performance of the opera took place at about 5.30pm and when it had finished I then caught the sleeper express back to Cornwall. It was all very well worthwhile.

A less dramatic but equally exciting appearance for the choir was The First Night of the Proms. The season of the Proms, ending with the well known Last Night of the Proms is always popular for music lovers some of whom may not be aware that there is also a first night of the Proms. The event took place in Trafalgar Square an hour or so before the performance at the Royal Albert Hall and the choir were invited to contribute to the performance.

Heathcote Education Trust

Even with careful planning there is always the possibility that an unknown factor may affect the successful outcome of an event and so it was with a concert to be given by the choir in Chingford. I had become friendly with Lloyd Davies, the head teacher of Heathcote school which co-incidentally had been the first school attended by Lloyd and Denise when we moved to London. His school boasted a children's choir and he put forward a suggestion as to whether it was possible for them to appear in a concert with the Police choir. The concert would be held in his school hall which had ample seating capacity and the Parents' Teachers Association would be anxious to assist in the preparation.

The Police choir members were agreeable to the proposal and it was arranged that our choir would start the performance and the school choir would make their contribution immediately before the interval and again immediately after the interval with the Police choir completing the evening's concert.

Everything went well with the sale of tickets and it was obvious that there would be strong support from the parents and friends in addition to our usual choir supporters. One week before the concert Lloyd received a call asking if there were any tickets for sale and when he said there were the caller identified himself as the borough Licensing Officer and that the school hall was not licenced for public performances. With only a few days before the concert the possibility of finding another venue was unlikely but by chance I learned that the local Assembly Hall had received a cancellation for the evening of our concert and the problem was solved. We arranged for large notices to be displayed at the school and re-arranged our plans.

The normal practice for the Police choir was that some members would make their own way to the concert venue whilst others would travel on a police coach from New Scotland Yard and an appropriate booking was made with transport department. Unfortunately the message was misconstrued and instead of the coach arriving at New Scotland Yard to take the choir to Chingford, it arrived at Chingford expecting to take the choir to New Scotland Yard.

Frantic telephone calls were made to reverse the mistake and we quickly altered the programme for the children's choir to make their contribution to the concert for the whole of the first part and the missing choir members arrived in time to commence the second part. Overall we considered the evening to be a success.

The friendship with Lloyd Davies was the basis of an ambitious project which I agreed to support under the title of Heathcote Education Trust. The object was threefold; to develop a Centre of Excellence for training teachers of deaf children; to develop sports facilities for students to be coached by professionals and to develop facilities for specialist music tuition. I was one of the trustees and appointed chairman of the Trust with Lord Tebbitt of Chingford our President. The launch of the Trust was on 23rd May 1996 by local Member of Parliament, Iain Duncan Smith Esq. with many persons present including school governors and other local dignitaries.

Not all of the objectives were achieved although a music recording studio was established in the school leading to a comment by Lord Tebbitt that although he didn't have a clue how to use the state-of- the-art studio, it looked amazing. Similarly facilities were provided for teaching profoundly deaf children to become skilled in IT procedures. The intention to build a gymnasium specifically to coach promising gymnasts was abandoned when the local council announced a huge rebuilding project for the school which effectively undermined our proposals.

The music recording studio which had been provided together with the specialised training for deaf children were lost in the massive development programme commissioned by the Borough but I was able to leave one lasting memento of my involvement with the school.

Ann and I presented a beautiful cut glass bowl suitably inscribed as "The Stowe Trophy" to be awarded annually for outstanding achievement.

Chairman of the Choir

In 1981 on promotion to Chief Superintendent the Chairman of he choir, Deputy Assistant Commissioner John Radley suggested that I should take on the chairman's role but I declined because I considered it would be more appropriate to continue as Vice Chairman. However, he did present me with several packing cases containing choir documents which he had considered consigning to the refuse collections. It was several months before I decided to sort through them and found so much of interest it would have been tantamount to sacrilege to have thrown them away.

Being in full time employment at Middle Temple Arbitration Rooms, it took several years for me to read through the documents, research aspects of the information and collate the information which finally resulted in a book of the history and development of the choir from 1945 when they were the Metropolitan Police Choral Society which I entitled 'London Medley'.

One feature of my research for the book revealed that in 1872 a group of police officers styling themselves "The Metropolitan Police Minstrels" had been formed and appeared with their faces blackened, performing many concerts and raising huge sums of money for police charities. I recorded the details in the book accompanied by a photograph of the group and when Ian Blair (later Sir Ian and then Lord Blair) was appointed Deputy Commissioner I sent one of the books to him inviting him to become our chairman. I received a message from his staff officer to the effect that the photograph was not acceptable and the book must be reprinted without it. I ignored the order on the premise that it was part of the history of the Metropolitan Police. When Sir Ian Blair became Commissioner his deputy was Bernard Hogan-Howe who also directed that the book was not accepted whilst it included the photograph and it must be re-printed. Again I ignored the directive and when Bernard Hogan-Howe left the Metropolitan Police to become Chief Constable of Merseyside I breathed a sigh of relief. How was I to know that he would subsequently return as Commissioner?

Unfortunately the disc on which the content of the book was recorded was lost when my employment with the Middle Temple ceased and the premises used for Arbitrations was cleared of its contents

Chapter 16. The International Police Association

One of my choir colleagues was Inspector Chris Barker who bore such a striking resemblance to the actor John Cleese famed for his characterisation of Basil in the comedy series Faulty Towers, that Chris was affectionately known as Basil. His ability to mimic his namesake was uncanny. Chris was a long time member of the International Police Association and for many years was the membership secretary of the New Scotland Yard Branch. In 1980 he persuaded me to join and in doing so opened another door of social involvement resulting in many new friendships.

The nature of IPA membership encourages foreign travel and Ann and I enjoyed visits to Germany, Austria, Switzerland, Ireland, Wales and Prague always in the company of a coach full of genuine friends. The chairman of the Branch was David Forder whose employment was driver and personal close protection officer for the Commissioner. As a result of his unique position at New Scotland Yard he was able to make personal contact with police officers literally all over the world. It seemed that whenever we undertook a foreign trip, David could find someone who knew him. Thus we were always treated as VIPs and the local IPA members would always ensure that we had favoured treatment.

The nature of IPA friendship is that on the visits which we made, the local IPA representatives would receive us and ensure that so far as possible, we would enjoy their social facilities and visits would be arranged for us not available to the usual tourist groups.

On a trip to Goslar in the Black Mountains of Germany the Head of the local Border Police escorted us to the border with East Germany and when asked if he thought there would ever be a reunification of Germany, his answer was an unequivocal "Never." His prophecy proved to be inaccurate however and a few weeks later, world news was dominated with scenes of demolition of the Berlin Wall and collapse of the Communist Regime.

Germany has a long tradition of Christmas Markets which are popular tourists' attractions. In 2001 our tour organiser arranged for such a visit and we welcomed the opportunity to join our friends. At 6.15am our coach collected passengers at Imber Court Police Club but we joined the group at the Warren Police Sports Club and then a new experience for us, travel by Eurotrain to Calais.

After an overnight stay in Leige, we travelled to Aachen to be greeted by the local branch of the IPA who arranged lunch and a tour of the town. We then continued our journey to Gimborn Castle 30 miles east of Cologne which for 50 years has been used by the IPA as a conference centre. The accommodation was basic but adequate and our meals were taken in an adjacent annex. The bar was well stocked but operated on an honesty basis with guests expected to serve themselves and leave the appropriate payment.

During the night when everyone was asleep, the fire alarm was activated and following the written instructions in the rooms, we all evacuated the castle in our night attire, standing in a light covering of snow. No official appeared to advise us what to do and it was 30 minutes before we realised that the resident caretaker was still in his room at the top of the castle and was not in the least perturbed, even expressing annoyance that we had wakened him. There was no fire; it was a false alarm.

The following day we visited Cologne Christmas Market returning to the castle for our evening meal where we entertained the Director of Gimborn and his wife. The highlight of the next day's activities was a guided tour of the Museum of History of the Federal Republic of Germany in Bonn.

One trip which probably had more unexpected elements than others was when we visited Prague. We were to travel by road and stop overnight in Liege. We did not appreciate before our arrival that the Bedford Hotel where we stayed was on the border of the local 'Red Light' district of the town. To stretch our legs before dinner, Ann and I, arm in arm, went for a short walk and when we had almost arrived back at the hotel we were both surprised when one of the local 'working girls' not only invited me into her boudoir but grabbed my arm to pull me inside. With Ann pulling me one way and the rather unattractive other woman pulling the other way it must have looked to any casual observer that something was seriously amiss.

It almost goes without saying that Ann won the contest but what we didn't know was that the tussle had been witnessed by some of the other members of our party and I was subjected to sustained teasing and ribald comments for two or three days.

On arrival in Prague we found that the prostitutes were a much better class and could be seen lounging in the foyer of our hotel but of course, all the men in our party were properly chaperoned by their wives and there were no embarrassing confrontations.

The first full day of our visit was when our schedule of visits started to go wrong. Our coach took us to the castle which is a principal attraction for tourists and the arrangements were that our coach would return after a suitable time to collect us and return to the hotel. At the appointed time, in our little group we waited for the coach and as time passed we became increasingly anxious. Eventually, the coach driver arrived in a taxi! He explained that a defect had occurred in the coach which would require urgent attention.

Fortunately our local IPA member and our guide, Marketa was married to a local coach operator who would arrange for our immediate needs. Marketa directed that we all wait in a nearby café and she would arrange for a fleet of taxis to collect us. She gave strict instructions as to what fare we were to pay to avoid us being overcharged. Our coach driver in the meantime had contacted his employers in Milton Keynes who agreed to send out a replacement coach whilst our original one would be repaired. Marketa was able to use her influence to arrange for the repairs to be carried out expeditiously.

That evening we were due to visit the police social club and agreed that we would all go by the local metro transport which we did. Having left the train we sauntered down the road, a group of about 30 persons and as we passed a bank night safe, David Forder felt a tug on his shoulder bag in which he carried his cine camera and shouted out in alarm. Suddenly one of two men by the night safe, pulled a gun and pointed it at David's head. We were all bewildered but our local police officers who were walking with us did not seem to be particularly perturbed and when we later questioned their lack of response, they explained that the two men thought they were being robbed and had taken defensive action.

The rest of the evening passed without incident but the following day, David's wife Sheila found that her purse and credit cards had been stolen. Although they were never recovered there was evidence in the next few days of the cards having been unlawfully used.

On the last day of our visit we left in the replacement coach whilst the original one had the necessary repairs completed. We were held up at the German border for 2 hours whilst the bureaucratic processes were completed and eventually reached Nuremberg where we were to stay overnight and where our repaired coach eventually caught up with us. The following morning we returned home passing through Lille and Dunkerque.

One aspect of the Czech Republic which we found interesting, amusing in fact, was the large number of garden gnomes which were to be seen alongside the road, on lay-bys, car parks and anywhere where a space was available.

On the IPA trips I had gained somewhat of a reputation for humorous verse which led me to compose the following:

> Come and see the Czech Republic, come and see our home sweet home
> Come and see our lovely glassware, come and see our garden gnomes
> Gnomes are guarding all approach roads, gnomes surrounding every stall
> Waiting like a mighty army marching forth to conquer all
> Gnomes stand watch at every corner; gnomes hide in the shops and loos
> Gnomes disguise themselves as lamp posts watching all you think or do.
> Did you sense someone was watching as you showered all alone?
> Did you check behind the mirror? You were spied on by a gnome.
> So farewell to Czech Republic and the kindness they have shown.
> Cross the border into Deutschland, where they welcome home sweet gnome.

When David Forder retired and moved from London the emphasis on foreign travel diminished and the final trip in which we were included was to Switzerland. On that occasion we flew by Easyjet whereas all other trips had involved lengthy coach journeys.

In addition to the visits to other countries, membership of the IPA provided the opportunity to participate in social events which included formal dinners, usually at New Scotland Yard. Many are the happy memories we have of our excursions with our friends. and the international contacts are still accessible to us if we wish to avail ourselves of the facilities.

Chapter 17. Holidays in Germany - Norbert Wolf

The visits to Germany with the choir and IPA had developed a fondness for the country and the people of Germany and Ann and I decided that we would take holidays ourselves without the restrictions or itineraries prepared for us by others.

On 15th May 1984 we travelled by Ferry to Hamburg following an invitation from Norbert Wolf to spend a holiday with him in his home. His house was typical of German houses, having a large basement area which he had converted into a self contained flat intended for rental and having received his assurance that we would be completely independent and would not interfere with his own household requirements, we had accepted.

Unfortunately he did not inform me that there had been problems with the local planning Regulations and the basement could not be used as he had intended. Consequently he and his wife vacated their bedroom to accommodate us for the duration of our visit. Whilst Ann and I were embarrassed that our visit had obviously caused inconvenience, we were very appreciative of their generosity.

Norbert was anxious to show off his friend from the London Metropolitan Police and I had agreed to take my uniform with me. I attended a formal luncheon with him on board a moored sailing vessel the "Passatt" where the main course was a local favourite – Labskaus. I realised there was a large sausage content but I could not identify the remainder of the stew like meal. I was interviewed by the Press who described me as an Officer of the Crown in the largest Police Force in the land, a somewhat grandiose title. I thought. The Press photograph of me sampling the meal with headlines in the local newspaper proclaimed "I like Labskaus very much."

Following the lunch there was a presentation ceremony for sailors who were honoured by the DLRG - the equivalent of our inshore rescue boats. The individuals were called forward individually and presented with a cap and I did not understand the full significance until my name was called, was handed a cap and informed that I was now an Honorary Captain of the DLRG. The cap sits with my other mementos in my study.

I was able to make a visit to the Rotary Club of Lübeck-Holstentor during my visit with my attendance appropriately recorded. Although I felt somewhat isolated among the other Rotarians, I was befriended by one of them who suggested that if I visited Germany on a future occasion I should visit his own club at Eutin, a few kilometres north of Hamburg.

25th May was Norbert's birthday and it was celebrated in grand style with many of his friends coming to his home and it seems that Ann and I attracted more attention than the birthday host. During the evening we realised that Norbert was missing and after a search found him fast asleep in his bedroom; hardly to be expected from the host.

We had made our travel arrangements with our friend Ille Ludlow, the proprietor of Travelcraft and our intentions were to make our homeward journey from the Belgian port of Zeebrugge. During the afternoon of the day before our intended departure I was listening to an English news broadcast on the car radio when I heard that the ferry

Company Townsend Thoresen were intending to strike at midnight. That immediately caused problems for me because that was the ferry Company which we had intended to use.

Because I was a member of the RAC I telephoned their local office in Frankfurt and the advice given to me was to contact the Automobile Association, hardly the response I had expected and not at all helpful. I then telephoned my friend Ille who confirmed that the ferry Company were intending to strike and the last ferry would leave Zeebrugge at 23.00 hours.

It was about 17.00 hours when I received that information and to drive over 300Km was out of the question. We decided that our only course of action was to drive to Hamburg the following morning and hope that we could be accommodated on one of their ferries.

We spent the evening with Renate one of Norbert's charming lady friends as the final social event of our holiday.

The following morning we set out for the ferry terminal, not entirely sure of our route but a very observant local car driver deserved a special commendation. He must have noticed my car displaying GB plates and my passenger, Ann, studying a road map when I pulled to the side of the road. I think he used his initiative and decided that a British car driver studying a road map in Hamburg was probably heading for the ferry terminal. He pulled alongside me, sounded his car horn and waved me forward. No words passed between us but he led us to the ferry, waved his goodbye and disappeared. We never saw him again.

As we queued to board some passengers leaving the vessel advised us that there was a strike at the port of Harwich where we expected to disembark but the warning proved groundless.

Sadly in the extra day taken for the altered travel arrangements, my mother died before we were back in England

Touring Germany

With increasing confidence in my linguistic prowess and driving competence on the continent, we decided to be more ambitious in our holidays abroad looking to the possibility of visiting several of our German friends in Hamburg, Bamberg and Coburg.

On 13th May 1990 we travelled by ferry to Hamburg, watching a film in the ferry's cinema during the journey. The film was "Shirley Valentine" but our enjoyment was marred a little in that a group of young women who had obviously seen it previously constantly commented to each other details of the story before we could watch it ourselves. However we saw the film on several occasions afterwards and always found it to be excellent entertainment.

We approached the port on the captain's bridge and could see riot police assembled dealing with a demonstration by anarchists. However, out friend Karoline was also there and after leaving the ferry she accompanied us to the hotel Kronprins where we had booked accommodation. Karoline treated us to afternoon tea at a local restaurant and then home where her mother Helga was waiting for us.

Ann and I felt quite comfortable making our way back to the hotel by tube experiencing no difficulties with the language or transport. Everyone with whom we came into contact seemed to go out of their way to help where necessary.

The following morning we visited the Rathaus, took a trip on a pleasure boat on the Alstersee and in the late afternoon, we were collected by the Polizeipresident's driver and taken to meet the man himself, Herr Dirk Reimers. In the evening, again we were guests at Helga's home with other friends whom we had met on a previous occasion and then visited the Plantembluhm Gardens to see the dancing waters.

Our next visit was to my friend from the Lübeck Police Choir, Gernot Seegar who lived in Hutsfeld several kilometres north of Hamburg. We stayed with Gernot and Erika, his wife for three days during which time I was able to visit Gernot's Rotary Club at Eutin. In my limited German I was able to announce greetings from my own Club President and felt reasonably pleased with my effort. A Japanese Rotarian then stood and in flawless German made a little speech most of which I could not understand but shortly afterwards a waiter entered with a tray of champagne glasses, giving one to everyone present. I assumed it was someone's birthday until the Japanese Rotarian said "And now we drink a toast to our friend from London." – me. I felt very honoured and humbled.

We were able to host Gernot and Erika in our home at a later date when they visited London on their way to join his fellow Rotarians whose club was linked with the Rotary Club of Redhill.

Our plans were then to visit Bamberg, some 500 Km south but we managed without any problems enjoying an impromptu rehearsal from a brass band who had broken down on their journey. About 20Km from our destination we had to make a phone call to our intended host, Ruth Schneider to give us directions to her home.

We stayed the whole of the following week with Ruth and her family, husband Herbie, and daughters Sonja and Sandra accompanied by their dachshund Hannibal. We were aware of some strained atmosphere in the house and assumed it was the fact of having strangers in the house but it was not until much later that we learned Herbie had left Ruth for another woman but to keep up appearances, returned to the house every morning to give us the appearance of normality in the household.

Another friend I was anxious to visit was the officer from the Border Police who had arranged the tour of Bavaria for the choir, Reinhard Kilian. Arriving in his home town of Coburg at a time when the communist regime had collapsed and East and West Germany were in the process of reunification.

Reinhard took us on a visit to what had been the border but instead of the fortifications we had witnessed previously, there was only a wide open gate in the fence. Reinhard, in his smart uniform driving his impressive BMW police car, drove through the gate to meet his counterpart on the other side. The comparison was still very obvious when meeting the East German policeman in his drab faded brown uniform with a Traban car and a police building which was no more than a small wooden shed. However, he greeted us warmly and I found later that he and Reinhard had been friends for a long time.

On 29th May we returned to Hamburg and arrived in Harwich the following day after one of our most enjoyable holidays up until that time.

The Bamberg Wedding

On a late evening in August 1998 Ann and I returned home to find a message on the telephone answering machine asking us to call our friend Ruth in Bamberg.. We did so and found that we were invited to the wedding of Ruth's eldest daughter, Sonja. due to take place a few days later. We explained that it would not be possible because I would not be able to take time off from my employment. A few days later we received another call insisting that we were invited and again we expressed concern but not to be thwarted, Ruth went to her local travel agent and arranged for our flight.

At 5.00am on 10th September we left in Ann's car for Stansted airport for our flight at 8.40am. We were due to fly on a 46 seat turbo-prop aircraft but due to strong winds over the channel, it was not allowed to take off until 11.40am which necessitated telephone calls to Ruth in Bamberg to explain our delay

Wearing a white carnation for identification, Sonja and her soon to be husband quickly located us at Nuremberg airport and we were amazed that the young school girl we had seen on our previous visit was now a very attractive young woman.

We spent the afternoon on the day of our arrival helping to buy last minute necessities including a large umbrella due to the continual rain but mainly as a safeguard for the wedding day. The only one Ruth could find was 30 marks but typical of Ann's reputation, for finding bargains, she found one at a mere price of 9 marks. The following day we engaged in more shopping but we were worried because we knew that Ruth and her partner Herman had many demands on their time at home, not least being to lay a new carpet.

The following day, Saturday, we had arranged to visit the family Dirauf in Hallstadt and we were delighted when Paul and his son Hilmar arrived to take us to their home where Paul's wife Theresa was waiting with their excitable little dachshund Choker. We were later joined by the younger son Marius who also had grown from a little boy to a mature young man. I have always had a deep affection for this family ever since our first visit nearly 20 years previously.

One of Paul's hobbies is making sausages and we enjoyed a meal of weiß wursts (white sausages) which Bavarian tradition insists must be eaten before the mid-day bells are heard. We were then taken to a concert in the cathedral in Bamberg but before doing so, we were given a small chocolate bird something like a wren. We were told it was the cathedral bird and local folk lore suggests that if anyone catches one it will have a good luck message. This one apparently had foretold our visit to the Dirauf family.

A late afternoon meal consisted of a variety of more sausages everyone of which we had to sample and did so to the delight of our hosts although Ann and I knew there was an evening meal planned when we returned to Ruth's home.

On the day of the wedding we realised that local procedures were far removed from what we would expect for an English wedding. Sonja was dressed in her bridal finery together with her three little attendants, 2 girls and a boy and at mid-day she was joined by her groom who arrived in a white Mercedes car adorned with a large floral arrangement on the bonnet and ribbons on the door handles.

We drove in a procession of many cars to the church continually sounding their horns until we arrived and joined the crowd of well wishers assembled outside. I didn't realise why but the bride's mother handed me a bag of coins but after the ceremony, the groom took the bag and threw all the coins on the church pathway for the children to scrabble and pick them up.

The reception was at a nearby schloss with a long table filled with typical German gateaux and other cakes, presumably to make sure we did not go hungry before the main meal. The bride and groom wandered away from their guests for photographs but there was no formal photo shoot arrangements as would have happened in an English wedding. It was shortly afterwards that we received information that the bride had been abducted but it was all part of their traditions. The longer it took for the groom to find his bride, presumably in a local hostelry, the higher the cost of the beers consumed by the abductors for which the groom would have to pay.

When the bride was safely restored to her guests, she was subjected to a "This is your Life" style presentation and gifts were announced. The gifts took the form of promises by the donor to carry out some function for the couple. "We will clean your house windows every week for one year" was one particular one I remember but it was all symbolic of the love and affection for the couple.

5.15am the following day Hilmar arrived to take us to the airport for our flight back to Stansted. I left Ann to struggle with our luggage back to her car whilst I boarded the Stansted Express train to Liverpool Street, then to the tube and arrived in my office at about 10.00am. We had crowded a lot of sightseeing and other activities into the weekend and I was only an hour or so later than my normal time to start work.

Die Einladung

In March 2004 I received a surprising item of postage. It was die Einladung, an invitation from my friend Paul Dirauf in Hallstadt (Bamberg) asking me to join him for his 60th birthday party which would take place on 15th May which would also be an occasion to mark his retirement from the police. Whilst I felt very honoured I did not consider that it would be practical for me to accept but Ann was insistent that I should do so. Her persuasiveness overcame my own reservations and I contacted Paul's son Hilmar with whom I corresponded regularly.

In the following days Hilmar and I agreed on the preparation for my visit and although I did not know at the time, he informed his mother, Theresa that I had accepted but did not tell Paul..

Consequently, flying by Air Berlin on 13th May I travelled to Nürmberg airport where Hilmar met me and drove to his home. It was very late in the evening but time for supper with his wife Melanie who was heavily pregnant with her first child. A little after midnight Hilmar explained that we should retire to bed because we were due to go to his parents' home the following day for breakfast. The following morning, Hilmar drove to his parents home, Melanie in the passenger seat and me in the rear seat. The plan was that we would all walk down the garden path and surprise Paul. Our plan did not evolve as intended because as we drew up outside the house, Paul appeared at the door with the little dachshund.

Hilmar jumped out to greet his father and prevent him walking towards the car where Melanie was hiding in the passenger seat well whilst I lay down flat in the rear seat. When they entered the house, Hilmar made some explanation that Melanie would follow shortly and when the door closed Melanie and I then went and rang the doorbell.

The surprise which had been planned for Paul then erupted in a show of affection as we embraced and we both shed a few tears of emotion. What I didn't know was that Paul had been annoyed with me that apparently I had not responded to his invitation and when he saw the breakfast table set for 6 persons, (Paul, Theresa, Hilmar, Melanie and his other son Marius) he had questioned who the sixth place was for. The family had explained that the girl friend of Marius may join them but Paul insisted that the sixth place should be removed. The secret which his family had kept from him added to the pleasure of the breakfast and the remainder of the day.

His birthday celebration continued throughout the day as friends and well wishers called bringing presents and sharing his wine until the late afternoon.

The family are devout Catholics and later that day they invited me to accompany them to the church where details of a Mass for his birthday were confirmed with the priest.

The following day, Saturday was taken up with preparations for the great party which would be preceded by Mass in the church. I was able to follow the Service and when Hilmar read a portion of scripture I was pleased to tell him afterwards that I had memorised that particular reading many years ago and had no difficulty in following it as he read.

After the Mass we adjourned to the adjacent church hall and as we entered, we were welcomed by a group dressed in traditional huntsmen's uniform playing hunting horns. This was to acknowledge Paul's keen interest in hunting. The Big Band of which Hilmar and Marius were members played as Paul greeted his guests and when we sat down for our meal, the Male Voice Choir sang. At one point the Musical Director announced that the next item was in honour of their guest from Scotland Yard. I felt enormously privileged to have been honoured in such a way.

When the party finished and we were to return home, Paul had received so many presents that four cars were required to transport them to his house.

Before I took my departure the following day, Paul showed me his extensive collection of rifles which he used for hunting and I left with so many bottles of his local wine, it was difficult to carry them all.

During the weekend there had been time to meet my friend Ruth and she took me to a church which apparently had many attractive features. Unfortunately we were not able to enter because a wedding was taking place. The doorway was covered with a large sheet with the outline of a heart; leading up to the door was a double line of young men and women all holding long stemmed roses. Suddenly the outline of the heart was burst open to reveal the bridegroom carrying his bride down the steps. Ahead of them was a large log on a trestle which they then proceeded to saw in half. The symbolic action was that they would face difficulties together and prove that with joint effort they would succeed.

Shortly afterwards, Melanie had her baby, a boy and subsequently two other children, also boys. Every year Hilmar sends us a calendar with photographs of the children on every page of the calendar months. It gives Ann and me much pleasure to send Christmas and birthday presents to the children who I like to think of as our surrogate grandchildren.

Chapter 18. Life as a Rotarian

Having joined the Rotary Club of Warminster I was quickly caught up with their activities but we never actually achieved any notable successes whilst I was with them. We were keen to establish a link with another Rotary Club and thought that Dundalk in the Irish Republic would be suitable. We did not realise that it was to become a hotbed of IRA activities and perhaps it was just as well that nothing came of it.

Another idea was to convene and organise a caravan rally at Longleat but again, our enthusiasm was not matched by experience and we would have been completely out of our depth if we had progressed beyond merely suggesting it.

We did however enjoy many social events with our Rotary colleagues one of which resulted from a suggestion by members of the club to organise a motor "Treasure Hunt" where participants drive round the area seeking clues as to where the next clue was to be found until eventually a winner would be identified. I was invited to enter into the discussions but my friends had not taken into account the legal restrictions and eventually the proposals were shelved. However the discussions were held at the home of one of our members, a solicitor where we enjoyed a lovely meal served on Royal Doulton china of country rose pattern. Ann and I were so impressed that we promised ourselves we would have similar china in our home. It took us many years buying a few pieces at a time until eventually we had a full set for eight places. On moving to Swindon I transferred to their Rotary Club which had a much larger membership than Warminster and again we enjoyed many social events with them

It was when we moved to Chingford that my Rotary activities developed and I became involved in many aspects of Rotary which were to broaden my horizons more than I could ever have experienced. Ann joined the ladies of the Inner Wheel and also became involved in their activities.

There was one little amusing consequence of my joining Chingford Rotary Club of which I was unaware until some considerable time afterwards. I had joined Chingford Club because it was local to where I lived and irrespective of where I worked, my membership of that club would be constant. It transpired that Ann was present at a function with other ladies from Inner Wheel Clubs and overheard a conversation that the new superintendent at Barkingside (me) had been expected to join the Rotary Club in that area and the nature of their comments suggested that my decision did not meet with their approval.

One of the regular activities undertaken by the Rotarians was collecting at Christmas whilst playing recorded Christmas music from static points. The money raised was used to purchase groceries for food parcels to be distributed to needy persons. The practice was well established but had two distinct disadvantages. The first was that using static points for 6 – 7 hours repeating the same music tended to generate complaints from shop keepers and residents in the close proximity and the second disadvantage was that we realised that the same persons to whom we donated our parcels were on the lists of other Organisations which meant they received several parcels when the people probably in greatest need were unknown to us.

We dealt with the first problem by constructing a sledge with loudspeakers on board powered by a car battery. which we pulled on a trolley To address the second problem we abandoned the parcel distribution and instead collected for nominated local charities.

The club members were allocated to various committees and within a year or so I was invited by the then President, Richard Miles, to take on the chairmanship of the community services committee. I felt highly honoured and undertook my responsibilities very seriously not only in the club but also at District level when I was invited to join the District Community Services Committee.

In 1979, scarcely 4 years since I joined the club I was elected to be President for one year which I regarded as a great honour. At that time there were about 90 Rotary Clubs in London, 5 of them in Waltham Forest and several other clubs near to Chingford in other boroughs. Social communication was a feature of all clubs and particularly for the Presidents with invitations to Presidents' Ladies' Festivals from other Rotary Clubs, the Round Table, Lions' Club, Inner Wheel Clubs and Chamber of Commerce.. The functions were always regarded as formal and evening dress was expected. Our own formal dinners were always the high point of our club activities.

In later years when most clubs experienced reduced memberships and costs of such events increased, the formal evenings were less commonplace and in some clubs ceased altogether. This being my first experience of Presidential duties, Ann and I kept an album of photographs, invitations and newspaper reports as a permanent memento of our year and at the end of the year I was presented with a pair of Rotary cuff links.

I remember very well the first formal dinner of my Rotary club which Ann and I attended. It was held at a functions room in Edmonton about 10 miles from home. It was after midnight as we left and approaching a cross roads where we would turn right, I saw a police car driving towards us from the opposite direction with his right indicator flashing. Not knowing if he intended to pass in front of me or behind, I stopped in the middle of the junction. The police car passed in front of me and I continued my turn. Seconds later the police car overtook me and pulled in front of me. The driver (police constable Y 799 – I will never forget his number) came to my driver's door and spoke to me in a most aggressive manner concerning my driving. I replied that I didn't know which way he had intended to go and that is why I stopped. He threatened to breathalise me which I urged him to do but he then said he couldn't waste time talking to me because he had a call to answer. I suggested he carry on and he left. I was a newly appointed superintendent in the Metropolitan Police but gave no indication to the constable and I thought perhaps his attitude was not typical of my fellow officers. Unfortunately experience in later years made me realise that I was mistaken

Every year in October the Rotary Clubs in London (District 113) held their conference in Eastbourne and the normal practice was for the Chingford contingent to take accommodation at one of the more expensive hotels, the Cavendish. The price range was really more than Ann and I could justify but for several years we accepted the collective decision until eventually we found a more suitable hotel, The New Wilmington which was less expensive and gave a better service. We patronised the New Wilmington for several years and for 3 years I served on the District Conference committee involved in the organisation of the conferences.

Although we always looked forward to the annual conferences, in 1987 we were unable to attend and perhaps that was fortunate for us because Britain suffered the worst storm of the century which caused considerable damage all over the country including Eastbourne.

In addition to formal social occasions, there were other events when clubs would be invited to participate in activities, usually for fund raising. One such invitation was extended to me as President of the Rotary Club to take part in a camel derby. The local Round Table had organised the event and borrowed from Chipperfields Circus were four camels for each race. I was asked to ride one of them and the Chairman of Round Table would ride another. With a little friendly rivalry, we wagered that we would pass the finishing line ahead of the other. By some miscalculation, when we reported for our race, there were 5 riders for 4 camels and he and I agreed to ride the same camel with me sitting in front of him. The race was like no other when we were given the "off". The camels took off with no control at all from their respective riders and were brought to a halt by their handlers grabbing their tails and digging their heels in. Of course, sitting in front of the Chairman, I crossed the finishing line ahead of him and won the wager.

When my Presidential year ended I handed the chain of office to John Williams, who with his wife Tricia were in our inner circle of friends and he was the principal contact in arranging what was to be a wonderful unexpected extension of our Rotary friendship – our visits to Sweden.

When I joined the Rotary Club of Chingford there was a membership of about 40 and the weekly meetings were held at a local restaurant at 1.00pm. Not only did we experience a steady decline in membership but working in central London I found it increasingly difficult to attend the meetings and at one point, reluctantly tendered my resignation. Other club members also experienced similar problems and it was decided to change to an evening meeting which allowed me to withdraw my resignations.. The change of time for meetings necessitated a change of venue and having used pubs and restaurants we eventually moved to the International Scouting Centre at Gilwell Park, on the outskirts of Chingford.

The move resulted in the resignation of some members and our numbers dropped to a worrying 15. I decided to do something about it and made strenuous efforts to recruit new members. There is no automatic entitlement to be accepted to membership of Rotary, depending rather on personal individual invitation. In subsequent years I invited 13 persons to become Rotarians and several years afterwards many of them were still serving in our club.

Although the office of President would normally be passed to a new President every year, with fewer members in some clubs, it was not usual for a Past President to be invited to take office on a subsequent occasion. It fell to my lot to be President of my club on no less than 6 occasions. One of those occasions was in the year 2000 and to celebrate the centenary we planted a copse of 100 trees in the grounds of Gilwell Park, our normal venue for club meetings. We also created a garden in the grounds of a local hospital utilising a space where buildings had been demolished leaving an area of rubble and weeds. The garden was used extensively by long term residents in the rehabilitation Unit of the hospital.

For some reason my fellow Rotarians considered that I was worthy of an honour peculiar to Rotary – a Paul Harris Fellowship given for outstanding Rotary service. On a subsequent occasion the Honour was upgraded to a Paul Harris with Sapphires. They also saw fit to nominate me for, and I was awarded a Commitment to Service certificate from the President of Rotary International and was one of only 5 given to clubs in the London District.

Although Ann and I regularly attended the District Conferences in Eastbourne, when the annual Rotary International Convention was held in Birmingham, we took the opportunity to join several thousand Rotarians from all over the world for a very memorable 3 day event. It was a wonderful experience but the selected venues for the annual Conventions were worldwide and it would have been impractical for us to consider attendance at future events.

One of the benefits of joining a Rotary club is that membership entitles the Rotarian to associated membership of every other Rotary Club in the world. Consequently I have visited many other clubs not only in London but throughout the United Kingdom, Sweden, Latvia, Germany, Irish Republic, Canada and Belgium.

Many Rotary clubs established regular contact with Rotary clubs in other countries referred to as 'Link Clubs'. Another local Rotary club near to Chingford is the Epping Club and they had arranged a visit to their link club in Sweden. They were hoping to benefit from concessions in the flight arrangements if they could guarantee a maximum number of persons on the aircraft. We were invited to join them and establish our own link club, the Rotary Club of Falsterbo-Vellinge.

Falsterbo/Vellinge Rotary Club – Sweden

Together with 11 other Chingford Rotarians and our wives on 30th April 1981 we commenced our holiday, travelling to Heathhrow airport where we were due to fly on an Airbus aircraft. Unfortunately due to industrial action by air traffic controllers in Copenhagen we were delayed 1 ½ hours which resulted in our being given lunch on board which we had not expected. After what seemed a very short flight we landed at Copenhagen airport and after passing through customs control we were greeted by one of our host Rotarians, Nils Harde. Travelling by coach and ferry to Malmo we were met by our individual hosts, Bo Hennby and his wife Kerstin (pronounced Shastin) with their delightful wire haired dachshund Stina. The standard of living in Sweden was obviously higher than in Britain and our hosts' home was a huge semi-bungalow, very spacious and having a swimming pool and sauna.

Falsterbo is a small town on the most southerly tip of Sweden with beautiful white, smooth beeches and a little way out in the sea was a life size statue of a nude female with her arms spread wide, looking out to sea. After touring the area we took lunch at the restaurant where the Rotary Club meet during the summer months after which we were taken to various places of interest. The evening was a formal dinner at the golf club with speeches by their President and our own President John Williams both of whom took turns to wear a Viking helmet complete with horns.

The ladies all received gifts of a pair of Skanör geese which were to remain with us as mementos of the visit for many years. There was a slight breach of protocol when the Swedish hosts proposed a toast to our Queen and (incorrectly) we responded by proposing a toast to the King of Sweden. It was after midnight when we left the golf club and returned to Bo's home where we talked until the small hours.

The following day Bo and Kirsten's son Toby took us to Malmo to view the shopping possibilities and later went to the home of other Rotarians, Stig Hjertström and his wife Gunborg who was dressed in national costume. We were very impressed by the typical Swedish welcome of small candles all along the wall on the entrance to their home. The high-light of the meal was our introduction to the 'Spit-coker' cake, a giant meringue creation about 18" high and of a lattice work pattern requiring 60 eggs to create. Apparently it is a traditional sweet in the Skanör district.

The following morning, Sunday, we were all taken in a coach for a tour of the coast area and one of our stops was at a little beach where we saw several people leaving a hut eating something from paper wrappers in much the same way as English folk may have eaten fish and chips. To satisfy our curiosity we went to the hut and realised the delicacies were herrings which some of us couldn't resist.

Shortly afterwards we arrived at SiMr.ishamii where we were to take lunch. On a large table there were plates of herring in every gastronomic preparation imaginable. We were urged to sample every variation and return for 'seconds' if we so wished. What we didn't realise was that it was not our lunch but merely a 'starter' and we were then expected to sit down to a proper meal. The hospitality of our hosts seemed to know no bounds and in the evening we went to another of the Rotarians' homes for a social evening but knowing that they would have to go to work the following day, we dispersed before midnight.

Our day of departure depended on Toby acting as chauffeur to the hydrofoil bound for Copenhagen then a 3 hour coach trip round the local area to give us a flavour of the nature of Denmark and ultimately to the airport. What we didn't realise at the time was that as we were boarding, 6 of our party were informed that the aircraft was full and they would have to make alternative arrangements. We had heard some sort of commotion as we sat in our seats and one of our party, Ille Ludlow, the owner of a travel firm in Chingford who had made all our arrangements went to investigate. Ille was a lovely lady but not someone to cross when discussing business. We never did learn what she told the official who had prevented our friends boarding but it was obviously unequivocal and direct because when we took off our party was complete.

Return Visit

Of course it was expected that our Swedish friends would want to taste our hospitality in Chingford and a return visit was arranged. We realised that we could not hope to match the level of their hosting but the whole of the Rotary Club were enthusiastic to make the visit memorable for our guests and ourselves.

The visit of the Swedish Rotarians co-incided with the 50th anniversary of our club's charter and we were determined to mark the occasion suitably. We arranged for a formal dinner at the Chanticleer restaurant which was within the building complex of Tottenham Football Club. Some of the club members expressed their reservations because the venue was situated in a notorious troublesome area but the restaurant proved to be excellent in every aspect. My friend Peter Bloor was invited to be President for the prestigious year and guests for the function included not only our Swedish guests but the Swedish Ambassador, the Worshipful the Mayor of Waltham Forest and as would be expected, Rotary dignitaries. I was required to propose a toast to the guests but when I rose to my feet I felt decidedly unwell and barely finished my speech before I was taken out into fresh air and for the first time in my life, drank brandy which restored my composure.

Another special feature of our club's celebration was to issue first day cover stamps to commemorate the occasion.

A dinner at our home with some of the Swedish visitors and some of our own Rotarians provided an amusing incident which we related many times afterwards as a party piece. The wife of one of our Rotarians was a very attractive woman who had won many beauty contests in earlier years. She was the proprietor of a florist's shop and her husband had a fresh fish business in the same premises. Our Swedish guests had brought with them the powerful Schnapps alcoholic drink. Our lady of the moment was not used to the effects and after several drinks was 'merry'. She related an incident where she and her husband had gone home for lunch and to exercise the dogs. Quite unabashed she explained that they had an uncontrollable urge to make love, went to the bedroom and satisfied their mutual needs and only then did she realise that her husband was still wearing his green wellies. We still smile whenever we relate the story.

A smaller group of the Chingford Rotarians returned to Falsterbo in April 1989, flying from Southend airport which was a very relaxed experience in comparison to the crowded hustle and bustle of Heathrow. A little way from the airport building, standing alone was a magnificent Vulcan bomber, truly a thoroughbred aircraft without equal.

I was President of the Rotary Club on this occasion and we were received by our hosts with the same degree of hospitality as previously and without saying anything to my fellow Rotarians I prepared a little surprise for the occasion of a formal dinner held at the golf club. At the time when their President made a speech of welcome to the guests – us, I rose to give my reply. To the amazement of my colleagues and to the undisguised delight of our hosts, I made my speech in Swedish. I had prepared what I wanted to say and my own host, Bo Henby had made a translation for me and carefully schooled me in pronunciation and presentation. My one and only attempt to speak in Swedish consisted only of a few sentences but was well received.

One aspect of our visit which was to remain in our memory for many years was a visit to a pig farm which on the face of it seems rather unattractive. However, this farm was rather unusual. The pigs were free-ranging and well fed but the manner of their slaughter was different to any other method of which we had knowledge. The pig farmer explained that if animals are stressed at the time of killing, the quality of their meat is adversely affected. When we went to the abattoir we were required to wear white overalls, white hats and white overshoes. The pigs entered the room two at a time with soothing music playing in the background and then as they passed side by side through a curtain, they were spontaneously electrocuted. The result was that at the time of death they were not stressed and the quality of their meat was enhanced.

Unfortunately on 1st May, Ann and I had to curtail our holiday ahead of our friends because on 2nd May the Police Male Voice Choir members were to receive members of the Bamberg Police Choir and we were committed to hosting arrangements in London.

The Swedish club made a second visit to London but the expense of hosting such a visit was more than we could reasonably sustain and the enthusiasm for continuing the link waned. Indeed the irresponsible arrangements of some events for the visitors seriously affected the club's financial stability resulting in strong criticism by members, some of whom resigned in protest.

However we did arrange some attractions for our visitors and a river trip on the Thames was arranged with a meal on board, the only problem being that our vessel did not have catering facilities. The solution was that the meal was prepared on another boat which drew alongside and the food transferred. To view the Thames Barrier was the ultimate intention of the river trip and our guests were suitably impressed.

On this occasion, the highlight of the visit of our Swedish visitors was a mediæval dinner at Hatfield House, a magnificent Manor House dating from 1480. The wearing of period costume was encouraged but not obligatory as the guests, seated at long wooden tables received their food and drink (mead) from serving wenches in typically low cut dresses. With music suitable for the historic past and Court Jesters adding to the atmosphere, there came a time when someone was selected from the assembled diners to assist in a light hearted presentation on the stage. Of all the persons present, who should be chosen but our own house guest, Bo Henby. It was a wonderful evening and a suitable conclusion for the visitors from Falsterbo.

The Group Study Exchange

The Rotary Foundation provides many educational projects including the Group Study Exchanges which allows teams of four young professional persons with a Rotarian leader to visit a foreign City where they are hosted for four weeks by Rotarians. The team members live with the host Rotarians and undertake visits to experience their own individual professional calling in a foreign land and talk to Rotary Clubs. On their return they make presentations to the 'home' Rotary clubs describing the benefits of their exchange visit.

For every exchange I canvassed for suitable candidates in the Metropolitan Police or Middle Temple and for eight or nine exchanges which occurred in alternate years, the Rotary Club of Chingford sponsored candidates on exchanges to Australia, Mexico, India, Canada, several cities in the USA China and Sweden.

Not only did Ann and I participate in the exchange procedure but I undertook some of the necessary organisation. The incoming team would spend one week in each of the four London Rotary Areas and as organiser I was responsible for arranging their accommodation and a schedule of visits for them. With 10 or 12 Clubs in the area and probably 200 – 300 Rotarians, it should have been relatively easy but in reality the bed and breakfast facilities usually devolved to 6 – 7 offers and suggestions for a programme of visits and work experience became the responsibility of 2 or 3 Rotarians.

For these visits, Ann and I hosted in our home, particularly if one of the visiting team members was a police officer. Some of the friendships initiated by the exchanges resulted in lasting friendships which is typical of Rotarian membership. The downside was that for Ann particularly there was an increase in her work load preparing meals, washing for the visitors and general housework. For myself , trying to make sure that the team members were always at the place at the time they were expected and pulling together all the strands of the arrangements all led us to the realisation that it was too tiring and we withdrew from the hosting and organising commitments.

For one intended exchange visit I decided to put myself forward to be the team leader. The exchange was to be with Nigeria and I spent many hours reading books on the political, cultural and economic details of that country. I thought that I would be able to acquit myself favourably on any interviewing panel.. I realised that there was considerable instability there but reasoned that living with fellow Rotarians, no harm would befall us. In the light of the deteriorating situation in subsequent years, perhaps it was just as well that the exchange was cancelled by the Nigerian authorities.

A Different View of Sweden and Latvia

One of the Group Study Exchanges had been with Sweden and Latvia and subsequently a suggestion was made that those of us who had been involved should take the opportunity to make a visit to those countries ourselves. Eight of us with our wives eventually made up a party for our visit.

The initial intention was that all 16 of our party would be hosted by Swedish Rotarians in their homes but various factors necessitated a change of plans. The revised arrangements were that we would travel to Stockholm, stay in a hotel for three nights, organise our own sight seeing, then travel to Riga in Latvia where we would stay for 4 days in a hotel arranged by a local Rotarian. Afterwards we would return to Sweden where 4 couples would be hosted by Rotarians and the other 4 would visit Gothenberg.

On 1st August 2001 we left Heathrow by SAS airlines after a minor security problem. I had decided to take 3 gifts of paper knives the handles of which were in the shape of Sherlock Holmes, a typical British figure. Carrying them in my hand luggage contravened the restriction on carrying knives which were removed from my luggage and consigned to the luggage hold for the duration of the flight to Arlanda airport. It seemed rather odd when collecting our luggage, the carousel brought the usual conglomeration of suitcases, holdalls, haversacks etc and one tiny plastic bag containing my knives.

In Stockholm we were unable to locate any local Rotarian Clubs but did experience visitor attractions including the Vasa, the flagship of the Swedish navy which sank on its inaugural sailing in 1628 but had been located in the harbour waters, raised and a museum was constructed round the ship preserving it virtually in its original condition. We decided to take a tour of the city on an open top trolley bus but became somewhat alarmed at the close proximity of the overhead power cables which seemed almost to brush against our heads when we stood up. However, logic dictated that our apprehensions were groundless.

On the return journey to our hotel, we were uncertain where we should alight but the 'bus driver could not have been more helpful, typifying the friendliness of the Swedish residents.

Flying by Baltic Airways we arrived in Riga on Saturday 4th August where we were greeted by Liene, a young lady who had been on the original Group Study Exchange and had subsequently joined the Rotary Club of Riga. She had arranged hotel accommodation and prepared a comprehensive programme for us including a concert of classical music in the Riga Dome Church.

The following day we were guests of Rotarians from Latvian clubs at a BBQ party held in one of Riga's principal restaurants and on Monday, were guests of the RIGA Hansa Rotary Club for lunch followed by a visit to the Aldaris Brewery for beer tasting. On the following day, yet another Rotary Club visit to Cēsis.

During the visit we were taken to a local orphanage and were so impressed by the work of those in charge with very primitive facilities that at a later date we provided funds for a Rotary Foundation Matching Grant which would provide valuable equipment for them.

We were impressed with a huge street market selling flowers, meat, fish and every conceivable item for purchase and with mild amusement, were interested to notice that young ladies on their way to evening entertainment carried their shoes rather than risk damaging them in the badly repaired roads and pavements. Altogether it was a wonderful few days with our hosts making every effort to ensure it was a visit to remember.

Following our visit to Riga we travelled to a town approximately 80Km south west of Stockholm, Norrköeping (pronounced Norshepping) a town which had been an important industrial centre at the turn of the century and was making determined efforts to be identified as a tourist attraction. Without the benefit of local Rotarians we would have been hard pressed to locate interesting local features. Ann and I were welcomed to the home of Bert and Karen-Margrette Eckman.

There was some degree of misunderstanding on the part of our own hosts who on many occasions had provided accommodation for young exchange students and didn't appreciate that we anticipated a little more comfort We found that our bedroom was in the basement of the house adjacent to the sauna and we slept in two-tier iron framed bunk beds. Other members of our party expressed their own views as to how they would have reacted but Ann and I merely accepted the situation without complaint.

On the first day of our visit we were guests of the Rotary Club of Norrkoeping-Kneippbaden for lunch and in the evening visited a local sculpture park for a concert of music and fireworks.

On the second day we visited a Glass factory, witnessed glass-blowing and bought souvenirs then in the evening participated in an activity which could have been dreamed up only by Rotarians. Our host family entertained all four couples and we were divided into two teams together with local Rotarians, given a menu (in Swedish) together with necessary ingredients and had to prepare the meal. My team was responsible for the main course — meat balls which are apparently a favourite with our hosts. The meal was a great success.

Arrangements had been made for us to visit another small town, Linkoeping (pronounced Linshepping) whose industries include the Nokia telecommunications and of particular interest to me, the Saab aircraft base with a fascinating museum. Our hosts for the day were Göran and Pagnhild Segner, owners of a delightful black Labrador dog. A visit to yet another Rotary Club, that of St Mars and then return to Norrkoeping for the final two days.

However before we left Linkoeping, we were with our hosts walking across a cobble stoned area when Ann tripped and fell breaking her spectacles. Bearing in mind it was late Saturday afternoon, the posssibility of having them repaired was very slim. However, Göran using his local knowledge and friendly persuasion found an optician who was able to restore them to their normal condition and what could have resulted in a distressing conclusion to our holiday was no more than a bad memory. The greater worry for me was that Ann was required to wear a neck support collar following earlier serious surgery and the fall could have had disastrous consequences but she suffered no more than some bruising and laddered tights.

On Sunday we travelled by a taxi boat to a small island for Sunday morning worship in a small chapel capable of seating about 80 but crammed with twice as many including a male voice choir. Our intended picnic lunch had to be taken in the sacristy due to the rain on that day.

Altogether, a very enjoyable and memorable visit to Sweden and Latvia and the glass apple in our display cabinet is a frequent reminder for us.

Hosting our Rotarian Friends from Norrkoeping

In September 2001 our Swedish friends came to London and we hosted Karen-Margarette and Bert in our home. Whilst our home is not unduly opulent we did form the impression that they felt just a little uncomfortable when they compared our accommodation and that which they had provided on our visit. However, nothing was ever said out loud and they were welcomed exactly as any other guests.

We took them to a lovely garden centre in Kent and then to the Clacton area where we had had our caravan sited. On the way home, late in the evening and when it was very dark I became concerned that the petrol gauge in my vehicle was registering almost empty and I was on tenterhooks that we would run out before reaching home but fortunately that did not happen.

We had made arrangements with other Rotarians who had been on the trip to Sweden that our guests would visit the Rotary Club of Battersea for lunch after a visit to the Houses of Parliament. After lunch I was intending to attend a meeting at New Scotland Yard to discuss details for a forthcoming police choir concert.

However, our plans did not materialise as we had intended.

Outside the Houses of Parliament, extensive alterations were taking place on the road to provide extra security and the building site was protected by a 6' high wire fence leaving only a minimum space for pedestrians to pass. Ann and I were concerned that other members of our party may have gone to the wrong agreed meeting place and I decided to look for them Trying to make my way along the crowded walk-way I tripped on one of the concrete supports of the fence, fell and in trying to save myself, my face scraped down the fence which acted in the same way that a cheese grater would.

My head and face were a mass of blood but within minutes, a motor cycle paramedic, two police officers and an ambulance were on the scene. With my head swathed in bandages I was taken to St Thomas's hospital where 13 stitches were inserted in the lacerations. The lunch appointment was out of the question but I did attend the concert committee meeting complete with the evidence of my recent surgery.

One request which had been made by our guests was that they should go and see the musical ABBA and we had obtained tickets. Although I enjoy the music for which the group were well known, it was played at a high volume and part way through the performance, the loud music and my head throbbing from the injury, I was forced to make a quick exit.

Before our guests ended their visit we were at dinner in our house and they cautiously asked how I had managed to slice the joint of meat so thinly. I explained that I had used an electric knife and then they produced the gift which they had brought for us – a carving knife made from the finest Swedish steel!

Rotary Youth Exchange

Another Rotary activity in which Ann and I took a keen interest was Youth Exchange. This was a project where foreign students in the equivalent of 6th form were given an opportunity to study for 12 months in this country, hosted by Rotarian families. At any one time there would be about 30 students in various parts of the country but on one weekend they would all come to London for their 'London Experience' and London Rotarians would be invited to host 2 students for about 4 days.

We took on the hosting of several of these visits and at various times, received students from Australia, Argentina, France, USA, Brazil and many other countries. Most of the students (always girls) were perfect guests but the American girl was the exception. Sullen (or perhaps homesick) she did not easily fit into our way of life and expectations.

She was paired for their visit with a young lady from Wales and on the Friday of their weekend visit, they visited Madame Tussauds, a popular tourist attraction. I arranged to meet the girls on their return at Walthamstow Central station, giving them very specific written instructions to identify the appropriate tube travel from central London to Walthamstow. At the appointed time I waited from them, becoming more anxious with their non-appearance. Not having a mobile phone, I asked one of the transport staff to watch for them whilst I ran across the road to make a telephone call to Ann to ascertain whether she had received any message which she hadn't. Back to the station and eventually my guests arrived explaining that someone else had given them directions and they had got lost. They hadn't even read my prepared instructions. Arriving home, we had arranged for other members of my Rotary Club to join us for a social evening and meet the girls. The Rotarians arrived, the girls were missing and we located them in their bedroom, resting because they were tired.

Some of the girls continued to send us Christmas cards and letters and when Anita, the Australian girl married, she brought her husband, Mark to visit us; a remarkable show of friendship to travel to the other side of the world to keep in touch.

Rotary Youth Makes Music

All Rotary Clubs are encouraged to support a wide range of activities intended to generate interest from young people. One such activity organised by the London Rotary clubs is Rotary Youth Makes Music, a concert every second year when every Rotary Club is encouraged to find young musicians with outstanding ability for a final selection to perform at one of the prestigious concert venues. The concerts have been held at the Albert Hall, the South Bank Festival Hall and the Barbican Centre.

It was an activity in which I took particular interest and for many of the concerts, I was able to identify and provide successful nominations. One such nomination was a young 11 year old boy, Cody Lee Smart whose skills in playing the piano justified him using the title "Boogie-Woogie Boy". I heard him playing at a local village fête and decided he was a worthy nomination. Not only was he selected but received a standing ovation when he played at the Barbican Centre and such was the appeal of his music, when I submitted a nomination for the concert two years later, again he was selected.

Having displayed his skills at the Barbican, he was encouraged by a professional jazz band to take on engagements with them and he also played at concerts of the Police Male Voice Choir organised by my Rotary Club. It is interesting that he developed his interest and competence when his mother was diagnosed with breast cancer and he determined to raise money for cancer research and other charities. In 4 – 5 years he was credited with raising over £40,000 and as a result, my Club nominated him for a Rotary Young Citizens' Award.

50 Years and Onward

Following the success of the 50th anniversary celebrations in 1993 we decided that we would hold a similar function for the club's 60th anniversary at which time once again I was President but the celebrations on that occasion though not as lavish as for the 50th, had a special significance for me because Ann was also President of the Inner Wheel Club. A dinner was arranged at the Waltham Forest College with the food prepared and served under supervision by students who were hoping to develop their career in catering. As a commemoration of the evening, on behalf of the Inner Wheel, Ann presented the Rotary Club with a plaque which depicted the emblem of the club.

With a lower membership the 70th anniversary was a rather low key but still an enjoyable occasion when we booked a suite of rooms at the Walthamstow dog track where we could enjoy our meal and look out over the track to watch the greyhound racing. We even had our own dedicated betting facilities.

80 years history behind us and to mark the occasion we invited Rotarians from our link club in Chepstow to join us for a special meal at our normal meeting place, Gilwell Park. Ann and I provided personal gifts for the ladies and goblets, suitably engraved for the men. As President I considered it important that I participated in the other activities which we had arranged for the visitors over the weekend although because I was still under hospital supervision following surgery 3 months previously, Ann was understandably very concerned for my well being.

Chapter 19. Chingford Association for the Physically Handicapped

When I transferred into the Chingford Rotary Club I participated in the established activities and commitments, one of which was to provide drivers for the Handicap Club's fortnightly meetings. The club had use of two mini buses, both of which were approaching their sell by date. The requirement was to collect club members from their homes, take them to their meeting place and return them, home afterwards.

The members of the club were of varying phases of disability but without exception were all pleasant to work with and very appreciative of the chance to leave the four walls of their homes for this modest social outing. We were fortunate that several members of the local branch of St John Ambulance Brigade were also involved with the club and provided skilled support when the occasions necessitated. Although the duty roster for Rotarian drivers expected only one driving session every few months, I frequently replaced drivers who were unavailable but I enjoyed the opportunity for extra duties.

In 1984, the chairman of the club Ron Watson died suddenly and unexpectedly, leaving the club without a chairman. Although I had not been a member of their club committee, I was invited to take on the chairmanship and agreed to do so. It was then my responsibility to co-ordinate the club's activities and arrange for weekly entertainment which frequently resorted to the well tried and popular Bingo.

Although the club members had enjoyed outings to various places before and during my association with them I decided to explore the possibility of taking them away for a holiday at the sea-side and was able to negotiate with a small family hotel in Cliftonville to have exclusive use of its facilities for one week. The venture proved a success and we were able to repeat the practice for several years until the situation arose where we had insufficient 'pushers' for the number of wheelchairs that we required. It was a sad acknowledgement that coping with more people in wheelchairs with too few able bodied people could not be sustained.

In addition to the week long holidays, we tried to maintain a policy of at least two outings each year, one of which would be to a seaside location. We also enjoyed river trips, visits to stately homes and a shire horse centre. Whenever possible we would dine out at restaurants which provided suitable facilities for wheelchairs. For their Christmas shopping trips we would use the benefits and facilities of the numerous shopping malls where all the shops are under one roof and we would not have the worry of adverse weather conditions

Whenever we planned an outing, Ann and I would make a 'dummy run' to check the route, suitable stopping places for 'comfort breaks' and most important, the suitability of the restaurant where we would take our lunch. The importance of careful preparation proved the point when one of the club members who was on holiday in Eastbourne agreed to make the necessary arrangements for our intended visit and I accepted the assurance I had been given. However on arrival we found that everything was not as we had anticipated. The coach we were using would have to unload in the centre of the road; the entrance to the restaurant was not accessible for wheel chairs; the dining room was on the first floor with no lift and to cap it all, the restaurant would not allow us in for lunch between 12 noon and 2.00-pm. Fortunately we quickly identified an alternative location for our lunch.

During my tenure as chairman we realised that our vehicles had seen better days and we made a determined effort to raise funds for replacements. Many avenues were explored and the Rotary Club made significant contributions for the purchase of the first vehicle which was achieved in 1994 It was a proud day for me when Ann and I travelled to Southampton to collect the vehicle where it had been modified with tail lift and fitted with removable seats which would allow for transportation of wheelchairs.

We donated the vehicle which it replaced to a local hospital inviting our local Member of Parliament, Iain Duncan-Smith to be present at the photo-shoot for the handover.

With one brand new vehicle, we still desperately needed a new second vehicle and I made application to the National Lottery for funding. I knew that many Organisations made applications, most of which were unsuccessful and following a perfectly legitimate practice, I visited the offices of the National Lottery to discuss the details required in the application. Not being very optimistic I was surprised late one evening to receive a telephone call from a lady at their offices to discuss the application and provide more information to support the application. It was a very happy day for me and the club members when I was informed that we had been awarded the necessary finance to purchase our second vehicle..

I continued as chairman of the club until 1999 when problems which had necessitated my hip replacements meant I was no longer able to take an active role in handling wheelchairs. It was a wrench to step down but there was no alternative and at the club's annual general meeting another chairman was elected and I was given the honorary title of President for Life. I was also presented with a beautiful pewter Quaich which is a replica of a domestic utensil originating in the West Highlands of Scotland used as a porridge bowl and also a cup for ale. Basically it is regarded as a 'Cup of Friendship'.

Unfortunately, not only the Handicap Club members themselves age and are less mobile and less inclined to venture out in the late evening, but the Rotarian drivers who, for many years were the mainstay of the club were not permitted to drive the ambulances when they reach the age of 75 years.

The nature of the Handicap club is that the membership gradually shrinks due to death and advancing frailty whilst new members are few and far between but for those who remain, the attraction of leaving their homes for a few hours to meet their friends will provide the stimulus to continue. I never ceased to be impressed by the members who, in spite of their disabilities and limitations always maintained a pleasant disposition

Chapter 20. Orion Harriers

When I arrived in Chingford in 1975 and realised that the house allocated to me was less than 100 yards from the trees of Epping Forest I realised the potential to rekindle my running interests. My chief superintendent at Barkingside, Bert Berry was the man who put me in touch with police sergeant Laurie Durrant and it was he who made the contact for me with Orion Harriers. The secretary was Harold Lee and I wrote to him suggestion that I would be an asset to the club even if only to sell programmes but in spite of my modest approach I was welcomed to the club and found myself one of about 10 other police officers in a membership of about 100.

Although my level of ability was far below that of most of the club runners, there were many club fixtures which enabled me to make a useful contribution. One of my favourite races was the 'Mob Matches' against other clubs in which the number of counting finishers would depend on how many the respective clubs could field. The consequence was that everyone had to run to finish because his position could well determine the winning team.

The forest provided every aspect of cross country running that any enthusiast could wish for and whatever time of the year, the magic of the changing seasons compensated for the mud, rain or snow. The principal race in the club's fixtures was the Orion 15; 15 miles of running up and down hills, through mud and streams with the winner likely to finish well inside 2 hours. I ran the race several times and for many years afterwards would still proudly wear my T shirt emblazoned with "I ran the Orion 15 – and survived". One occasion when I finished soaking wet and covered with mud, my only thought was to enjoy a hot shower. In those days the changing accommodation did not cater for women competitors who were expected to go home to change and shower. However, as I stripped off and turned towards the showers, I realised that the runner next to me who had also stripped off was a young woman. She was probably as exhausted as I was and although I will never forget the experience, I wouldn't recognise her even if we met again in identical circumstances.

Having regained my enthusiasm for running I was not averse to using the distance from home to office for my training schedules and whatever my police colleagues thought, I was blissfully unaware. It was many years later in a hospital waiting room, long after I had retired that I was approached by a man who I didn't recognise. He obviously knew me and when he introduced himself I realise he had been a constable under my supervision over 30 years previously. He informed me that I had been referred to as 'the governor who ran to work in shorts'. At least I was remembered for something.

As a member of Orion Harriers I was soon caught up with the enthusiasm of marathon running and applied to compete in the London Marathon. I was not successful on my first application because there was a strange selection procedure. Applications from London applicants were held back whilst applications from other areas were dealt with. The following year I was struck by misfortune when it became necessary to have an operation on my left big toe and it was suggested I would never be able to run again.

Undeterred, I applied the following year, was accepted and completed the course with an official time of 3 hours 45 minutes and 2 seconds. I was so elated that I made a phone call to the surgeon who had performed the operation, Mr. Richards, to tell him. As a result of the operation my left big toe was noticeably shorter than the right one and one day when I was changing in the club house, one of my club colleagues asked me to explain. Another runner was listening and then he told me that he was also an orthopaedic surgeon and he would have told his patients that they wouldn't be able to run after such an operation. I thought little more of that conversation until several years later when it became necessary for me to have a replacement hip operation and who was my consultant surgeon? Tom McAuliffe, my fellow Orion Harrier. He also carried out a similar operation 2 years later on my other hip and 20 years later I was still denying the experts who had told me such replacement hip joints would only last 15 years maximum.

I completed 3 other London marathons, 2 Torbay marathons and one in Swindon, every one in a similar time. The first Torbay marathon was particularly memorable because it coincided with a Superintendents' Association conference in Torquay and Ann and I went one day early for me to compete. The course commenced in Paignton, on to Torquay then up a long climb to Newton Abbot where we turned and ran back over the same roads to Paignton. Ann had sent me off on the race with her good wishes but in the time I was running she had gone to a jeweller's shop, purchased a trophy cup and had it engraved so that as I ran across the finishing line, she presented me with a very personal trophy.

In my first marathon when my daughter asked what had been my finishing position, I rather embarrassingly mentioned that it had been about 10,000. Her rather more encouraging reply was that there were about 20,000 who finished behind me. Although most runners regard their medals as cherished trophies when one of our Church ministers was due to leave she announced that she would have loved to own a London marathon medal. I gave her mine.

During my active athletic life, I often adopted training practices which, on reflection may have been considered eccentric. It was not unknown for Ann and me to visit friends and I would leave her to travel home either by public transport or by car whilst I ran home. In early days before we had children as a factor in our lives she would ride her bicycle to "pace" me but before long she decided I always ran faster than she could ride and the pacing was discontinued.

Sadly my running career came to an abrupt close in 1992. I had been accepted for the London Marathon in that year and my planned preparation would be to run the club's 10 mile handicap race, followed by a half marathon, then the Essex 20 mile road championship and then the marathon. There was no suspicion of what was to come until the Essex Twenty. It was a 2 lap race each of 10 miles and during the first lap I realised something was wrong but struggled to complete the lap and joined the spectators to watch the finish.

When the time came to return to the club house, I realised I could not move until two of my colleagues supporting me under each armpit helped me to stagger back. There was no argument when Ann realised what had happened and demanded I visit my GP, Dr. Judith Fisher. She diagnosed arthritis in my hip and decided that I should be referred to a consultant – Mr. McAuliffe! After the subsequent operation his advice was that I should forget about running.

I never anticipated one consequence of the change of what had been an integral part of my life but the emotional stress of not being able to run was such that I could not bear even to watch athletics on the television. I found out later that the change of condition by which the body had become used to regular running was in fact a medical rather than a mental factor which affected many runners. Not to be entirely deprived of the pleasure of Epping Forest, I bought a mountain bike to cycle with my friends on their training runs. Unfortunately it was a mental condition that eventually made me realise that riders on bicycles could not leap over ditches and streams as did the runners and I took many tumbles before the penny dropped.

When the disappointment of not running eventually worked out of my system I maintained my interest by acting as a marshal for local races

Orion Harriers formed an elite "Club 25" which consisted of all club members who had been with them for 25 years or more. Every year those members enjoyed a dinner at which they could renew acquaintances and recall their own past experiences. In 2011 Orion celebrated their Centenary and included in the entertainment for the evening the Orion Choir performed some humorous songs under the musical direction of - Leslie Stowe!

Chapter 21. The Sea Cadets

When Lloyd expressed his wish to join the Royal Navy, where we lived in Warminster there were no facilities to encourage him but in Swindon there was a Sea Cadet Unit. When we moved to London our home was barely ½ mile from a Sea Cadet Unit, TS Acorn and it was only a matter of time before I was invited to join the Unit management committee under the chairmanship of James Shadbolt, a local businessman who had had a distinguished naval career during the war serving on board motor torpedo boats.

The Unit had become progressively more popular with the cadets resulting in an increase in numbers which exceeded the capacity of the building itself. In 1992 the committee had decided to expand and develop a new "main deck" even though at that time the expected cost was more than the available funds would justify. However the enthusiasm and commitment of all concerned resulted in an extended building sufficient for the needs of the Unit at that time.

London Area of the Sea Cadets consisted of about 60 Units stretching from Richmond in Surrey to Walton-on-the-Naze in Essex. The Area was divided into 4 Districts and after a few years, having been appointed Vice Chairman of the Unit, I was asked to accept the chairmanship of the District Chairmen. I was thus in the strange relationship of being deputy to James but senior to him in District committees.

In due course, James realised that having been chairman of the Unit since he returned to civilian life, it was time to hand over to another chairman and he was appointed to be President for Life whilst I became chairman of the Unit. I was fortunate that the treasurer of the Unit was Neale Miller, a retired bank manager who, as would be expected was fastidious in recording and controlling the accounts.

In 1997 I was elected to be the London Area chairman., a position I held for 7 years during which time I attended many prestigious events with high ranking naval officers but eventually I became disenchanted with the manner in which the Organisation was developing and stood down. The duties of the Area Chairman required that I not only visit other Units from time to time but if their administrative competence was in doubt I would be asked to take on the Unit temporarily until stability was restored. Over a period of time I accepted the responsibility for 7 – 8 Units including Clapton & Hackney where I remained for 3 years. Whilst here I was able to persuade the Jack Petchey Foundation * to assist in the purchase of a minibus for use by the cadets .

TS Acorn had again reached the situation where the available building space was inadequate for the activities and numbers of cadets and it was decided to expand again. Neale was skilled in making applications for grants which would provide the necessary funds and eventually at a cost of about £40,000 an annex comprising 9 classrooms was built and suitably named "The James Shadbolt Annex" to acknowledge his contributions over many years.

Transport for the cadets was a vital factor in their activities and together with Neale I made application to the Jack Petchey Foundation* for assistance to purchase a new mini bus and with contributions from other sources we were able to finance the purchase at a total of £25,000 followed shortly afterwards by the purchase of a trailer for their equipment. We had deliberated whether to buy a new minibus first or build a new garage and then buy the vehicle. We decided that it was more important to provide the garage which cost just over £20,000.

The hall of the Unit (the main deck) was frequently hired for birthday parties, wedding receptions and other events but probably the most interesting were the Civic Nationality ceremonies. Frequently I was invited as one of the VIP guests to officiate when 50 – 60 persons from other countries would be officially sworn in as British Citizens. The other VIPs included the Mayor of the Borough, the Deputy Lieutenant or persons of similar status.

When the Chingford Green Indoor Bowling club, mainly retired persons, could no longer use the venue which had been their home for several years, I made arrangements for them to use the facilities of the Unit on three mornings every week. It enabled them to continue their very popular pastime and increased the income for the Unit.

Although there has always been friendly rivalry between Sea Cadets and Sea Scouts, when the Sea Scouts were required to vacate their headquarters whilst refurbishment was undertaken, we opened the doors of TS Acorn and allowed its use for them when not required by the Cadets. The Sea Scouts were quickly followed by a Girl Guides' group who were similarly required to find alternative temporary accommodation. Not only did these arrangements increase our finances but ensured that the Unit was occupied more or less constantly which increased its security aspect.

In November 2010 I decided that I no longer wished to have the responsibility of chairman of the Unit but remained as a committee member and another chairman was appointed.

In recognition of my involvement with the Sea Cadets, in 1988 and again in 1991 I was given certificates by the Council of the Sea Cadets Corps for "valuable and unselfish service to training of youth in the Sea Cadets". In May 2008 together with Ann, I was hosted for afternoon tea by the Mayor of Waltham Forest and at a full Council meeting, presented with a "Civic Award for Outstanding Service to the Community", particularly my work with the Sea Cadets.

The certificates hang on my study wall and my name is inscribed in gold letters on the Honours Board of the Town Hall.

The Jack Petchey Foundation was founded in 1999 by Jack Petchey, a self made millionaire who decided to use his fortune to benefit young people in the London Area and has donated over £42M to youth Organisations. In 2010 he was awarded a CBE

Chapter 22. Holidays at Home

In the later years of my police service, we had often accepted invitations from our friends Peter and Joy Bloor to use their caravan on a permanent site at Weeley, a small village near Clacton, Essex.

We had never given any thought to purchasing a caravan ourselves but following retirement, we decided that having made modest investments during the previous years, it was perhaps time to take advantage and so we decided to buy a luxury static caravan. It was near enough to our home to make spontaneous decisions to spend a few days there and it was literally home from home.

The owners of the site and the staff were all very pleasant and we were quite content to spend days or weeks there, inviting many of our friends to visit us. The holiday resorts of Clacton, Frinton and Walton were only minutes away if we wished to see the sea and I spent many happy hours with jig saw puzzles and running through the Essex countryside although the opportunities to participate in competitive cross country running were very limited.

Although we enjoyed our visits to the caravan where we were able to relax completely, in hindsight one visit did not fulfil our intentions as planned. We decided to spend a few days immediately after Christmas Day but that necessitated some co-operation from the site managers. Whenever the caravan was shut up for the winter months, the water supply had to be shut down, a task undertaken by an employee of the site and when the caravan was to be taken into use again, the water had to be turned on. For our out of season visit, Christmas Day fell on Saturday which meant that Boxing Day was postponed until Monday.

We notified the site manager that we would arrive on Boxing Day for a few days and would require the water to be turned on. Of course we meant the day after Christmas Day but he interpreted our request to mean the official Boxing Day – Monday. When we arrived we had no water and in zero temperatures it was several hours before we could make contact to provide the comforts of home life – a cup of tea.

Over the next ten years the ownership of the site changed several times resulting in the introduction of new policies and restrictions. One of the changes was the 'Ten Year Rule' introduced to persuade caravan owners to buy new ones. It was eleven years before we received an offer to take advantage of 'end of season sales' offering new caravans at reduced prices. Such were the restrictions of having a caravan on a pitch at the site that rent demands for the following year would only be issued to owners of caravans which were considered suitable to be on the site. No caravans over 10 years old would be considered suitable and the consequence was that it was the owner's responsibility to remove their caravan from the site or sell it. The cost for an owner to remove a caravan would have been exorbitant even if an alternative location could be found. The pressures were increased because the site owners insisted on having the initial offer to purchase the caravans which would be at a price probably one tenth of what the owner had paid for it.

We decided that enough was enough and although we had spent many happy days in our mobile home, we decided to sell. Our caravan was probably moved to another site to be rented to casual visitors making enormous profits for the site owners.

The Orient Express Experience

When we moved to London, there was a public house called "The Horseless Carriage". The name was appropriate because on the forecourt was a railway restaurant car dating from the days when railway lines were run by private Companies and competed with each other by providing more attractive services. The restaurant car was in chocolate and cream livery typical of the Southern Railway Companies. It was in regular use by the pub and we took our children there for their birthday meal outing within months of arriving in Chingford.

Shortly afterwards the pub changed hands and "The Horseless Carriage" became "The Wheelwrights". The railway restaurant car disappeared.

It was not until nearly 30 years later that I would see the horseless carriage restaurant car again and certainly not in circumstances which I expected.

I retired from the Middle Temple in September 2001 and to mark my retirement and as a belated birthday gift, Ann arranged a surprise for me and keeping her secret until the last moment, she insisted that on 15th October we would have to go to Victoria Railway Station. She had booked 2 tickets for a journey on the Orient Express for an excursion to Chester.

The Venice Simplon-Orient Express Company had been formed to recapture the splendour and opulence of the renowned railway and in addition to continental journeys also arranged domestic journeys. Our trip had the added attraction that our train would be hauled by the famous Flying Scotsman steam engine although for the initial part of the journey our locomotive would be a diesel engine.

The train consisted of about 8 Pullman parlour carriages all in chocolate and cream colours each one having its own history of previous service with details of its restoration. Having been greeted with a red carpet and bucks fizz drinks as we boarded, we wandered through the carriages, admiring the impeccable restoration work. One of the carriages had a plaque with the following inscription:

Gwen

First class kitchen car, 20 seats. Built 1932 by Metropolitan Cammel
Carriage & Wagon Co. Ltd. For the Brighton Belle. In 1948 was used
With sister car Mona, to convey HM Queen Elizabeth (later the Queen
Mother) to Brighton. Brighton Belle service withdrawn in 1972.
Preserved as a restaurant at The Horseless Carriage, Chingford,
Essex and later at the Colne Valley Railway, Castle Hedingham, Essex.
Acquired by VSOE in 1988 and joined British Pullman train in 1999.

It was almost like greeting an old friend.

The excursion did not materialise as we had expected. The itinerary provided that we would travel to Chester to arrive there in time for a short walking tour. One of the attractions of this particular journey was that the train would be pulled by the famous Flying Scotsman steam engine but on departure from Victoria, our locomotive was a normal diesel engine and we did not connect with the Flying Scotsman until we arrived at Banbury in Oxfordshire where we waited for about an hour, giving many of us an opportunity to be photographed on the footplate of the famous engine. When looking at the photographs afterwards I realised that my face still bore the scars from the accident in Parliament Square a few weeks previously.*

Special itinerary excursions have to be routed so that they do not interfere with scheduled services on the railways and consequently our journey took a roundabout route and was much longer than we had expected. The original plan was that any passengers who wished to do so could leave the train at Stafford for an excursion to the Wedgewood Pottery factory and they would be taken by coach to rejoin the train at Crewe.

Much to our surprise, and probably more so for those who had opted for the Wedgewood visit, we passed through Stafford without stopping until we reached Crewe. All passengers then left the train and boarded buses to Chester where we arrived approximately 20 minutes prior to our departure time to return to Crewe. Although we were due to leave promptly at 6.00pm it was nearer to 7.00pm when we left which justified the provision of dinner on board, which had not been in the original plans.

In spite of the unexpected alterations to the prepared plans, the quality of the menu and the very personalised service by the attendants resulted in a very enjoyable day's excursion and we decided to wait for another occasion to walk round Chester.

It was not the last occasion to travel on the Orient Express and for my birthday in 2005 Ann again surprised me by booking a trip to Winchester on the famous train. From Winchester we travelled by coach to Southampton where we were able to view the new gigantic luxury liner, Queen Mary 2, towering above the dockside.

Chapter 23. South Chingford Methodist Church

When we took up residence in Chingford we were approximately one mile from the Methodist Church in North Chingford but when we purchased our house it was only 200-300 yards from South Chingford Methodist Church and it was more practical for us to regard that Church as the one to attend.

Although we made many friends at the Church, neither Ann or I engaged in Church responsibilities for the first year or so but then I was persuaded to take on the Covenant Secretary's duties which required me to invite Church members to sign documents which enabled the Church to recover tax paid by the Church member under the Gift Aid Scheme. Gift Aid is very beneficial to the charity concerned (including our Church) and increased the value of the donation by 28% at no additional cost to the donor. Without consciously realising it we both became involved in the Church activities.

The most dramatic period evolved from the time when our minister was The Reverend Elizabeth Rundle. The church had been built in 1933 and the building was becoming a matter of concern in respect of the structural stability and a decision was made to cease all "lettings" rather than face the risk of accident.

Elizabeth set up a small committee and invited me to be a member. The brief was to consider the future of the Church and every course of action would be considered. We identified the committee as the "Crossroads Committee" which had a double significance because the Church was at its own crossroads in life and it was geographically at the crossroads of two busy thoroughfares. At the first meeting it was necessary to appoint a chairman and in the absence of any other nominee, I was given the role.

As a committee we considered several options including closure of the church and rumours circulating in the locality suggested that we had actually done so but there were other avenues to explore. There was a strong representation from a local branch of the YMCA that we could enter into some type of partnership but after extensive discussions, it was apparent that they had lost interest.

There was a scheme involving several Churches in the area which provided overnight accommodation for homeless persons but only for one night at a time and then another church would open its doors for one night. A suggestion put to my committee was that our church could be used more or less on a permanent basis. I made enquiries with the Local Authority and discovered that planning permission would be required, fire safety requirements would have to be taken into consideration and it became evident that the suggestion could not be developed.

However as the result of the lengthy discussions and contacts made I linked up with an Organisation CREST.(an ecumenical Christian charity working in Waltham Forest) who were anxious to open a branch for their work in Chingford and again it seemed that a partnership was a possibility. For various reasons that was not to be but a development was that a lady named Patty Gurman who was involved with the Chingford Hall Children's Centre wanted to use our church premises. Patty was in effect the turning point for the

Church using the hall 3 mornings each week and some of her clients asked to use the hall for birthday parties.

I had previously made an application to the Church Circuit funds for £10,000 to lay a concrete path round the rear of the church halls and we then decided to find funds to provide new floors in each of the three halls. The necessary work lasted for 4 – 5 weeks at a cost of £70,000 part of which was a £3,000 grant from Waltham Forest Borough obtained by Patty Gurman. With the new floors the attraction of the halls had increased dramatically and in addition to established Church activities and Patty's requirements, a Dance School, singing classes, karate instruction and yoga sessions were regular users.

When the time came for the next round of applications for Borough Grants, Patty was required to attend the meeting and explain how the money she had received had been used. She asked me to accompany her and when those present were invited to submit applications for further funds she suggested to me that we apply for money to create a sensory garden. I wasn't sure what that entailed but submitted a sketchy application and did not expect to hear anything further. Much to my surprise a few weeks later I was asked to provide a detailed, fully costed application. I asked for £5,047 to create a safe play area for children with a play house, sand pit, other suitable equipment and planting troughs for flowers.

What I had not appreciated was that every ward in the borough of Waltham Forest had £10,000 available to sponsor a suitable community project. However, money would not be donated to a church and I had to quickly think up a name for the organisation on whose behalf I was making the application. Living in the Larkswood Ward I decided that we were 'The Friends of Larkswood' and all my subsequent correspondence was on suitably headed notepaper. Selection for a project was by a majority vote by persons attending a ward meeting and my project won the day.

The purchases were eventually delivered and volunteers from the International bankers Goldman Sachs gave their time and energy for one full day to undertake much of the physical work with some help from Church members. What, for many years had been an overgrown neglected rubbish area was transformed into a beautiful garden and a safe play area for children. When completed, the garden included a play house for the children, a sandpit, a pergola with climbing plants, several waist high 'planters' with an impressive array of flowers, bench seats and a picnic table all enclosed with a large grass area.

In June 2010 when the basic work had been completed to establish the garden, the Sunday morning Church Service, including communion was held in the garden. The sun was shining, the birds were singing and it was a wonderful atmosphere.

> "The kiss of the sun for pardon; the song of the birds for mirth;
> You're nearer God's heart in a garden than anywhere else on earth."
>
> (Dorothy Frances Gurney 1858-1932)

The facilities of the garden and the halls increased the popularity and use of the premises and in February 2011 an approach was made from the Borough (Community Learning and

Skills Service) to conduct adult education classes in the halls. As a result we opened our doors for English language classes, computer courses, cake decoration, floristry and many other activities in addition to the many other uses which by that time were well established. Whereas 6 years previously, the church halls had been in use for 3 – 4 hours each week, we had reached the situation that every day from 8.30am until late evening, the halls were a hive of activity. As a result, the income for the Church was substantially increased to the point where we budgeted for £40,000 income which was a substantial improvement over a period of 6 years previously when we received nothing from lettings.

The extensive use of the church premises necessitated for me, the preparation of invoices and associated correspondence; frequent visits to the church, usually 3 – 4 times every day to open or close the premises; undertaking mundane duties of building maintenance; ensuring adequate supplies of toilet rolls, kitchen rolls and hand wash, putting out the rubbish bins to be emptied; arranging for gardening to be carried out etc.. Some Church members suggested that we employ a caretaker but my own view was that it would not have been practical and I was prepared to carry on with the business which I had built up. I was back in full time employment

When addressing the Church Council meetings, whereas initially I emulated Dr Martin Luther King with his challenging "I have a dream" speech I was able to announce that my dream had become reality and our Church was now the centre of vibrant community activities. Although the congregations of Church members did not noticeably increase, the premises were extensively used for birthday parties and by followers of many faiths including Moslem, Sikh and Hindu for their celebratory functions.

Chapter 24. Our Own Home

Within 12 months of moving to London we had decided that we must buy a house which would be our own and for the first time in our married lives not be dependent on accommodation provided by the police Authority. We decided that we would remain in the Chingford area and looked at many houses on offer from the estate agents but none really appealed to us. That is, not until we viewed 15 Brook Crescent, a house which stood empty after the previous occupants had died. It was 3 bedroom semi-detached with a small garage standing slightly separated from the house. It had the definite feel that this was the one. The garage was only wide enough for our car to be driven in but not sufficient space to open the car door. This was resolved by having a door adjacent to the car door which could be lifted off, the car door opened and then the removable door replaced. The purchase of the house took every pound of our financial resources but proved well worthwhile for the future.

As we gradually established our residence various aspects of the house were altered to our needs including the important feature of central heating to replace the electric storage heaters and electric fires. In due course we converted one of the fire places into an alcove in which we could display our ever increasing collection of figurines and other porcelain treasures on glass shelves with a mirror to reflect the items and concealed lighting. Our collection gradually grew from the Beswick animals started in 1960 to Royal Doulton figures, Lladro, Royal Crown Derby and vases commemorating Nelson's battles and the Battle of Britain.

In addition, my interest in aircraft was in evidence with many aircraft featured on wall plates and pictures. These were the embellishments which made our house our home.

As our 25th wedding anniversary approached we decided that to celebrate we would take out an additional mortgage and invest in major alterations which consisted of an extended kitchen, a sun lounge, utility room and the garage would be demolished then rebuilt as an integral part of the house with a connecting door. The work was undertaken by a building firm the proprietor of which was one of my Fellow Rotarians whom I trusted to make sure there would be no cause for complaint. We did not fully appreciate the upheaval which would be necessary and at one time, everything movable in the kitchen was in the living room and the kitchen was no more than 4 walls, a floor and the rafters of the bedrooms above.

However, we lived through the days of endless dusting, eating meals wherever and whenever we could until eventually the work was completed and we were able to enjoy the improvements.

We had not appreciated that the employees of the firm all had their own specific responsibilities which may have been to dig the foundations, build the walls, arrange the plumbing or electrics, tiling the walls etc. When they had completed their own particular jobs, they would move on to another job and they never saw the completed alterations from start to finish.

We decided to create a precedent and invited all the workmen and their wives to a celebratory evening when everything was finished. It was a happy event, greatly appreciated by all the workmen, one of whom presented us with a beautiful mantel clock as a lasting memento.

Over the next few years we hosted many social occasions for our friends from Rotary and the Inner Wheel but in 1988 we were overtaken by events which resulted in a change of lifestyle.

In July 1987 I was in my office when I received a telephone call from a neighbour of Ann's mother and father in Birmingham to the effect that her mother had suffered a stroke and had been taken to Heartlands hospital. I telephoned Ann but she was not at home but I was able to contact Denise who lived 2 – 3 minutes away from where we lived. I told her to go to our house, wait for Ann to arrive and instruct her that I was on my way home and we would leave immediately for Birmingham. We drove as quickly as was legally possible and arrived with only minutes to spare before Ann's mother died.

Her parents had been totally devoted to each other and we doubted whether her father would survive on his own. Consequently it was not unexpected when he phoned a few days after the funeral to say he wanted to come and live in London, which was another way of saying could he come and live with us.

There was no question that we would not agree and considered how best to provide accommodation for him. We looked at various options but the most suitable was to convert the garage into a bedroom which would include his own bedroom and lounge area and we put the work of the alterations in the hands of my builder Rotarian friend. Eventually father moved to our home but such was his nature that when his Birmingham house was sold, everything was left in place; beds made up ready for sleeping; crockery and cooking utensils in the kitchen just as though when he closed the door, he could walk back in and everything would be as he left it.

His room included his bed and bedside cabinet, separated from his washing facilities by a flexible room divider, wardrobe, a toilet next to his room and we felt that he had his own little domain where he could watch television, look out of the window and watch people passing by and be as happy as possible in his final years. He was able to continue his association with the Salvation Army and I would take him to the Services on Sunday morning before our own Church Service then collect him afterwards. He lived with us for 10 years and gradually it became apparent that Parkinson's disease was gradually worsening and sadly, although we did not realise it at the time, he also suffered from Alzheimer's disease. When he died his funeral cortege was preceded by a Salvation Army flag which was a fitting tribute to a gentleman and devout life-long Salvationist.

The bedroom which had been father's home then provided a much needed study in which I could store my books and later computer, to undertake all the administrative duties which filled my daily life. My collection of model cars, model ships, choir mementos, pictures and the ceremonial sword presented to me by colleagues on my retirement from police service all created for me my own personal space.

In Sickness and in Health

It is almost certain that in a marriage which continues for 30, 40, 50 or more years there will be occasions when the health of the partners will make extra demands on the love of each other. Unfortunately neither Ann or I have enjoyed a life where we have been strangers to hospitals. Ann's first major surgery was early in 1956 when two years into her training as a nurse she was diagnosed with tuberculosis which caused considerable distress to her thinking it would affect our future relationship. Of course her worries were groundless. It was not until we had been married 3 or 4 years that gynaecological problems were identified resulting in increasingly invasive fertility tests and surgery for her.

However shortly after we moved into our first police house, it became obvious that she required extensive dental treatment and it must have been very distressing for a young woman of her age to realise that she would have all her teeth extracted and full dentures fitted. I remember that when she returned from the dentist's surgery she ate some ice cream which was all she could manage but it really was not suitable and she was violently sick. At times like that it is comforting to have a loved one close by to give physical and mental comfort. It wasn't long before she accepted the dentures and at party times on many occasions she provided hilarious amusement for her guests by removing her teeth and dressing up as an old woman. The transformation was so complete that invariably she was unrecognisable.

There was one particular occasion at Christmas time we called on a friend who owned a little West Highland terrier. Ann went to his door and rang the bell whilst I hid out of sight. The door was opened and she pleaded for a crust of bread because she was hungry. She kept her head bowed and as he stooped to try and hear what she was saying, Ann stooped lower and I could scarcely contain my laughter as both Ann and our friend stooped lower and lower whilst the little dog who had immediately recognised Ann was wagging his tail furiously demanding her attention.

Her ability to portray an old woman dressed in a black shawl and carrying a bird cage, also enabled her to perform a party piece and sing "My old man said follow the van and don't dilly dally on the way." At times, she could be extremely extrovert whilst the other side of her nature suggested a shy introvert. I benefited from both aspects.

Ann's dental treatment resulted in an unexpected consequence for me. Having neglected my own teeth she urged me to seek treatment before I suffered the same effect as she had experienced. I went to the same dental surgeon who had treated her who advised me that extensive work was required. The first session which was to require drilling commenced with an injection and I immediately passed out. I remember being brought back to consciousness resting on the bosom of his attractive nurse. The next appointment followed the same pattern – injection, fainting, revival by his nurse. On the third visit, the dentist made it quite clear to me that he would not give me an injection if the sole purpose was to enable me to be revived by his nurse and I never had another injection unless it was for an extraction. I still have my teeth which have a higher percentage of metal than calcium.

In the later years of married life Ann developed worrying dietary limitations associated with ceoliac and lactose intolerance. Before the true nature of the situation had been identified she had been subjected to many tests including the removal of her gall bladder. Great care had to be taken to ensure that she did not eat anything which would cause unfortunate consequences and careful scrutiny of food packaging labels was necessary to identify potential harmful additives, including monosodium glutamate which seemed to be in almost all food products. In spite of meticulous planning for meals, there were occasions when without warning she would lose consciousness. One evening, having attended a formal dinner at New Scotland Yard and on the way home we had to leave the tube before the end of our journey because Ann was so ill. None of the other passengers on the platform offered help but fortunately it wasn't long before we were able to complete the journey.

Eventually Ann's metabolism stabilised and she was able to relax the rigid diet requirements but another medical condition slowly became more noticeable for her; arthritis. It became more noticeable with increasing discomfort in her neck and eventually she was recommended to a consultant who reluctantly suggested that surgery may provide long term relief. Any operation on the spine is inherently hazardous but after considering the options, she agreed and in March 2002 a bone splint was taken from her hip to supplement the titanium splint and 8 screws used to strengthen cervical vertebrae which were fused together. It was essential to stabilise her neck with a collar support which she was obliged to wear at all times. Before taking her home from the hospital I carefully surveyed the route so that so far as possible I could avoid road bumps and other hazards so as to reduce to a minimum any jolting for her.

Gradually as the wound healed she was able to reduce the number of hours when she was obliged to wear the collar but the need remained. A physiotherapist explained that the human head weighs 11lb – 12lb and therefore the weakened neck depended on additional support. If we thought that Ann would not be subjected to any further medical problems, we were sadly disillusioned on 28th September 2010.

Ann had visited her friend Shirley in Derbyshire for a few days and returned on Tuesday 28th September. I had met her from the train, escorted her home and then, as was normal went to my Rotary Club meeting. When I returned in the late evening, we sat and chatted until she visited the toilet. There was no indication that she was unwell but I heard a loud bang and found her lying in the hallway unconscious. Although it was 11.45pm I telephoned my neighbours, Gary and Nicola who arrived almost immediately and Nicola did what I should have done in the first instance – dialled 999.

It was only minutes before an ambulance arrived and Ann was taken to Whipps Cross Hospital with me accompanying her and Gary and Nicola following in their car. Nicola stayed with me throughout the night while Ann was taken for scans and x-ray examination. At 5.30am Gary returned to the hospital and took Nicola and me home while Ann was taken to an assessment ward. Later that day she was transferred to the National Neurological and Neurosurgical Hospital where she was diagnosed with subarachnoid haemorrhage and remained there for one week then later transferred back to Whipps Cross Hospital.

Unfortunately the excellent treatment she had received on her first admission to Whipps Cross and similarly at the Hospital for Neurosurgery was not repeated on this occasion. Much to my concern and Ann's distress, the other patients in the ward all appeared to be in various stages of dementia and the nursing staff with one or two exceptions did not display the level of professionalism expected. Ann became increasingly distressed and restless, pleading with me to take her home and it was a great relief to do so three weeks later. As would be expected from any husband, I remained with Ann every minute of the permitted visiting hours and I will be forever grateful for friends and neighbours who insisted on providing transport for me to and from the hospital. There were many days when, returning home I was invited by Nicola and Gary to spend some time with them and they didn't mind at all that I frequently lost my composure and sobbed like a child.

In the fall she had broken her spectacles and It was necessary for her to visit her optician and also attend the hospital clinic for follow up tests from a psychologist . Whilst she received a clean bill of health from the latter, the injury had caused double vision and as a result she was unable to renew her driving licence for 12 months. We were both very relieved when the consultants at the Neurological Hospital and Eye Clinic decided that there was no need for further treatment.

Although the fall had caused serious concern for her long term recovery, there was one unexpected benefit. It was not until several months after the event that she realised she no longer needed to wear the neck support collar and only 12- 15 months afterwards that she recommenced its use and then only rarely rather than permanently.

Sadly, misfortune visited Ann again on 12th 12th 12 – twelfth of December 2012. She was making her way to the local shops when she tripped and fell resulting in a double fracture of the left wrist and a fracture to the right knee cap. An immediate visit to the A & E department of Whipps Cross Hospital was followed by several visits to the fracture clinic and eventually, surgery on her left wrist. For nearly three months she had her left arm and right leg encased in plaster and it was necessary to use an arm crutch to assist her mobility.

Of course whilst I was very concerned about Ann's medical problems and gave her all the love and support I could, there were many occasions when I benefited from her support with inherent nursing skills and compassion. Other than days of being off colour or upset tummies, in 1967 I experienced what was to be the first of many abdominal hernias and was treated at one of Birmingham's "cottage" hospitals in Rubery. I was an inspector at the time and had recently commenced my studies for a Law degree. I recall lying in my hospital bed studying the complexities of Roman Law and a nurse, knowing that I was a police officer jokingly suggested that my inspector would be surprised if he visited me. I think she was the one to be surprised when I told her that I was the inspector!

Shortly afterwards I experienced the pain of sciatica which caused me considerable discomfort when sitting, standing or walking. The only relief was when I was running and in spite of numerous pleas from Ann to visit the doctor, I stubbornly refused until eventually there was no alternative but to agree and he diagnosed the problem – running! He recommended complete rest and although that wasn't practical, I did ease off with my running and eventually I woke one morning and realised there was something different – no sciatica. It had disappeared completely and unexpectedly.

It was not until we had moved to London that my medical problems resulted in further hospitalisation and each occasion seemed to have some association with my running activities. In 1982 a necessary operation on my left big toe had restricted my normal running but in spite of scepticism from some of my friends, it was possible for me to complete my first London marathon 12 months after the surgery. I was so pleased that I telephoned the surgeon who had operated on my foot to tell him what a good job he had done.

My problems leading up to the 1992 marathon proved to be more permanent. Following several consultations by my friend Mr. McAuliffe he was not anxious to perform a hip replacement until he was satisfied that the time was appropriate. It was not until April 1994 that the decision was made and I was admitted to Holly House Hospital when I inadvertently caused some concern to the staff. My normal pulse rate was about 46 per minute and probably due to my eagerness to leave nothing undone which should have been done and the dash to arrive at the hospital on time, my pulse rate on arrival and on the first check was about 78.

A few hours later when I had been resting in bed my pulse was taken and immediately the nurse left the room and returned with the nursing Sister who took my pulse again. I was asked if I was feeling alright and after a few more routine tests and conversation it transpired that my pulse had dropped back to my normal rate of 46 and the drop from that on my admission had given the impression I was slowly dying!

The operation was a total success and the second hip replacement was carried out in July 1999. Although the result was having one leg slightly shorter than the other the difference was easily rectified by having an extra ¼" on the heel of one shoe. I had never experienced the pain and discomfort experienced by many other persons who required hip replacements, and I realised how very fortunate I was. Although some of my running club contemporaries continued their running activities after joint replacements, I followed my consultant's advice and never ran again. As he explained, the replacement joints were not designed to go pounding the streets of London. .In spite of suggestions that the replacements would only last for about 10 years, after 18 years mine seemed to be as effective as when originally implanted.

Perhaps the effectiveness of the hip operations encouraged me to overlook the fact that I did have some physical limitations but it was a previous hernia repair which came back to haunt me. I had frequently used my vehicle to collect supplies for the Sea Cadets' "stand easy" on parade nights. In August 2010 together with one of the Unit helpers I had delivered our purchases to the Unit and then I returned home. Ann was not there but within minutes I experienced excruciating abdominal pains and when Ann did return about 20 minutes later, I was writhing on the floor almost incoherent. She dialled 999 and within minutes I was on my way to hospital with sirens and flashing blue lights.

Whatever criticisms of the NHS which may be justified on occasions, the treatment which I received was excellent and I felt justified in writing a complimentary letter to the Hospital Chief Executive. The injury which led to my hospital admission was a ruptured hernia which had become infected.

Perhaps the most serious medical problem for me occurred in May 2013. Having experienced what I regarded as an upset tummy for two or three weeks, I visited my GP who referred me to a consultant at Whipps Cross Hospital who directed that I should have an MR.I scan and colonoscopy. Those tests revealed 'something nasty' as the doctor explained to me. The 'something nasty' was identified as cancer of the rectum and on 5th June, I was admitted for surgery which removed the cancer but the experience required a revised outlook on life and a moderation in the activities I had previously regarded as normal.

Chapter 25. 50 Golden Years

We had invested in home improvements to celebrate our Silver Jubilee wedding anniversary but for 50years we decided that it would be in keeping for the occasion to treat ourselves more personally. We decided on a 3 week tour of Canada organised by Titan Travel but that would not take place in our wedding anniversary month of February but April 2007.

23rd February fell on Friday of that year and on Sunday 25th there was a special Church Service when Ann and I took communion independently of the other members of the congregation and we presented two golden roses to every lady present.

On 3rd March we held a party at our home or rather two parties. In the afternoon we welcomed our Church friends, neighbours and elderly friends and then in the evening our Rotarian friends and others who didn't mind being out late in the evening. The catering arrangements were undertaken by our son Lloyd's partner Jo with some of her catering friends. By the end of the evening probably 100 had shared the festivities with us.

What we considered to be the probability of experiencing the holiday of a life time began on 24th April when we were collected from home by a Titan Travel mini bus to take us to Heathrow for a flight by Air Canada to Montreal. Whilst that airline has a very good record of punctuality on this occasion, our 7 ½ hours flight was delayed for 4 hours, taking off at 7.30pm.

Montreal is a fascinating city, predominantly French speaking but in many establishments English was spoken and we encountered no problems. I was even able to use my very limited French vocabulary when ordering coffee for our breakfast in a patisserie near to our hotel.

Quite unique in our experience was the underground city. Over 20 miles of shopping malls underneath the above-ground city. Completely independent from everything above, the underground city is accessible from many public buildings and in 2006 a marathon was run through its 'streets'. The spoil taken from the tunnelling operation was used to construct an artificial island in the St Lawrence waterway which was used for the Expo 67 and is now an integral part of the city. One unexpected benefit for us was that to celebrate 40 years since Montreal hosted Expo 67 and the final settlement of the debts which had been incurred, the tube travel for the whole of our weekend there was free.

In 1976 Montreal hosted the Olympic Summer Games and we were able to visit the Olympic site which now incorporates the area used for the Canadian Grand Prix Formula 1 race track. In our 50 seater coach we drove round the track and will now watch for the Canadian GP to compare the racing cars travelling at 200 mph compared with our lap of honour. (Watching the Canadian Grand Prix on TV a few months later, the track with safety barriers, pit lanes and advertising hordings bore no resemblance at all to the track when we drove round it!)

We were left to our own devices in the afternoon and returned to the Olympic site where we enjoyed 2 hours or so in the Biodome. This is a building so constructed to allow visitors to wander through tropical rainforests and other habitats where birds, animals including monkeys, sloth bears Canadian Lynx and reptiles (Cayman) lived without restriction. The most interesting part was the arctic area where we passed what appeared to be a huge aquarium but when we went up the steps to a higher level we found that we were in the icy waters of the arctic with penguins, sea birds and the Canadian Lynx. (Penguins are not found in the arctic but they couldn't put polar bears in the area.)

On a cold rainy day we visited Quebec City which is only one of the two walled cities in the North American Continent. The walls of the city are carefully preserved and still adorned with many cannons on the balustrades. Not only is the first language French but we were informed that the law requires all public notices to be in French. It was all part of our holiday but we were not particularly impressed.

On to Ottawa, the seat of Federal Government, the parliament building of which bore a striking resemblance to our own Palace of Westminster.

Next stop was Toronto and a visit to the CN Tower which at that time was the highest freestanding structure in the world (1,815 ft) The viewing platform is 1,136 ft high and has a glass floor at one point where those who are not faint hearted can gaze down to the street below. As would be expected there are magnificent views including overlooking a small airport similar to our own City airport where aircraft land on an approach over the sea.

Following a tour we travelled to Niagara which must be one of the most stunning examples of water power in the world. Our hotel was the Sheraton on the Falls, literally overlooking the Falls but our bedroom overlooked the area behind the waterfront. That view and the whole of the area was a disappointment containing so many amusement arcades and Blackpool type tourist attractions that it is definitely not worth visiting.

One aspect of Niagara which was a complete surprise to us was the transport facilities on offer. None other than a big 6 wheeler, scarlet painted, diesel engined, 97 horse power London Transport omnibus. Yes there in all its nostalgic glory was a Routemaster London 'bus. The vehicle was one of three which we saw whilst we were at Niagara and they provided a trip to a suburb, Niagara on the Lake.

Having seen the Falls 'in the flesh' so to speak, in the early evening we visited the Imax theatre where we saw a film on a screen which must have been 30 ft high and probably twice as wide with multi stereophonic sound giving the history together with myths and legend of the Falls. We bought a DVD so that we can play it at home.

Our evening meal was in the hotel and was a self service buffet like no other we had ever experienced. The servery was about 60 ft long with an amazing selection of food to suit every palate. Ann even managed metaphorically to twist the arm of the chef to find her some cheesecake. The dining room overlooked the Falls which were illuminated by spotlights when darkness fell.

We were disappointed that our intended 'Maid of the Mist' boat trip which would have taken us behind the pounding water of the falls could not take place because there was too much ice on the river. However we did take a helicopter flight over the falls and were able to take many aerial photographs. We even had a photograph and certificate to prove that we had flown.

We returned to Toronto airport for our flight over the Rocky Mountains to Vancouver .and it was interesting to see the large number of lakes and islands. Apparently Canada has 20% of the world's fresh water.

Landing at Vancouver we adjusted our watches back 3 hours and were taken to The Marriott Pinnacle hotel. As in the USA, Canadian roads seem to be long and straight and driving towards Granville Bridge, gradually descending a long hill, we could see the harbour where our hotel was located, way in the distance.

The accommodation was just as impressive as the other hotels on our itinerary and we noticed that there was always a uniformed person on the door to welcome the guests. As soon as one of the doormen moved away perhaps to call a cab, immediately another person took his place. Another example of the friendliness of the Canadians.

We had arranged to take an evening meal at the Aqua Viva – a privately run restaurant with the first floor dining room overlooking the harbour and a 15 minutes gentle stroll from the hotel. As we had been promised, the meal was excellent and afterwards, we visited the Observation Tower and were able to view the whole of the city and harbour even though it was late in the evening. We could almost transpose the words of 'London by Night is a wonderful sight, there is magic abroad in the air. Most people say they love London by day but Lovers love London by night.' Certainly the night lights of Vancouver were very romantic.

A familiarisation tour of the city gave us opportunity to gain an overall impression and it was very impressive. Apart from the harbour with cruise liners there were float planes taking off and landing every few minutes and I had a special treat when I took a floatplane trip for half an hour flying in a De Havilland Beaver over the harbour and out towards Vancouver Island. I sat next to the pilot and watching him using the controls, the aircraft appeared to be very uncomplicated to fly.

Our guided tour included a visit to Stanley Park which was particularly interesting. The cedars and massive pines dominate the wooded areas but sadly, there was still much evidence of the 120mph storm winds Vancouver experienced in February 2007, 3 months before our visit. Totem poles have an important historic association all over Canada and Stanley Park has a large number of them. Their origin and purpose was explained to us that they have a similar significance as our own tradition of coat of arms with their symbolic emblems.

Not to be missed was a visit to Grouse Mountain including a ride in the Sky Ride cable car to the top where we were hoping to see the two resident Grizzly Bears Cooler and Grinder but they were still coming out of hibernation and not active. We did see the resident wolves and enjoyed the magnificent views from the snow covered peak. (There had been a significant fall of snow the previous evening.)

Leaving Grouse Mountain we then went to the Capilano Centre with its famous suspension bridge over the Capilano Canyon, 230 ft over the river. It was exhilarating if not a little frightening to walk the 450 ft on the swaying rope and plank footway for which we eventually qualified for a certificate to record our bravery! We were told that when the region was struck by the severe wind storms in February, many of the huge trees had been uprooted. One of them had fallen across the suspension bridge but in spite of the immense weight of the tree the bridge had not been damaged. However when one of the workmen on the bridge removed the tree by cutting it, it suddenly fell into the canyon and the rope supports of the bridge, released from the pressure, reacted like a catapult and had it not been for his safety harness, the workman would have been shot into the air like a missile.

We visited Vancouver Island which like mainland Vancouver almost seemed more British than England in some respects, then afterwards, returning to the mainland, continued our journey by coach through the magnificent scenic countryside to the small town, Hope which has a population of just over 3,000. The name 'Hope' has several origins – one is that it was at the centre of the gold rush in the 1800s when every prospector hoped to make his fortune.

The town has been used extensively for film making and some of the war epics supposedly taking place in the Far East were actually filmed in Hope. The town was also used as an internment camp for Japanese Nationals during the Second World War and there is a Peace Garden in their memory. Most notable aspect of the town for us was the magnificent avenue of chain saw wood carvings on both sides of the main road, converting tree stumps into very impressive works of art.

Our itinerary then took us to Kamloops (where the rivers meet) and much of the road which seemed to cling precariously to the mountains ran alongside the valley where the railway lines are located. On occasions we caught sight of trains on the other side of the deep gorge including the Rocky Mountaineer which was travelling to Kamloops. The freight trains were very impressive with at least 2 power units hauling large numbers of trucks (the largest number I counted was 145 which would have made a total length of about 1 mile). On the journey we passed a small town, Ashcroft and there at the side of the highway was the well known 'Rotary 'wheel.

Our hotel in Kamloops was the Executive Hotel which displayed a plaque on the wall 'The Rotary Club of Kamloops meets here Mondays at 12.15pm'. We arrived on Sunday evening and left on Monday morning so that was the nearest I came to making a visit to a Rotary Club.

Leaving Kamloops We continued to the town of Jasper through Yellowhead Pass* and the Jasper National Park with its beautiful lakes and mountains including Mount Robson which is the highest peak in the Rockies (12,972 ft). Not exactly a monument but in the town centre there is a huge cartoon character bear called Jasper which has been adopted by the town. There is also a vintage steam engine in the main street.

*Yellowhead Pass is named after an Iroquois Indian Pierre Hatsination who was an employee of the Hudson Bay Company and had blond hair. He made the first crossing of the mountains through this Pass.

Many of the lakes in the area have a distinctive green or blue appearance as the result of rock flour – where the constant action of the glacier waters gradually wear away the rock and deposit the fine particles in the lakes.

Our journey included a visit to Dutch Lake (Contracted from the original Deutsch Lake as a result of German immigration in earlier times). We enjoyed a pleasant 30 minute trip round the lake in a stern paddle boat but Ann's experience was spoiled when she found herself literally crawling with ants after she stood on a convenient spot to take photographs, not realising she was standing on an ants' nest.

We drove through Jasper National Park on to Banff and Yoho National Parks, the whole journey through countryside as breathtaking as we had experienced for the previous few days.

One of the high points of our holiday both factually and for our memories must be the visit to the Columbia Ice Field. We boarded a coach to take us to the Athabasca Glacier, part of the Columbia Ice Field which covers an area of approximately 125 square miles and is up to 1,200 ft thick. From the high point, there is a unique geophysical feature. Water from the glacier drains into three oceans, the Arctic, Pacific and Atlantic.

To gain access to the glacier itself, we boarded an Ice Explorer bus, 50 seats and 6 wheels with tyres 7ft in diameter and a width of about 2 ft. Our driver/guide was a young woman with an effervescent personality - Vanessa who was quite justified in her frequent expression of 'awesome' when describing the various features of the glacier. Accepting her competence in driving the vehicle, she surprised me when she told me that she had received only 2 test drives before her competency test on the vehicle.

When we left the Ice field we continued to our next destination – Banff.

The unspoiled beauty and sheer wonder of the mountains, canyons and rivers continued to amaze us and the small town of Field was yet another example. Lying below the Kicking Horse Pass it was the point where the Canadian Pacific Railway descended a dangerous incline much greater than the safety limits would normally allow. To provide a safer alternative, the Spiral Tunnels, one each side of the Kicking Horse river, were constructed through which the railway line now passes and with particularly long trains (freight trains can be up to a mile in length) it is possible to see the head of the train emerge from the tunnel and cross over its own rear portion so that front and rear of the same train are visible travelling in the opposite direction.

Banff is a town of many features. Situated alongside the Bow River it was developed from the time when hot sulphur springs were discovered in the 1800s and led to the building of Banff Springs Hotel We joined our fellow travellers on the gondola ride to the 7,500 ft summit of Sulphur Mountain which provides a spectacular view point and stunning views. On the observation platform cities of the world are identified with their direction and miles distant (London is 4,419 miles in direction NE 38.8 degrees.) Our journey then took us away from Banff towards Calgary leaving the mountainous scenery behind us and moving towards the lowlands and prairies. We were now more likely to see cattle rather than Elk or Moose.

On the approach to Calgary, our ultimate destination, we arrived at the site of the 1988 winter Olympics and many of the facilities constructed at that time have been retained and are in use for community activities. We were particularly impressed that our visit coincided with the first week-end of the season when hundreds of youngsters with their mountain bikes were availing themselves of the facilities originally constructed for he bob-sleigh competitions.

Dominating the sky-line of Calgary was the 621 ft high Calgary Tower which would be the point of our departure on the Rocky Mountaineer.

The Rocky Mountaineer

We were due at the Rocky Mountaineer at 5.45am and booked a cab in time to make the ½ mile journey. Unfortunately the Calgary marathon was due to be run and the route took in the streets where we had to go to the Calgary Tower. Our cab driver warned us that we may have to take a diversionary route but as a police car passed, he tucked in behind it and followed the police car through No Entry signs and an underground car park, delivering us in good time to book in for the Rocky Mountaineer.

Two gigantic engines linked together would be our motive power and 11 cars each about 50 yards long, some with the observation upper deck and 3 providing the cooking and catering requirements. Because there are no station platforms on the railway, steps were provided and to complete the red carpet treatment – a red carpet had been rolled out for us as we were welcomed aboard by staff who would be our close companions for the journey.

We left Calgary with only about 25 passengers in our car and within a few minutes were called to take breakfast with a superb choice of menu, the food all served nouvelle cuisine style. Our choice was fruit followed by smoked salmon on scrambled egg with caviar – more or less what I am used to at home!

On returning to the observation lounge it wasn't long before we heard the call 'bear on the left' and there it was, about 50 yards away sitting on the railway line which had branched off the line on which we were travelling. We had been told that the railway line is a favourite haunt of bears, particularly the black bears because they scavenge for the grain which spills from the many railway trucks as they are hauled from the grain areas of Alberta. Shortly afterwards alongside a lake we saw an osprey actually take a fish from the water.

Having enjoyed our relaxed breakfast it was almost time to make a stop at Banff where the remainder of our passengers boarded and it was then their turn to settle in and have their breakfast. This staggered feeding arrangement meant that we were first for lunch and by the time the Banff passenger took their lunch it was late afternoon. On day 2 the roster was changed so that we were the late diners.

On leaving Banff we were at the highest point of our journey – 5,300 feet and the river flow changed from Atlantic direction to Pacific direction. We also altered our watches from Mountain Time to Pacific Time, making a total variation of 8 hours over British Time.

Throughout our journey we were constantly pampered by the staff, feeding us Bucks Fizz, freshly baked muffins and cookies, giving us commentaries on interesting features of the scenery and generally tending to all our needs and requests.

Our journey was strange in some respects because we were now travelling the reverse route of the one travelled on the previous 2 days by road coach and we were able to view the beautiful scenery from a different perspective. Indeed at one point we could see the Trans Canadian Highway hundreds of feet above us, with a massive build up of traffic. It was only later that we learned a landslide had blocked the road and we quietly thanked providence that had we not travelled the road 2 days later it could so have easily been our journey which had been interrupted.

On the first day of our Rocky Mountaineer we passed through the spiral tunnels at Kicking Horse pass and then passed Craigellachie, where a small stone cairn marks the place where the last spike of the Canadian Pacific Railway was driven home on 7th November 1885 to join up the railroad built from the east and that built from the west. Although a very small township, Craigellachie is very important in Canadian history and alongside the stone cairn, flags of all eight provinces fly to commemorate the joining of the eastern provinces to British Columbia creating a united Canada.

At one point the general manager of the train came into the car and presented every lady with a chocolate rose, all nicely wrapped in cellophane. The significance was that this was Mothers' Day in Canada. At the end of our first day we were due to stay overnight in Kamloops and as the train eased into the station, a small group of 'Mounties' were there on horseback to welcome us. They were not actually police officers but dressed in a not dissimilar uniform and it was a good PR exercise we thought.

At our hotel, we collected our room key, found the room on the first floor and were truly amazed. On entering, the bathroom was on the right; ahead of us was a huge Jacuzzi; to the left was a breakfast bar with high stools; beyond the Jacuzzi was a lounge area with 2 settees and an armchair together with a large TV; round to the left was a huge bed, at least 6'6" wide; at the side of the bed was a door leading to a balcony which had a table and 4 chairs and was overlooking the hotel swimming pool alongside ornamental gardens and a waterfall.

Because it was in the late evening – 8.00pm or thereabouts we could not do more than change and freshen up because we were due at a musical evening with a meal. Fortunately it was in the hotel, taking us only 5 minutes to arrive and even so we were the last ones to be seated. There were something like 200 diners, 10 to a table and we helped ourselves to our meal from a sumptuous buffet with drinks etc served to us by waitresses in 19th century period costume.

The entertainment was light hearted, a cross between Country Western and pantomime re-enacting a famous train robbery committed in 1906 by a bandit named Billy Miners. Unfortunately his notoriety appears to be commemorated by his incompetence rather than as an accomplished train robber. Having held up the train, he chose the wrong wagon and instead of gold, found that his haul was $15 and a box of liver pills. He was sentenced to life imprisonment but escaped and set up his robbery business in the USA.

The evening's entertainment and excellent meal was finalised when the female compère announced to everyone that it was our Golden Wedding Anniversary. On return to the hotel we queried with the reception staff why we had such a luxurious room and we were told it was the Bridal Suite!

The following day we continued our journey, relaxed and continuing to wonder at so many points of interest but we realised that it would eventually end. However there were still one or two surprises in store. At one point, one of our attendants, Lleilah made an announcement "Is there a Mr. and Mrs. Stowe on board?" Of course we admitted who we were and she then announced it was our Golden Wedding anniversary, everyone applauded and the staff presented us with a book of the Rocky Mountaineer, autographed by all the attendants.

One thought had passed through my mind without really thinking of the possibility of what would happen if the single track line became blocked. Of course it was never likely to occur even when, 25 miles from Vancouver, the train slowed and crawled along before finally stopping. Then came an announcement we had not expected. A freight train ahead of us had suffered a derailment and we were unable to continue.

Although there are two railway lines, we were on the Canadian Pacific Railway and the other was the Canadian National Railway. Apparently there is no automatic presumption to switch to the other track and our attendants excelled themselves in making sure that we did not become bored or frustrated.

Negotiating for the re-routing lasted a full 4 hours, but eventually we arrived in Vancouver and we were interested to see a Salvation Army van at the point of arrival. We were told that all the unused food on the train was passed to the Army for distribution. It must have been something like a five star hotel soup run.

There were as many cabs as were required and within half an hour we were back at the Marriot Pinnacle Hotel.

The following morning we relaxed with a little sight-seeing before setting off to the airport. We actually booked in for our flight at the hotel which saved time and inconvenience. We were able to look at the seating plan on the aircraft and choose which seats we wanted. Our flight was due to takeoff at 17.50 local time and with the 8 hours time difference in addition to an 8 hour flight we expected to feel a little jaded when we did eventually land.

We had an uneventful flight, landing a little ahead of schedule, greeted by the Titan Tour mini-bus and an equally uneventful road journey home. The holiday was over and even 75 e-mails, 23 answer-phone messages and a pile of mail waiting for us, could not detract from the memories of our best ever holiday, full of new experiences and pleasures.

Chapter 26. Broadening Our Horizons

Having enjoyed our Canadian holiday with Titan Travel, of course we were then on their mailing list resulting in numerous offers and invitations to participate in other holidays but we remained unconvinced that cruising holidays would be of interest to us.

However it was not until we received an invitation from the Company to celebrate their 30th Anniversary for a weekend in Rouen during the August bank holiday in 2009 that we decided to accept their offer. They had joined with another tour Company, Fred Olsen and although we had never been attracted to cruise holidays, we decided to accept for the relatively short cruise lasting overall only 4 days.

Rouen is where Joan of Arc (Jeanne d'Arc), the maid of Orléans was martyred on 30th May 1431 when she was burned at the stake.

Other than the obvious hours on board as we sailed across the English Channel, we were not tied to a time table for sightseeing arranged by the tour operator and were able to wander round the town at our own pace. The church adjacent to the spot where she was burned was of modern architecture, relatively small but very light and airy, giving a feeling of peace and tranquillity.

We toured the town in a motorised train, like the ones we would see in England carrying visitors along the seaside promenade and altogether we considered Rouen to be a delightful town.

Our first experience of cruising on the MV Braemar made us realise why some of our friends consider it to be the ideal holiday. We were invited to a cocktail party and formal dinner where we were encouraged to dress appropriately. The food on board both in quality and presentation was of the standard expected at a 5-star hotel with crew members anxious to attend to every requirement of the passengers. Whereas previously we had never been attracted to a cruising holiday, on our return we had changed our minds and considered that perhaps sometime in the future, we may be persuaded

Norway with Saga Holidays

In May 2010 we decided to commit ourselves to a 7 day cruise aboard the MS "Saga Ruby" to visit the Norwegian Fjords a holiday which had often crossed our minds but which we had never actually undertaken. Unlike Titan holidays where door to door transport can be included, on this occasion we made our own arrangements for a car to take us to Southampton where we boarded the cruise liner but we had a trouble free journey and arrived in good time although recent awareness of terrorist threats resulted in a long queuing session to pass through security and passport control.

My first observation when we were on board was that most of the passengers were elderly until I rationalised my thoughts and remembered that we were of the same age group.

As with all holiday sea cruises, the service on board and quality of food was excellent and although for the first day we were at sea with just the occasional oil rig on the horizon to break the image of endless sea, we were not bored, making our own enjoyment without the organised facilities.

First port of call was Stavanger but with only 8 hours ashore, we were only able to visit the immediate locality of the port with a mixture of modern shopping facilities and the old town with its traditional wooden houses dating from 18th and 19th centuries. The 12th century Cathedral was particularly interesting with its beautiful panelling on the walls and especially on the pulpit.

All aboard then to travel to the delightful small town of Flâm and whilst the immediate vicinity of the port seemed to be so peaceful and almost deserted, its importance is mainly historical. The railway line high in the mountains from Oslo to Bergen, required a connection to a deep water port. The connection was provided by the railway which took us on a beautiful scenic journey high into the mountains stopping for a photo shoot at the magnificent Kjosfossen waterfall. Local folklore claims that a mysterious maiden would appear out of the mist created by the falling water and lure men to their deaths, perhaps much the same as the German legend of the Lorelei.

Tourism being what it is of course, we did see the maiden standing on a rock high in the waterfall accompanied by haunting music. Neither I or any of the other men ventured towards her because we only had a few minutes before the train continued its journey up the mountain where, in a hotel we enjoyed coffee and Norwegian pancakes before returning to Flâm. We were in port throughout the day and were able to visit the local tourist shops and a delightful railway museum before we returned to the ship for our evening meal.

The next stopping point was a pretty village of Skjolden at the head of Norway's longest Fjord. Whereas cruise ships had previously moored out in the Fjord and ferried the passengers ashore, we were informed that our ship was the first to have the benefit of a new jetty constructed with money provided by a local philanthropist. We were greeted in the entrance hall by several, attractive young women in traditional Norwegian costumes. Unfortunately we were not allowed to take one home as a souvenir.

Not only was there a newly built jetty but new houses were under construction nearby and much of the area had the appearance of a building site. However we were able to visit a glacier high in the mountains travelling by coach which clung to the narrow road as it spiralled upwards with high rock faces on one side and drops of hundreds of feet on the other. On the glacier although it was covered with snow, we wandered about in shirt sleeves because the temperature was so mild. Whilst we were there we were treated to the sight of a convoy of high powered sports cars driven by members of a local motoring club just out for a 200 -300 miles or so spin for the day. They had stopped to stretch their legs which allowed us time to admire their cars.

We were intrigued to see at various points small houses, clinging to the mountainside and it was explained that originally they would have been occupied by herdsmen or wood cutters perhaps but would now provide a facility for anyone requiring temporary shelter when crossing the mountains.

Norway's second city of Bergen was our final port of call and we had a full 10 hours in which to see the sights and browse through the shopping and market area. Ann even managed to persuade me to buy a rather expensive woollen jacket designed to defy the coldest temperatures. We took a short guided coach tour which included a visit to the birthplace of the composer Edvard Greig whose home is now preserved as a museum. In a concert hall built in the grounds of the house we enjoyed a piano concert of some of his music.

We returned to Southampton on June 1st and quite unexpectedly I was about to have a very pleasant surprise.

Passengers had been requested to assemble in the lounges to await instructions for disembarkation. We sat at a table which would normally allow 6 persons to be seated and a man and his wife asked if they could join us. After a little while of normal conversation, he said "I think I know you." He then identified himself as John Walmsley, one of the young police officers included in the Special Course at the Police College nearly 50 years before. * Either he had a very good memory or my appearance had not changed greatly but whatever, it provided for me a very enjoyable finale to the holiday.

Although we had enjoyed the cruise, both Ann and I agreed that 7 – 8 days was sufficient and we would probably start to get bored with a longer period.

• *John later became Assistant Chief Constable of Derbyshire Constabulary.*

Guernsey

In August 2010 I was admitted for an emergency operation at Whipps Cross Hospital. Although only in hospital for 4 days, I felt less than 100% fit for a week or so after discharge. However, we had booked to go on another mini cruise over the August Bank holiday period to visit Guernsey and Honfleur in France. Ann agreed to regard it as a convalescence for me and we joined the Fred Olsen cruise ship MS Braemar at Dover. We had often thought of visiting the Channel Islands but, like Norway, had never actually managed to do so.

The tour of Guernsey revealed aspects of the occupation by Germany during the Second World War which had been preserved as tourist attractions or possibly as reminders to the present population that there was a dark shadow in its history. Gun emplacement sites and concrete anti invasion blocks were amongst the more idyllic aspects of the present day holiday resort. There were many other tourist attractions including a very tiny chapel which was over-crowded if more than 4 persons entered at the same time.

The founder of the much publicised "Specs Savers" business empire is a resident on the island, a personalised example of an entrepreneur spotting a niche in the market and using initiative and determination to become a multi-millionaire. However I did not require her spectacles to see a pair of lovely pearl ear rings for Ann as a memento of our visit.

Leaving Guernsey we sailed to Honfluer, the principal attraction being a visit to and tour of the Château du Breuil, the Calvados distillery and cellars. The Château dates from the 16th century and stands in extensive grounds with 42 hectares of orchards. A tasting session of the liqueur accompanied by local cheeses was the high-light of the tour. Our guide for the occasion was a lady who had lived through the war years when France had been an occupied country. She led us to believe that there were many of her generation who could not completely forget that period of their history.

The 4 day cruise which allowed us to relax completely served as an ideal recuperation for me which was to stand me in good stead in just a few short weeks when my medical problems faded into insignificance compared with the accident which happened to Ann a few weeks later resulting in her head injury.

Nürnberg

Prior to Ann's accident we had planned to hold a function in our home for the Rotarians. It was obvious to everyone that such an event had to be postponed but in her confused state whilst in hospital and for weeks after her discharge, she insisted that she had to keep her promise. In the same way that I had benefited by days away from home for my convalescence, Ann also needed time without stress to recharge her batteries and we decided to take the opportunity to go away for the Christmas period. There was a two-fold justification, the first being to have a break from the traditional stay at home and second, the package tour holiday to Nürnberg including a visit to Bamberg which has so many lovely memories for me.

Unfortunately in the weeks prior to departure, we experienced some of the most severe winter weather for many years resulting in transport disruption on rail road and air. We were due to fly from Heathrow and be collected from home at 7.00am but we received a call from the tour operator the day before departure to say the pickup time would be brought forward to 6.00am.

In the late afternoon the day before our planned departure, with deep snow wherever we looked, I telephoned the Company to ask if our flight would still take place and was assured that it would. That evening we were at a Rotary function and returning home at about 11.00pm there was a message on the answer phone asking us to contact the tour Company urgently. We were offered two alternatives; either cancel altogether and have a refund of our money or accept an alternative arrangement. Instead of flying from Heathrow to Nürnberg we could fly from Gatwick to Frankfurt and then by coach to Nürnberg. We agreed to accept the alternative because we needed the break and our suitcases were packed ready to depart.

Our departure from Gatwick was in early afternoon and landing at Frankfurt in the early evening, we had not realised how long a journey it was going to be on the coach. It was not until 4.00am that we arrived at our hotel, about 12 hours later than we would have been if the travel arrangements had not been altered. We effectively lost the whole morning for sightseeing and our visit to Rothenberg later in the day allowed us only 2 – 3 hours to visit the Christmas market and other places of interest.

The following day, Christmas Eve there had been a heavy fall of snow and we were surprised to see mini-snow ploughs on the pavements clearing the snow almost as soon as it fell. We had hoped to visit the Nürnberg Christmas market but Christmas Eve in Germany has a much greater significance for giving presents and celebrations than in this country and we found that the stalls and other attractions were closing down before we really had chance to explore.

The meals in the hotel were of the highest standard and Christmas day lunch was well received after we had taken a guided walking tour of the snow covered town. After the evening meal, Ann and I went for a walk by ourselves but taking a wrong turning back to the hotel with the snow gently falling we encountered a delightful diversion in the almost deserted street. A nativity scene with life size figures of the Holy Family and shepherds etc together with live animals, including a camel all of which was illuminated with floodlights.

The following day was Boxing Day and again heavy snow falls created difficult driving conditions for our coach driver taking us to Bamberg. As a consequence, we arrived later than originally expected leaving us barely 2 hours for sightseeing. However that was somewhat academic because the streets and public areas were covered in snow and there were no shops open for shopping.

Ann and I decided to visit the Cathedral but with a Mass in progress it was not possible to enter merely for sightseeing. We chose to walk round the building and as we struggled through the snow we heard a woman's voice shouting "Leslie, Leslie." It was my friend Theresa Dirauf with her husband Paul, son Hilmar his wife Melanie and their 3 children. Knowing that we were making the brief visit to Bavaria, they had checked the itinerary on the internet, identified when we would be in Bamberg and travelled through the snow, hoping to meet us.

It was a wonderful surprise and for me the highlight of our Bavarian holiday. Paul even recommended where we should take our lunch and by co-incidence, it was the one where our tour Company had arranged for us to dine.

After lunch the itinerary anticipated a visit to the Levi Strauss museum in a small village. The museum was no more than the preserved house where the founder of denim jeans was born and after 20 minutes or so, most of our group trudged through the snow to a nearby pub where there was a huge log fire burning.

Our return flight to bring us home was from Munich airport which was completely free of snow.

Chapter 27. Family Ties Come Full Circle

In my early childhood and teen age years, there was a special bond with my sister Violet. She provided the greater part of my pocket money, much more than I received from my father and I learned much later that she assisted with the financial requirements of attending grammar school. During my developing years, she encouraged me to accompany her attendance at various churches. I also learned from her the protocol of escorting a young lady. I used to wait for her near to Fort Dunlop where she worked and walk home with her. Even when she married in 1948 I was still able to share special moments with her. I remember when she lived in a flat, I visited her and she instructed me into making flaky pastry. Unfortunately I never developed the skill beyond the initial rolling the pastry.

At one time, her husband Laurence was a heavy goods vehicle driver and he often allowed me to accompany him on his deliveries. There was an occasion when he was delivering gas cylinders to a factory and anxious to assist, I tried to move one of the heavy cylinders and squashed my fingers causing such pain I fainted. There were no serious consequences but it was the last time I went on such trips.

Vi and Laurence were frequent visitors to our homes and one occasion when we lived in Warminster, Ann had planned for us to have roast pork for lunch. Keen to use the facility of a timer to preset the oven to start cooking, the timer was mis-programmed and we woke in the morning to the smell of over cooked pork. The oven had switched on during the night instead of in the morning and the joint was ruined. Never mind; accidents happen in the best regulated households.

Vi and Laurence celebrated their 50th wedding anniversary, inviting many of the family members but it was not long afterwards that he died and Vi increasingly turned to me for advice when previously it would have been her husband with whom she would discuss problems.

Vi found it stressful to live alone in her three bedroom detached house and decided to find a flat. She constantly asked my opinion and when she informed me that she had decided to move into an apartment on the opposite side of Birmingham which was one of 60 in a block supervised by a house manager, I was not convinced that it was appropriate, anticipating that she would become insular and lonely without the close contact of lifelong friends and regular social activities.

Following Vi's move to her new home, Pat, my other sister who lived about 10 miles away from Vi visited regularly, often taking Vi on coach excursions, even buying a wheelchair when Vi's mobility made it tiring to walk. After 10 years or so living in the apartment Vi expressed a wish to move and Pat identified a bungalow for sale less than half a mile from her own home. Vi considered it suitable for her requirements and moved in but within days, Pat made a visit and found Vi lying on the floor unable to regain her feet. She was admitted to a local hospital for observation but was discharged later the same day.

Unfortunately a similar incident occurred a few days later, co-incidentally on a day when Ann and I were visiting. Social workers were also present when we arrived and it was decided that Vi should be sent to hospital again because she was unable to stand unaided. The social workers concluded that it would be necessary for VI to receive help if she was to continue living alone. Vi's address was in the Dudley Borough but it was decided to take her to a hospital in the adjacent Sandwell Borough where she remained for 5 weeks.

The hospital administrator would not discharge Vi until a care package was arranged for her but because she lived in another borough, it was not possible for them to make appropriate arrangements. Dudley Borough on the other hand insisted that because she was in a hospital in another borough, they were unable to make suitable arrangements. Consequently it was necessary to make private arrangements for her care but after two or three weeks it was becoming increasingly difficult to convince VI that there was no alterative to have visits to assist her. She was becoming increasingly frustrated and It was obvious that she could not settle. After six months I made arrangements for her to return to the apartment which fortunately had not been sold.

Sadly another incident occurred and once again Vi was found lying on the floor unable to move. She was admitted to a hospital near to her home, this time for six weeks. Fortunately when her mobility was sufficiently restored there were no complications in arranging for a care package because it was part of the hospital's remit. Knowing that she was receiving regular visits several times each day in her home was reassuring not only for me but also for sister Pat who still visited her whenever possible.

By this time I was becoming increasingly involved in dealing with her financial affairs and eventually took a Power of Attorney to regularise all her domestic financial arrangements and necessary correspondence. Although Vi expressed her appreciation I explained that so far as I was concerned, the support and guidance I had received from her in my early years more than justified relieving her of day to day problems so far as I was able to do so.

Chapter 28. What Next?

So, a miscellany of memories; a chronicle of events and decisions that set me on the path of life. It can only be a matter of speculation how any one of those decisions, had it not been taken, could have resulted in – who knows?

When I was 13 years old it was suggested to me that I consider the Police as a career. At that time I had not even thought of such a possibility but having done so, until the day of my reluctant retirement, never regretted for one moment taking that advice.

Accepting an invitation to join a running club in Birmingham encouraged me to develop skills which otherwise may have remained dormant and denied me the pleasure of athletic achievement and the many friendships which resulted from competitions.

Having risen to the rank of Chief Inspector and appointed as the officer in charge of the Warminster sub-division of the Wiltshire Constabulary the two men who invited me to join Rotary, changed the course of my life so dramatically that I could never have anticipated the consequences. A whole new world of experiences and friendship with new horizons to explore was the overriding benefit of Rotary Service. I have mentally thanked those two men a thousand times for their invitation.

The many hours of study to gain a Bachelor of Laws degree brought personal satisfaction and fully justified the commitment to study. As far as I know the degree did not overtly affect my career advancement.

The decision to move to London resulted in my involvement with the Superintendents' Association where my responsibilities brought me into contact with chief officers of police, Local Government officials, Ministers of the Crown and Royalty. I never regretted the move.

As an executive member of the Police Superintendents' Association I was involved in political discussions affecting the whole of the police service and when President strongly opposed the establishment of the Crown Prosecution Service. My status resulted in an invitations for Ann and me to many prestigious events including one of the annual garden parties at Buckingham Palace. I was selected to represent the Metropolitan Police at formal celebrations in Hamburg.

The decision to join the Metropolitan Police Male Voice Choir brought me many new friends in this country, Germany and Holland, encouraging me to learn to speak German which enabled me to act as spokesman for the choir when visiting other countries to sing in concerts and gave me confidence to tour Germany for holidays. Similarly joining the International Police Association opened the door to other holidays abroad and an ever widening circle of friends.

As a Rotarian in Chingford my close connections with the Chingford Association for the Physically Handicapped, resulted in forming many new friendships enjoying outings and holidays with them. Following the appointment as chairman and later when appointed President for Life, I was able to lead fund raising to purchase two mini buses for their use.

Encouraging my son to join the Sea Cadets resulted in appointment as chairman of the local Unit and later, chairman of the whole London Area comprising 70 + Units which also resulted in discussions with high ranking naval personnel and invitations to prestigious events.

The decision to apply for an appointment with the General Council of the Bar and later, the Honourable Society of the Middle Temple resulted in job satisfaction which would have been the envy of many other people.

I have often been asked why I was awarded an MBE? I honestly do not know. I had never considered my involvement in community affairs to have been more commendable than that of thousands of other people. Appointment as National President of the Police Superintendents' Association of England and Wales was not unique and I was preceded and followed by others who were not similarly acknowledged.

We can never know completely how our actions or words may have affected other peoples' lives. More than once I have met people with whom in previous years I had been closely associated and they have said "If it hadn't been for you………." I would like to think that those persons' lives were affected favourably rather than detrimentally.

No one knows what the future holds and looking back over the years it is easy to wonder whether a different decision would have altered the path of life. Certainly the decisions which I made individually resulted in a life of fulfilment, satisfaction, anxiety and determination but I wouldn't have wanted to change anything.

Definitely, I would not have wanted to change the choice of my life long partner Ann. Our marriage has survived the distress and anxieties of our respective medical problems, financial worries and domestic difficulties which has cemented more firmly our love for each other. The momentous decision to adopt twin babies has never been regretted.

If there is one period of my life which I would not wish to relive it is that of the war years and the build up to war where hunger and deprivation were common place. Even so, in those years of austerity we learned to economise, avoid waste and use skills of innovation to reduce hardship; valuable lessons for later life.

Trying to foretell the future has no attraction for me. Looking back over a life of fulfillment has much more significance.

Epilogue

As others see us

Take the book down from the shelf, the book entitled 'Know yourself';
Let's look together as we read to find the stimulus that we need.
"I've read the book times by the score, I know myself, there is no more."
But wait, as turns a page or two, should we take another view?
"Chapters and the verse are dead, there's nothing new to fill my head.
The book has nothing new for me, just filled with fading memories.
I feel so very ordinary but when they look what do others see?"
As life's path we've passed along, have we cheered someone with word or song?
Have we always given a smile or sometimes gone that extra mile?
Have we ever made our mark or gladdened some poor saddened heart?
We can say "What will be will be and nothing's changed, at least by me."
But you see that is not true for things do get changed by what we do.

© Leslie Stowe 1990